T0356273

Up and In

THE LIFE OF A
DODGERS LEGEND

Up and In

THE LIFE OF A
DODGERS LEGEND

Mark Whicker

TRIUMPH
B O O K S

Library of Congress Cataloging-in-Publication Data

Names: Whicker, Mark, author.
Title: Up and in: the life of a Dodgers legend / Mark Whicker.
Description: Chicago, Illinois: Triumph Books, [2024] | Includes
    bibliographical references.
Identifiers: LCCN 2023050369 | ISBN 9781637275740 (cloth)
Subjects: LCSH: Drysdale, Don. | Pitchers (Baseball)—United
    States—Biography. | Los Angeles Dodgers (Baseball team)—History.
Classification: LCC GV865.D7 W55 2024 | DDC 796.357092
    [B]—dc23/eng/20231122
LC record available at https://lccn.loc.gov/2023050369

This book is available in quantity at special discounts for your group or organization. For further information, contact:
    Triumph Books LLC
    814 North Franklin Street
    Chicago, Illinois 60610
    (312) 337-0747
    www.triumphbooks.com

Printed in U.S.A.
ISBN: 978-1-63727-574-0
Design by Nord Compo

To Pete and Alice Whicker because they allowed me to follow the ball

CONTENTS

FOREWORD

In my heart I was a Dodger a long time before I ever put on the uniform. Don Drysdale was good enough, and fortunate enough, to wear that uniform his entire career. He wore it with the highest distinction. My connection with that uniform began when I was seven years old. It was in late March of 1956, when the Dodgers came to the Gulf Coast to play the New York Yankees. I'll never forget anything about that day. My dad, Joe, drove a Greyhound bus. He took a lot of major league teams around Florida for exhibition games in the Grapefruit League. One day he came up to me and said, "Do you want to skip school tomorrow?"

I didn't know what to say. He was going to pick up the Dodgers at the Tampa, Florida, airport and take them to St. Petersburg to play the Yankees. He and my mom, Millie, were from New York, and he was a Dodgers fan, and she was a Yankees fan. I guess he was gloating a little bit because the Dodgers had just beaten the Yankees in the World Series. But that was the day I fell in love with the Dodgers. Off the plane came Pee Wee Reese, Duke Snider, Gil Hodges, Jackie Robinson, Roy Campanella, all of them. I was standing there with my eight Topps baseball cards.

Don was right there among them, towering over some of them. That would be his first year as a starting pitcher in the big leagues, and he was really emerging. I was sitting there, like the only child that I was, taught to listen a lot more than speak. I got to spend my share of time around them over the years. Sometimes they were kidding around. Sometimes they were very engaged in what they were about to do. Over the years they would keep up with how I was doing. I had been kind of pudgy, but then I started getting more athletic and leaner and I was starting to get a little power. Dad told them I had thrown a no-hitter. Don and the guys would say, "Throw strikes, don't throw breaking balls, and keep that elbow up."

Of course, Don never kept his elbow up. The Dodgers drafted me out of Michigan State in 1968, the year Don broke Walter Johnson's record for most consecutive scoreless innings. The next year he slipped, reached up, grabbed a dugout railing, and hurt his shoulder. That led to the end of his career, but by then Don and Sandy Koufax already had become arguably the greatest 1–2 pitching combination in the history of baseball. And because Don was from the L.A. area, I thought he was always symbolic of the Dodgers' move out west. Then they had that great run into the middle of the 1960s.

I was fortunate enough to be part of Dodgers teams that put together great seasons in the 1970s and 1980s as well. Sandy had methodical power and grace. Don was intimidating with that three-quarters delivery and that tailing fastball. They truly owned the plate. I played in the era where you could get knocked down quite a bit. People talked about Sandy and Bob Gibson of the St. Louis Cardinals, but Don was right there. He would have been the No. 1 pitcher for almost any other team and in 1962 he won the Cy Young Award. Twenty-two years later, he was inducted into the National Baseball Hall of Fame. He made that transition from the playing field to the broadcast booth and he was a natural at it. He was always engaging and knowledgeable.

He was a leader, too, even after he finished playing. If you wanted someone to stand up and cut through the situation, he could do it. He could be a loud voice of reason. His size and presence were something special and certainly made an impression on me. I didn't want to be tall. Being smaller meant that my strike zone was smaller, and I liked that. When people would come up to me in the airport and say they didn't realize I was so short, I'd always say, "Thank you!"

But Don was so big and tall that he made the opposite impression. He and Ann Meyers were a great couple, and they complemented each other so well. I vividly remember the day he died in 1993. I was in the Philadelphia area, playing golf at Pine Valley in New Jersey with some friends. I remember getting into the car, turning the radio on, and hearing about it. I told my friends, "Look, can we just pause a minute here?"

It took me a while to gather myself. Don was a great example of a man and a father and a professional. He was certainly a man for all seasons. It's important to keep alive the stories of the best players in the game, particularly ones like Don who meant so much to so many fans—and not just fans of the Dodgers. I hope you enjoy these stories as well.

—***Steve Garvey*** *played 14 years for the Los Angeles Dodgers and five for the San Diego Padres. He was the National League's Most Valuable Player in 1974. He was a 10-time All-Star and won four Gold Gloves at first base. From 1975 through 1980, he played at least 160 games every regular season. He led the league in hits twice and had 200 or more hits six different times. Garvey also drove in at least 100 runs five different times. Overall, he had 2,599 hits with a career average of .294 and he hit .338 with 11 home runs in 55 postseason games.*

COME FLY WITH ME

When Don Drysdale entered a room, the room knew it. When Drysdale walked to the top of a mound, it seemed to grow and rise, and everyone in the ballpark knew anything was possible or at least memorable.

He grew up in the late 1940s and 1950s, when America did its best to forget wartime and deprivation and division. The best place to do that was Southern California, where rows of houses began to flourish and surround Los Angeles like concentric circles. Towns like Drysdale's home of Van Nuys just sprung up from imagination and money without any colonial reference points. As he became one of the best pitchers in one of the best eras of pitching baseball has ever seen, Drysdale linked baseball's menacing past to California's sunny future.

The guy, who threw baseballs at the heads of hitters who had the gall to stand too close to his plate, was also the kindly idol who made Beaver Cleaver's day by answering his phone call. Television was the new force in American life, rooting tens of millions of families to their chairs and sofas, persuading them to eat TV dinners on TV trays. On many nights you could find Drysdale on those TVs from Dodger Stadium and Television City alike. Whether he was playing himself or some outlaw's henchman, the networks accepted him when he merely played himself. Thanks to his persona and success, his life had become its own entertainment showcase.

When the game was over and the night was still young and you were in Drysdale's circle, you also knew the possibilities. Hanging loose was the best option.

After his 14-year career with the Dodgers ended, Drysdale was the TV analyst for occasional games with the Montreal Expos in 1970 and 1971. Dave Van Horne was the play-by-play man. Drysdale entered the Hall of Fame as a pitcher in 1984. Van Horne received the Ford Frick Award for distinguished broadcasting in 2011, which earned him a place in Cooperstown right down the hall from Drysdale's plaque. One day they were in Shea Stadium for a game against the New York Mets. When they got back to the New York Sheraton, Drysdale turned to Van Horne and said, "I'm going upstairs to change. Meet me back in the lobby in 15 minutes."

Van Horne agreed and asked no questions. He knew adventure was afoot.

They boarded a cab and headed to Lower Manhattan. They got out at Sparks Steak House on East 18th Street. Sparks was and is a prestigious restaurant with a famous wine cellar and it moved to East 46th Street, where it had one infamous moment: the late afternoon in December of 1985 when Mafia boss Paul Castellano was shot to death in front of the doorway at rush hour. There was a chalk outline on the sidewalk, and it was there long after Castellano was buried.

On this night, in the original location, the place was packed. Van Horne braced for a long wait. Then the attendants guided Van Horne and Drysdale to an empty table with a "reserved" sign. A minute went by, and suddenly a handkerchief landed in Drysdale's face from somewhere. Drysdale blinked. Van Horne braced again. Only bad things were possible when Big D was provoked. Drysdale looked up and suddenly laughed. The handkerchief had come from the hand of his good friend, Francis Albert Sinatra. For the rest of the evening, Van Horne ate, drank, listened, laughed, and rarely spoke. Drysdale and Sinatra told stories that extended past closing time.

Van Horne and Drysdale returned to the hotel unsteady but still flying high. It was 3:00 AM when Van Horne telephoned Josee, his wife. "What's wrong?" she asked.

"Nothing," Van Horne said. "I just want you to know that I've been out all night. We were on the town with Frank Sinatra."

"Go to sleep," she replied and hung up.

Alphas tend to run with alphas—in a Rat Pack or a baseball clubhouse.

Drysdale retired as the Dodgers' pitching leader in wins. He died in 1993 at 56. His shrinking list of contemporaries remember him as the man around whom everything else rotated with a smile as immense as the sun—and sometimes as infernal. He was the center of the field where he pitched, the fulcrum of his franchise at all other times. Those friends use one phrase again and again. "Don was the epitome of a man's man," said Ken Harrelson, his broadcast partner with the Chicago White Sox.

"I know it sounds bad this day and time, and it's definitely politically incorrect," said Bill Bavasi, who was the general manager of two major league teams, and whose father Buzzie was Drysdale's GM with the Dodgers. "But he was a man's man."

"I really enjoyed his man's man comments," said Orel Hershiser, who would break Drysdale's 20-year-old scoreless-innings record in 1988.

A man's man. What exactly does that mean?

Drysdale stood 6'5 ½". Certainly, he was prone to testosterone over-load at times, particularly when he was a younger pitcher and felt victim-ized by the dimensions of the Los Angeles Coliseum. At one point Buzzie Bavasi was so tired of Drysdale's tantrums that he presented Drysdale with a plaque that read: "To Be Seen—Stand Up. To Be Heard—Speak Up. To Be Appreciated—Shut Up!" Fresco Thompson was Bavasi's farm director and later the Dodgers' general manager. "He's the hardest loser I ever saw," Thompson said of Drysdale. "When he gets knocked around, everything goes black. He says and does things he might regret later but can't very well take back. He's just too much of a competitor for his own good."

"Sandy Koufax and Don were different," said teammate Joe Moeller. "I remember sitting on the bus with Sandy after a game. He was saying, 'You know, I really shouldn't have left that fastball up. I got away with that one. And then there was another one to Cookie Rojas.' He said it about a couple of other pitches."

As he sat there on the bus, Moeller would smile to himself. Koufax was doing all this self-flagellation after he had thrown a no-hitter against the Philadelphia Phillies. "The difference with Don is that he would just get mad after he lost," Moeller said. "I made the mistake of being the first guy into the clubhouse after Don had gone in there. A table went flying by my head. I didn't do that again."

"I guess I'm a perfectionist," Drysdale said. "When I throw a curve that hangs and it goes for a hit, I want to chew up my glove. I want to bite nails in half. I want to stop time and make the pitch over, but I can't. And that makes me madder than ever."

But even then Drysdale had a certain magnetism, an ability to swallow all that bile after a decent interval and become the life of the party—even if he had to invent the party. He had a big head, a big voice, a big swing with the bat. He had big ambitions and saw big pictures and he believed in big gestures. *Halfway* was not a word that applied. He needed a big room sometimes, to be sure, but nobody would dispute the dimensions of his heart.

"He was the Pied Piper," said Vin Scully, the former Dodgers broadcaster. "Typically, Sandy would go out with Dick Tracewski and Doug Camilli if he went out at all. If Don went out, the whole team went out with him."

Much later, a Hall of Fame basketball player named Ann Meyers would become smitten by Drysdale's assurance and his ability to listen. "He was just so comfortable to be around," Meyers said.

There was a certain decisiveness, too, as in the night Drysdale said to Meyers, "What would you think if I asked you to marry me?" They had been acquaintances for three days.

Meyers turned that proposal down and several others that followed, primarily because Drysdale was still married at the time. Eventually, they did get married, had three children, and, by all accounts, enjoyed the happiest years of their lives.

*   *   *

It all comes down to presence. Pitchers weren't usually as big as Don Drysdale. In 1962 when Drysdale won 25 games and the Cy Young Award, fellow pitchers Joe Moeller and Stan Williams were 6'5", and Sandy Koufax was 6'2". On the 2023 roster, the Dodgers had six pitchers who were 6'5" or taller, and Clayton Kershaw was 6'4". In the first round of the 2022 Major League Baseball Draft, five pitchers were taken who were 6'4" or taller, including Noah Schultz of the Chicago White Sox, who is 6'9".

Most of the other top pitchers of the 1960s were all human beings of walking-around size: Whitey Ford at 5'10", Warren Spahn and Juan Marichal at 6'0", and Bob Gibson at 6'1". Since the Dodger Stadium mound was always high, Drysdale resembled a gargoyle, especially to righthanded hitters.

But his identifying characteristic was the acreage of his smile and its flip side. It usually transmitted joy and familiarity. It could also turn a hitter's bravado into tapioca, which is why the word "intimidating" is on his Hall of Fame plaque. More than one batter would turn and ask Dodgers catcher Jeff Torborg, "Why is he smiling at me like that?"

"He's not smiling," Torborg would reply.

Today we hear the term "good teammate," signifying a player who is aware of his surroundings, can feel when a teammate is struggling or angry, and cares enough to help. It's a quality devoted to the young ones, who need to learn the major league life and the customs and hazards within. Drysdale had been one of those young ones. He graduated from Van Nuys High in 1954 and started a game for the major league Dodgers 22 months later at Brooklyn's Ebbets Field. He was 19, surrounded by the aging remnants of the Boys of Summer.

His first roommate on the road was Gil Hodges, who had also played his first Dodgers game when he was 19, back in 1943. Hodges finally was voted into the Hall of Fame in 2022 after a series of campaigns by his fans and rejections by the Veterans Committee.

Hodges, like manager Walter Alston, was strong and nearly silent, leaving teammates and opponents to speculate nervously about what a true explosion would bring. When Drysdale needed to let loose a primal scream, Hodges would give him his distance and then bring him in for a landing. When Drysdale felt like going out with the boys, he noticed that Hodges almost always spent the nights in his room, ordering a brownie à la mode right before bedtime. When Drysdale left a tip that seemed too meager, Hodges would patiently ask him if he was sure that's what he meant to do. All of which caused Drysdale to refer to Hodges as "my second father" when he wrote his only book, *Once a Bum, Always a Dodger* with Bob Verdi in 1990. When Hodges died of a heart attack at age 47, Drysdale was broadcasting for the Texas Rangers. "I just flew apart," Drysdale said. "It absolutely shattered me."

By then Hodges had long since convinced Drysdale of the significance of an older shoulder. For the rest of his career, Drysdale was the big brother for all Dodgers around him, no matter how heavy. He not only looked out for the other Dodgers. He saw them.

Torborg was in spring training in 1964. Drysdale insisted that Torborg catch all his starts in Florida. Not once did he shake off a sign Torborg gave him. It wasn't a question of trying to get Torborg on the team because the Dodgers had given him a $100,000 bonus the previous year. That meant he was automatically on the roster. But it meant something when Drysdale walked over to Torborg's car one afternoon in Vero Beach, Florida, and told Torborg's wife, Susie, "The staff wants him to play, I want him to play. Don't worry. He's going to be fine. I'll take care of him." Torborg was in the majors for 10 seasons.

Don Sutton was a rookie in 1966, the year that Drysdale and Koufax held out in tandem for record-breaking contracts. The two signed near the end of exhibition season. Koufax sailed along as if he'd been pitching all year. Drysdale pitched miserably in the first half. Fans and reporters became less tolerant with each week.

Still, Drysdale was able to get outside of his own head. He befriended Sutton, who was 21 years old, from Clio, Alabama, near the Florida line. Sutton would go 12–12 in the first of his 23 big league seasons, which culminated with 324 victories and a place in the Hall of Fame. "Don found out I had a blind date one night," Sutton said. "He said, 'Take her to the

Coconut Grove.' The Righteous Brothers were playing that night. They were very big then. So Don called the Righteous Brothers, and they got us a couple of seats. In fact, the maître d' called me and told me I had the best seats in the house. He also said Mr. Drysdale was picking up the tab. That's what he did. I can't tell you how many times he picked up the tab. I was a socially inept kid from outside of Pensacola. I was in the big leagues after playing just one year of minor league baseball. I had one suit, and it wasn't very up to date. Don had a very kind way of letting me know about it without being sarcastic. It was a great quality of his."

Drysdale was the source of nicknames. Torborg, who played at the state university of New Jersey, was "Rudy Rutgers." From the very beginning, Sutton was "Elmer." When Sutton first prepared to face the Braves, Drysdale asked him if there was anything he needed. Sutton said he had a pretty good plan for everyone but Hank Aaron, which certainly wasn't unusual. "That's no problem," Drysdale said. "Bust him inside twice, then throw the slider away."

"That's fine," Sutton replied, "except I haven't got a slider."

Drysdale recoiled. "Elmer, you can't pitch up here!" he shouted.

Aaron went 2-for-4 against Sutton that day, hitting one of his 755 home runs. "At that point," Sutton said, "I was willing to take that."

The Dodgers once had a rookie whose name made him sound too good to be true. Unfortunately, Sandy Vance was not an amalgam of Sandy Koufax and Dazzy Vance, two of the Dodgers' Hall of Fame pitchers. Drysdale took one look at Vance's shopworn shoes and said, "Who gave you those, Ty Cobb?" Then he went inside and fetched Vance a new pair.

He once took new sweatshirts to the minor league clubhouse at Vero Beach for the attendants there. When the Dodgers threw a surprise birthday party for Anastasia Plucker, the Dodgertown nurse, Drysdale was the one who put her in a convertible and drove her to the site. "Drysdale was always comfortable, even as a rookie," said 96-year-old Carl Erskine, the oldest surviving Brooklyn Dodger. "Very self-assured. He was much further along than Koufax because he'd played in the minor leagues. Sandy didn't really know to hold runners on, wasn't very polished at all. Don wasn't like a rookie. He really didn't have a rookie year."

Koufax himself echoed that observation. "I met Don in spring training of 1956," Koufax said. "I didn't deserve to be there. I was only with the big club because of that bonus rule. Don got to pitch a lot more than I did that year. That's the way it should have been. But basically we grew up together."

Jim Murray, the revered columnist of the *Los Angeles Times*, was hanging out in the Dodgers' room in San Francisco in 1963. Drysdale was involved in his usual bridge game when another reporter eased up to the table and told Drysdale that a couple was outside the door and wanted to see him. They were deaf mutes and communicated to the writer how much they loved the Dodgers. They also communicated that they were distantly related to Drysdale, who abandoned the game and went outside to meet them. He exchanged written messages, acknowledged their stories. When they said they had remodeled their bedroom and put up new curtains, Drysdale asked what color the curtains were. When they said they always put out the cat when they made waffles, Drysdale said he liked waffles and cats alike. He was with them for 45 minutes. Oh, and Drysdale was the starting pitcher that night. "Most ballplayers in this league would have told the couple to get lost—in sign language," Murray wrote. "I had the feeling Drysdale would have stayed there until it was time for him to go pitch."

Kelly Fieux is a sergeant in the Palm Springs, California, police department. He is also Drysdale's nephew, the son of his sister Nancy. Drysdale was the broadcast analyst for the White Sox when the Fieux family visited. A trip to Texas was upcoming. "He calls my mom and says, 'Why don't you let him come to Texas with us?'" Fieux said. "I didn't have enough clothes, but he took care of that. We had a great time. We went to the mall, he got clothes for me, and then we'd go to McDonald's, which he always enjoyed. People would come up to us while we're eating, and he was generous with his time. He'd finally say he'd take care of everyone after we were finished, and he did. That's when I realized just who he was. Years later I was a reserve officer in San Diego. That was a volunteer position. You volunteer your time, but you don't get paid. He said, 'Why don't you apply at Palm Springs?' He and Annie were living in Rancho Mirage. He said I could stay with them as long as I wanted. One day he made a call. He hung up and said, 'You start work on Monday.'"

Dennis Lamp grew up in Long Beach, California. He grew up watching Drysdale or listening to Vin Scully describe him. In 1959 his dad took him to the Los Angeles Coliseum for a game, but Dennis didn't see Drysdale until there were two out in the ninth, and Drysdale relieved Danny McDevitt and retired Pittsburgh Pirates third baseman Don Hoak for the win. In early June of 1968, Lamp was busy studying for final exams at St. John Bosco High in nearby Bellflower. "I remember the night he pitched, and Bobby Kennedy won the California primary, and then he was assassinated," Lamp said. "Throughout that time we were following Don's scoreless streak. We would always find time to listen to it."

Lamp started with the Chicago Cubs organization. He asked for and wore No. 53, Drysdale's number, with the Chicago White Sox and Toronto

Blue Jays and went 11–0 for Toronto in 1985. He didn't get to wear No. 53 with the White Sox, but he did get Drysdale in person when Drysdale was the White Sox' TV analyst. On nights Carlton Fisk was not catching, the White Sox coaches were calling pitches for Lamp. "I was struggling," Lamp said. "Three straight games in that situation, I was getting my brains beat in."

The next game was a Saturday matinee against the Oakland A's. Beforehand, Drysdale came down to the field with a cup of coffee in hand. "You might want to think about calling your own game today," he told Lamp.

"I won 7–2," Lamp said. "I saw him later, and we just started laughing. It really put me on track. He helped me a lot in those years. His big thing was to get all nine of the leadoff men. Those were the nine most important outs. I had to bear down on those. And he said, 'Look: your pitches go to the catcher's left knee and his right knee. Think about an X and pitch to the bottom of that X.' If I did throw the ball up, make sure it was up and in. Up and in, down and away. I had to make my living inside and get them to chase away. But I could always go to him."

When Torborg was managing the Cleveland Indians, Drysdale was broadcasting California Angels games. Torborg remembered their days as teammates and particularly a spin pickoff move to second base that worked more often than it should have. He asked Drysdale to show it to his own pitchers. This was a little complicated because Drysdale didn't want to be seen helping the enemy. He needed a clandestine place for this clinic. "So Don took all these young pitchers into the shower and he was in there showing them all that footwork in his stocking feet," Torborg said, laughing. "I wish I'd taken a picture of that."

For Wes Parker, the Dodgers' first baseman for nine years, the best Drysdale moments came postgame, particularly on the road and particularly after a win. "We always had a seat reserved in the back of the bus," Parker said. "He would stretch his feet out on the aisle. He'd bring a six-pack with him and he'd start passing out those cans. We'd get back in the last four rows. He'd start telling stories. Nobody wanted to miss any of them. Then, on the plane, he was part of the bridge game. It was Don and me and Jim Gilliam, who could really play, and Wally Moon, and sometimes Bill Singer and Tom Haller would join in. One time we were flying cross-country and had to refuel in Grand Island, Nebraska. The trip took seven-and-a-half hours. We talked about how it was a tripleheader. But we played cards the whole way. He was one great human being. He loved people. I've had so many people say, 'Yeah, I met Don, at the bar at the airport.'"

A bar was not an unlikely place to meet Drysdale or many other Dodgers for that matter. This just in: ballplayers enjoyed drinking. Since Drysdale lived so disproportionately, he was known as an All-Star drinker. This might have been somewhat unfair because if 20 people see a ballplayer drinking one beer, the general impression will be that the player had 20 beers. It wasn't all that inaccurate either. As in all things, he had a high capacity.

One night the Montreal Expos played at the Philadelphia Phillies and then retreated to the Marriott on City Line Avenue. There was a Polynesian restaurant in the hotel. Drysdale and Dave Van Horne were there until closing time, which Van Horne was happy to see as best he could tell. "Then a big tray of Mai Tais comes to the table just as they're turning the lights on," Van Horne said. "I'm saying, 'What's this?' Don says, 'Hey, let's go out and sit by the pool and finish these off.' I'm wondering how we're going to do that, but, of course, we did."

"You know what Drysdale would have for breakfast?" Ken Harrelson asked. "Liver and onions and two Heinekens, I kid you not."

"We'd go to his restaurant [Drysdale's Dugout in Van Nuys] every once in a while," said Frank Howard, the 6'7" slugger whom the Dodgers traded to the Washington Senators after the 1964 season. "It was good for our togetherness, our unity. But you'd need track shoes to run with those guys."

Not that Howard was unfamiliar with nocturnal running. Drysdale told a story about Howard downing "a dozen banana daiquiris like they were water."

The size of Drysdale's table was elastic, depending on the night. His drink of choice was usually red wine or Dewar's and water. Two regulars were relief pitchers Ron Perranoski and Bob Miller. Stan Williams was usually there, too, in the early 1960s. He was a hulking, 6'5" righthander who pitched with more destructive intent than Drysdale. In 1990 he was the pitching coach of the Cincinnati Reds, who featured a bullpen of Norm Charlton, Rob Dibble, and Randy Myers known as the "Nasty Boys." Every night they pitched as if their nickname depended on it. "With the Dodgers we had places to go in every city," Williams said. "I remember the whole pitching staff going to the New Yorker in Milwaukee. A little guy at the end of the bar was there, too, and we said, 'Well, Walt's spy is on the scene.' We'd do that every night. But the rule we had was at midnight the next day's starter gets kicked out of the bar."

By then Pee Wee Reese had retired and was Dizzy Dean's sidekick on the CBS Game of the Week, which happened on Saturday afternoons, and for much of America, that was the only exposure to live Major League Baseball until the World Series. Reese went out with the boys one night and said not to worry about a thing, that he'd take care of the tab. After all, he was on expenses. "The bill came, and Pee Wee looked at it and said, 'Hey, guys, there's no way I can turn this in,'" Williams said. "We said, 'Hey, Pee Wee, you're the one that invited us.' So we ended up kicking in $20 apiece like we always did."

"I wasn't into going out at night with those guys," Moeller said. "I did it one night, and after two drinks, they put me in a cab and sent me back to the hotel. But Don would always throw a $20 bill on the table and say, 'Keep 'em coming until that runs out.' Of course, back then the beers were $1 each."

*   *   *

When Don Drysdale and Ken Harrelson were televising Chicago White Sox games, the TV booth was barely big enough. Their opinions, wing-spans, and personalities were all extra large. So were they. Harrelson was 6'2", a feared hitter with the Cleveland Indians and Boston Red Sox, and was a skilled enough golfer to play in periodic PGA Tour events. Known as "The Hawk," Harrelson also won a Frick Award. When Harry Caray left the White Sox booth, owner Jerry Reinsdorf interviewed Drysdale and Harrelson, couldn't figure out who he liked better, and hired them both. "Don was very knowledgeable, and our fans reacted to that," Reinsdorf said. "We didn't want any of these homer-happy announcers. That's what they want on the North Side. Once Don left, Hawk got to be more that way."

Indeed, Harrelson would razz opposing players when they struck out. "Grab some bench," he'd say, or "He gone."

As a player Harrelson dressed in Nehru jackets, owned 80 pairs of shoes, raked in the endorsements, turned Boston's Kenmore Square into his own personal rec room, and had two significant brushes with baseball history. When Kansas City A's owner Charlie Finley released Harrelson after a player revolt, he made The Hawk a de facto free agent, as several clubs in the U.S.

and Japan pursued him. Harrelson had been playing for $12,000 but signed with the Red Sox for $150,000 in what some people saw as a dress rehearsal for the really big money. Harrelson also blistered up his hands one day on the golf course with a ballgame to play that night. To grip the bat, he wore golf gloves, which seemed odd until he got a few hits. His teammates began wearing gloves, too. Now it's rare to see a player without them.

As broadcasters, Harrelson and Drysdale shared a view that baseball should be played with dirt under the fingernails—and for keeps. The 1970s had become the 1980s, and there was real money in the game. Players were changing. Big D and The Hawk were not. "He'd get down on players," Harrelson said. "I'd say, 'Goddamnit, cut him some slack. He's just a baby.' He'd say, 'Fuck him. He ought to know better.' If you didn't represent the game, if you didn't play the way he thought you should play, he didn't have time for you. We'd go out and argue about players, and he'd hit the sauce pretty good. But he was also more knowledgeable than anybody I was ever around. He knew the game from every angle. He would have made a great general manager. We had a group that was going to get a franchise in Orlando, and he was going to be the GM. But there was some subterfuge involved, and we didn't get it. We'd eat dinner every night on the road. I was Tom Paciorek's partner for 10 years, and we might have gone to dinner three times. Yet Don and I never talked politics or money or family. All we talked about was baseball. It could be a turbulent relationship. We'd get into arguments on the air, usually about players. The commercial break would come, and sometimes we wouldn't say a word to each other and then we'd go back on the air and we'd start arguing again."

Harrelson and Drysdale drained a couple of bottles of wine after a game in Cleveland one night. As they headed back to the hotel, one of those in-game arguments flared up again. Eventually, Harrelson, the driver, pulled the car over and said, "You want to go? Let's go."

The fact that they were on the breakdown lane of an interstate highway did not affect their fight plans. But when Harrelson got out and walked to the passenger's side, Drysdale opened the door and rose slowly and pleasantly. "He was smiling," Harrelson said. "I have to say: it was the most beautiful smile I ever saw because it meant I didn't have to fight him."

Sometimes it was unavoidable. Joe Moeller remembered the trip back from Baltimore after the Dodgers had been swept by the Orioles in the 1966 World Series. It wasn't a cheery flight, though the card game was ongoing. "I wasn't involved in the card games that often," Moeller said. "This time a lot of guys had been drinking. For some reason, Don's wife, Ginger, and my wife were supposed to get together in Baltimore, and something went wrong, and they couldn't. Don brought that up. All of a sudden, we're swinging at each other, and the other guys are breaking it up."

Another retreat from Baltimore in 1979 led to another confrontation. Drysdale was broadcasting for the California Angels, and they were headed home after losing the first two games of a best-of-five American League Championship Series, their first ever trip to the postseason. Pitcher Jim Barr was out with a hand injury, and Drysdale, well lubricated, began challenging him. "People have to remember that Drysdale never missed a start," Harrelson said. "He pitched one whole year with a broken bone in his left hand."

Drysdale and Barr began to square off when manager Jim Fregosi and others interceded. As it turned out, Barr really was hurt, and Drysdale later apologized.

What surprised people was Drysdale's fastidious side. Gene Mauch, a Dodgers player for a while and the manager of four major league teams, was one of Drysdale's closest friends, the best man at his wedding to Ann Meyers. Mauch was also an enthusiastic cigarette smoker, as Drysdale and Koufax once had been. When Mauch and Harrelson visited the Drysdale home one night, Drysdale would empty the ashtray after every dead cigarette. "And we probably went through a pack apiece that night," Harrelson said.

"He and Bob Uecker used to have this thing," Meyers Drysdale said. "Donnie would always have the coasters out. Ueckie would put his drink down on the table, just outside the coaster. Donnie would wipe off the table with a towel and put Ueckie's drink back on the coaster. Then Ueckie would take another drink and put it on the table again. That went on and on. Don got him back one day when Ueckie was in the guest room, sleeping a little too late. Don made up the bed. With Ueckie in it."

"I think that was a Drysdale trait," Kelly Fieux said. "My grandmother was so meticulous. Everything had to be spotless. The same traits filtered down to my brother and I."

Drysdale's mom, Verna, also made sure the house, whichever one it was, had a healthy rose garden outside. "So Donnie was adamant that we had to have roses," Meyers Drysdale said.

Drysdale was married to Ginger Dubberly for 12 years, some of them tempestuous. He was the young athlete on the make. She was the model and the beauty pageant contestant. On the surface they were the made-for-Van Nuys sitcom couple. But they didn't fall into traditional roles. Ginger handled the finances for the couple, including their horse racing business. Her husband, in many ways, was the domestic engineer. "He helps me around the house, does the dishes, tends to the baby, waxes the floor, and I don't have to say a thing," Ginger told the *Los Angeles Times* in 1960. "He just sees it and does it. He took one look at the asphalt tile floor in the den and went to work. First, he washed it, then he paste waxed it, then he polished it. It looked like one of those floors you see in one of those *House Beautiful* ads when he finished."

When Drysdale and Meyers Drysdale planned a house in Rancho Mirage, he threw himself into every detail, shopping for the granite, picking out windows and then changing them, devising the floor plan, picking the furniture. There was abstract art on the walls, a few baseball pictures, and a desert vista in a frame that dominated the main room. And, also, a photo of the Brooklyn Bridge. "That same night when Gene [Mauch] and I were over at his house, he's in the kitchen cooking dinner," Harrelson said. "Here's the king of macho in a very macho age in baseball, big 6'6" guy. And here he is wearing an apron. It was hilarious."

When the game ended for Drysdale in 1969, he found new teams. There were the broadcasters and technicians in Montreal, Texas, the Angels, Chicago, and the Dodgers. There was the ABC crew with Uecker, Al Michaels, and Howard Cosell with Keith Jackson and sometimes Tim McCarver. Drysdale did national telecasts, including the postseason, for 10 years, beginning in 1977. The guys on the ABC crew called him "The Winder," after his sidewinding delivery. He was nominated for the Frick Award, the same one Dave Van Horne had won in 2011 but didn't win. "He could broadcast anything," McCarver said. "I think he was the first guy I ever heard talk about being 'wild in the strike zone.'"

"Near the end of his career he knew that's what he wanted to do," Don Sutton said. "He'd get a little tape recorder and sit in his hotel room and practice doing play-by-play. And he would encourage me to do the same thing." Sutton did and became the TV analyst for the Atlanta Braves on Ted Turner's Superstation.

The best evidence of Drysdale's near-universal appeal was his peaceful relationship with Cosell, who thought nothing of criticizing Michaels and Frank Gifford in public. Michaels was critical of Cosell's spirited drinking and called him a "cruel, evil, and vicious person."

Of course, Michaels also enjoyed telling the story of Cosell's introduction to a young Bob Costas. "I know you," Cosell said, staring down at the young broadcaster. "You're the child who rhapsodizes about the infield fly rule. I'm sure you'll have a great career."

But Cosell didn't mess with Drysdale. He called him "Twin D" and treated him respectfully and sometimes thoughtfully.

In January of 1984, Drysdale was preparing to play in the Bob Hope Desert Classic as one of Lee Elder's pro-am partners. But before that he played in Cosell's charity golf tournament at the Club at Morningside near Palm Springs, California. That was the day of the Baseball Hall of Fame announcement, and Drysdale was in his 10th year of a 15-year candidacy window. He was getting closer every year, so he talked to Jack Lang, the secretary of the Baseball Writers Association of America. Lang told him to call at his convenience in the morning, and Drysdale said he would do so from the clubhouse.

As it turned out, Drysdale teed off on the 10th hole. When he finished the 18th, he ducked in and called Lang, who told Drysdale he'd made it. Then he went to the first tee to finish the round, and Cosell had assumed the position of narrator. "Donald Scott Drysdale," he said, "won 25 games and the National League Cy Young Award in 1962; broke Walter Johnson's record for the longest streak of scoreless innings pitched in 1968, won 209 games, and was a part of three World Series championship teams and hit 29 home runs during his career; made his first major league start for the Brooklyn Dodgers in 1956 and defeated the Philadelphia Phillies at age 19."

Cosell paused. "I want you people here today to be the first to know," he proclaimed. "Don Drysdale has been elected to the Baseball Hall of Fame."

"Well, I almost dropped," Drysdale wrote in his autobiography. "I got a little misty. How he got the news so fast, I'll never know."

Drysdale was sentimental but also good for a prank. Maybe it was Drysdale's investment in people, compounding daily in his account. He noticed things. It showed through pranks and helping hands alike.

When Drysdale got married to Ginger, Carl Erskine told him to bring back a pineapple ukelele from their honeymoon in Hawaii. That was in 1958. He assumed Drysdale knew he was joking. When the Dodgers reconvened at Vero Beach in 1959, Drysdale walked into the clubhouse with a bag of pineapple ukeleles and dumped them at the foot of Erskine's locker. "Here," he said, "I've been carrying these around all winter."

When Jim Campanis was trying to make the Dodgers as a reserve catcher in 1967, Drysdale saw him drinking an orange juice from the players' table. Not kosher, Drysdale told him. You only get to do that when you make the major leagues. In the 1989 movie *Major League*, a scene featured the locker ritual, in which a player would open the door in mortal fear that he would see a red tag, meaning he was cut. At the end of that spring, Campanis nervously opened that door. He didn't see a red tag. He did see a small bottle of orange juice, courtesy of Drysdale. He had made the team.

When the Dodgers played in Philadelphia, Torborg would stay at his home in New Jersey. Drysdale noticed that Torborg was out of the clubhouse a lot quicker on those Philly nights, and that the catcher would grab a sandwich or two from the spread for the drive home. "One night I'm driving and I take a big bite out of that sandwich," Jeff Torborg said, "and I almost threw up. There was a used sanitary sock in there right on top of the meat. I came back the next day and wanted to know who did that. Nobody said anything. But Don gave me that smile of his."

"He was this big kid," said Dick Tracewski, the backup shortstop. "He was the talented, blue-collar guy. He was the guy everybody played jokes on. If you were going to throw ice on somebody, it was going to be him."

Wes Parker, who could pass for 55 even though he turned 83 in 2023, sat at a restaurant on Pico Boulevard, spooning down a bowl of soup on a fiercely rainy March afternoon. He thought of those bridge hands, those nights in the back of the bus, that wide two-dimensional smile. "He was just a natural leader," Parker said. "Now, Sandy was better. But Don was our heart. He really was the Dodgers' heart."

2

ANYTHING GOES

Joey Amalfitano played Major League Baseball for 10 years, managed in parts of three others, was a major league coach for 31 more, and became a minor league instructor. When most baseball people had either forgotten the fundamentals of the sacrifice bunt or condemned it altogether, Amalfitano was teaching them to minor league teenagers. He could tell you how to make any play at second or third base and he knew when to wave in runners or hold them from the third-base coaching box.

The key was knowing who he was. As a player he hit .244 with nine home runs—total. He wasn't a real threat to Don Drysdale. But one day in 1964, Amalfitano stepped into the box at Wrigley Field and smacked a long line drive off Drysdale. "I thought, *Hey, I caught one off this guy*," he said. But Tommy Davis, the Dodgers' left fielder, leaped and grabbed it.

Amalfitano jogged past Drysdale on the way back to the Chicago Cubs' dugout. "Joe, you're swinging the bat pretty hard," Drysdale said.

"I didn't think anything about it," Amalfitano said.

The next time they met, Drysdale slung a fastball at him. "The ball went through my left sleeve and then through my right sleeve," Amalfitano said. "Down I went."

That night Amalfitano went out to dinner in Chicago. Drysdale waved him over to his table with his customary smile. "Why don't you have dinner with me?" Drysdale asked him.

Amalfitano sat down. After a drink or two, he asked, "What did you do that for?"

Drysdale laughed. "You were swinging the bat pretty good," he said.

"I was only hitting .250," said Amalfitano, who hit .150 against Drysdale. "But that was just him. He was going to intimidate you if he could."

Drysdale pitched in 518 major league games and hit 154 batters. That ranks 20th all time. Of the 19 pitchers ahead of him, only 12 pitched exclusively in the 20th or 21st centuries. Of those, Walter Johnson is the leader with 205—15 more than Randy Johnson and Eddie Plank. Two others, Tim Wakefield (186) and Charlie Hough (174), were knuckleball pitchers whose success depended on a pitch that behaved irrationally and independently. The only active pitcher who has surpassed Drysdale is Charlie Morton, who is in 12th place with 168. Ten of those 19 are in the Hall of Fame, and Roger Clemens (159) would assuredly be there if not for his suspected involvement with performance-enhancing drugs.

The all-time leader is Gus Weyhing, who hit 277 batters, 79 of them in 1886 and 1887, his first two seasons. His career ended after the 1901 season. For much of his career, pitchers stood 50 feet away from the batter instead of the standard 60 feet, six inches. Weyhing was also famous for marrying Lou Gehrig's cousin, Mamie, and for becoming the final pitcher to agree to wear a glove. He ranks fifth all time in wild pitches.

Throwing at hitters is the most dangerous part of baseball or used to be. Beanballs have ended careers and in one case ended a life. Drysdale never hurt anyone seriously. But he was the pitcher most associated with the high, hard one. He personified the art, even though many of his contemporaries were just as aggressive. Throughout baseball and particularly the National League, there were times in the 1960s and 1970s when all hitters knew that a knockdown pitch was coming. The difference with Drysdale was emphasis and lack of concern. He and Bob Gibson announced their contempt for a hitter's mere existence. But Gibson wasn't as tall and didn't throw from such an extreme angle that the release point to right-handed hitters appeared to be centered over the Santa Monica Pier. "I hate hitters," Drysdale said. "I start the game mad and I stay that way."

Drysdale always denied that he drilled hitters on purpose, maintaining that his control was good enough to put the HBP (hit-by-pitch) record out of sight had he chosen to. But he never denied the use of the inside pitch as a preemptive weapon. Anger was part of the equation. Drysdale's mood was never fouler than in the Dodgers' first four years in Los Angeles, when they played in the Los Angeles Coliseum, and Drysdale felt the left-field fence pressing at his back. Beginning in 1958 Drysdale hit 14, 18, 10, and 20 hitters, leading the National League each year. Those were the Coliseum years. "I'd get so mad that I'd get tired," Drysdale told the *Los Angeles Times*. "Later in my career, I realized I was getting tired of getting mad."

In 1956 and 1957, his first two years with the Dodgers and their final two years in Brooklyn, he had hit only 10 batters in 320 innings. The Dodgers moved into Dodger Stadium in 1962, where the air was cool, and the fences were only faintly visible. Visiting pitcher Frank Funk would call it "pitching at an airport." Suddenly Drysdale was the best pitcher in baseball, winning 25, losing nine, posting an ERA of 2.83, leading the league in innings and strikeouts, winning the Cy Young Award, and finishing fifth in the Most Valuable Player Award voting. In those 321 and one-third innings, Drysdale hit only 11 batters. Bob Purkey of the Cincinnati Reds was the league leader with 14.

The endgame for Drysdale was to deny comfort. Like many successful pitchers, he used an arrhythmic delivery to his advantage. He maximized his height by firing from the side, and right-handers couldn't see the baseball as quickly. Their feet were notably light already.

Catcher Jeff Torborg remembers a game in which Willie Mays walked into the batter's box and started digging in. Mays had not looked toward the mound yet. "Willie, you do know who's pitching today, don't you?" Torborg asked.

Mays looked up, saw those familiar teeth, and frantically started trying to fill the hole. Too late. Drysdale floored him anyway. "Threw it right under his chin," Torborg said. "Willie had that high-pitched voice. He got up and started yelling: 'You don't have to do that!'"

Mays' slugging teammate Orlando Cepeda would join Mays and Drysdale in the Hall of Fame. "The best advice," Cepeda said of Drysdale, "is to hit him before he hits you."

"He throws baseballs like they were knives and he will lose his letter if he misses," said Jim Brosnan, the Cincinnati right-hander famous for writing *The Long Season*, a precursor to *Ball Four*, the 1970 expose by Jim Bouton. "His idea of a 'waste pitch' is a strike."

In the beginning Drysdale thrived on two pitches. One was a fastball that rode into the right-handers and was responsible for many of the unintentional HBPs. The other was a breaking ball that dove toward the outside corner and stayed down. That one made Drysdale a ground-ball artist.

Joe Becker was Drysdale's first pitching coach with the Dodgers. He got Drysdale to throw the curveball from a three-quarters delivery so he could "get on top" of the pitch and make it break downward. Then he doctored Drysdale's change-up. Because Drysdale threw with a "stiff wrist," Becker had him spin it from the inside of his fingertips, a motion that was most associated with screwball pitchers. "Except it won't act like a screwball," Becker said. "It'll just slow up." More than anything, Becker recognized the unique mix of elements. There was delivery, there was speed, there was assertion. "Tight to right-handers, away from left-handers," Becker told him. "That's your strength."

Years later, Phil Regan joined the Dodgers and showed Drysdale a different ingredient. Drysdale was able to reach into the cabinet and put together what Torborg would call "the super sinker." In English that was a spitball.

It caused major theatrics at times, involving the umpires and opposing managers, and Drysdale promoted the legend of the super sinker, figuring it planted one more apprehension in the hitter's mind. Giants manager Herman Franks was a frequent accuser, but he saw opportunities in it, too. In 1968 Franks made a Vitalis hair tonic commercial with Drysdale. It began with Drysdale rubbing his hair before he stepped on the rubber. Franks roared out of the dugout. "It's a greaseball, it's illegal," Franks charged.

Exasperated, Drysdale walked into the clubhouse as the fans booed, then came back and held up a bottle of Vitalis to the crowd, who cheered. "Vitalis has no grease," the announcer said, as Franks shook his head and left the field.

When Milwaukee's players, particularly pitcher Lew Burdette, began the chorus, Drysdale replied, "I don't throw it. What they say isn't the gospel truth. What I throw is a knuckle forkball."

In his book Drysdale wrote that he'd actually learned the mystery pitch during his one Triple A year in Montreal. Drysdale saw Emilio Cueche loading it up without really pretending he wasn't. So Drysdale got a crash course from his Montreal catcher Johnny Bucha.

Drysdale also chewed tablets that came from the bark of slippery elm trees. They were intended to soothe inflammation. "All it was…was a piece of wood," Torborg said. But it activated saliva and made it easier to load up. "He wanted me to try it one time. You know that warm feeling you get right before you throw up? That's what it felt like when I had it in my mouth. He was laughing at me. But it never bothered him one bit."

Ken Harrelson faced Drysdale in the 1968 All-Star Game in Houston. Drysdale broke the super knuckle forkball sinker or whatever he was calling it. "I took strike one and I'd never seen anything like it in my life," Harrelson said. "The ball seemed to go up on its way in. Then it broke straight down. He'd given me the slippery elm. I guess the expression on my face was so aghast that Drysdale had to put his glove over his mouth to keep from laughing. Strike two was the same way. Then he gave me a hanging slider, and I almost knocked it out, and Curt Flood caught it at the wall, and I jogged by Drysdale and told him he was a lucky SOB."

"I threw some spitters in my career," Drysdale admitted in his book, which he wrote in 1990 with Chicago columnist Bob Verdi. "Some days I threw 20, some days 10, some days maybe five. I didn't have all the weapons I needed against left-handed hitters, so I used the spitter mostly on them. But I always figured it never hurt to wet one early and then let them look for moisture the rest of the game."

But Drysdale was more famous for the "purpose pitch" and, because of the Dodgers' prominence and his own delivery, he embodied it. Today's baseball fans would be shocked to learn that the hitters basically took Drysdale's up-and-in medicine and went about the business of the day.

The only serious brawl involving his brushback pitch came at Brooklyn's Ebbets Field on June 13, 1957, with Milwaukee in town. Johnny Logan was the Braves' shortstop. He was the first player to win a World Series in the U.S (with Milwaukee) and Japan (with the Nankai Hawks). Logan became a Milwaukee institution, operating the radar gun at County Stadium and becoming known for his attacks on the English language. "Rome wasn't born in a day," he once said and is credited for asking a waitress for an order of pie à la mode, "and put a little ice cream on it."

But Logan was all business on the field and a little belligerent, too, and he wasn't shrinking from this impudent, 20-year-old string bean in a Dodgers uniform. Maybe Logan didn't realize Drysdale had already learned the National League codes of misconduct at such an early age. But when Bill Bruton slammed a home run to lead off the game and Logan followed with a single, Drysdale tried to hit Logan with a pickoff throw, which turned into an error. In the second inning, Bruton hit another home run. Then Logan was wearing a blinking red light. "He was strutting around up there, showing me his teeth," Drysdale said. "A charge came over me. I thought I'd show him who's boss."

Drysdale hammered him in the back with a fastball.

Logan did not invade the mound area, not right away. He walked down the base line for a while, bat in hand. But, on his way, he couldn't resist yelling at the kid. "I'll see you when you get to second base," Logan told Drysdale.

"Damn second base," Drysdale said. "Let's do it right here."

And there they went. Logan got the first blow, Drysdale answered with a left and a right, Milwaukee's Eddie Mathews and Carl Sawatzki joined in, and eventually Brooklyn's Gil Hodges had to rescue his young roommate.

He pulled Mathews off the pile. "It looked like a scene from *High Noon*," Dick Young wrote in the *New York Daily News*, "with Drysdale in the role of Gary Cooper."

The Braves won 8–5, and Drysdale was removed with two out in the second inning. Beyond that, there were no serious confrontations. "The catcher's job," Torborg said, "was to make sure the hitter didn't charge the mound. With Drysdale that was never a problem. He'd throw at you and knock you down and then he'd come to the front of the mound and look at you, just to make sure you knew what he had just done."

Later, Logan would admit, "I don't see how anybody hits that guy."

*   *   *

Johnny Edwards came up to the Cincinnati Reds on June 27, 1961, the first day of a 14-year career. He would win two Gold Gloves as a catcher and was an All-Star three times. He had been an engineering student at Ohio State, but his arm and his toughness led him to a different line of work, and he knew how to think along with pitchers. When his Triple A manager Cot Deal called him in and told him, "I can't play you anymore," Edwards bristled. Surely, he wasn't going back to Double A. Then Deal told him he was going to Cincinnati instead.

He was joining a team that would win the National League pennant by four games over the Dodgers. On July 9 Edwards sat in a steaming dugout at the Los Angeles Coliseum. Cincinnati was in the midst of a 14–3 win, and the Dodgers had to reach deep into their pitching staff. Drysdale, who had given up a game-tying home run to Frank Robinson a few weeks earlier, got the call in the fifth inning. He brought a bad mood with him.

The Dodgers fell behind 5–2 when pitcher Joey Jay cranked a double off Drysdale. In the sixth Drysdale threw underneath Don Blasingame's chin and knocked him down. Blasingame popped out. Drysdale then decked Vada Pinson twice. Pinson doubled.

Robinson was the next hitter. He would win the National League Most Valuable Player award in 1961. Like Drysdale, he played on a full tank of bile. Walter Alston, the Dodgers' manager, ordered an intentional walk, which would have been Drysdale's third walk of the outing. *Enough of that*, Drysdale thought. *Hit Robinson and get it over with*. But it took a while. Drysdale sent down Robinson twice. He hit him on the third pitch. Umpire Dusty Boggess then ejected Drysdale from a game in which he didn't seem particularly interested in participating. As Robinson noted, Boggess yelled, "You're gone" before he stepped out from behind the plate.

Edwards, the new guy, watched all this with a slack jaw. *Man,* he said to himself. *This is sort of a tough league.*

The next day, National League president Warren Giles suspended Drysdale for five games and fined him $100. Drysdale fumed, raged, and then finally paid the fine—with a bag of pennies. Giles returned the bag to Drysdale with a note: "When the fine is paid in its proper form, you will be reinstated."

Later, Drysdale admitted how lucky he was to have saved the paper rolls. He stacked up the pennies, put them in the rolls, and sealed them up.

The fine and the suspension didn't soothe the Reds. Jay, who was 6'4", said he didn't know Drysdale personally. "And I don't want to know him," Jay said. "But anytime he wants to meet me, he can name the place, and I'll walk to it."

"I'll be around all season," Drysdale replied.

"He isn't a major league pitcher," Reds pitcher Bob Purkey said. "He's gutless and bush."

When Robinson was asked how it felt to be in the shooting gallery, he grunted. "I don't think he's that wild. Put it that way," he said.

Meanwhile, Rene Lachemann was doing odd jobs in the visitors' clubhouse at the Coliseum. He was 16. Batboys and clubhouse attendants often were aspiring young players, like Lachemann and Jim Lefebvre. Lefty Phillips, who had been the Dodgers' scout when Drysdale signed, recruited them. Lachemann and Lefebvre often worked out with the Dodgers, and Lachemann, who would catch for three years in the majors and then manage four major league teams, sometimes caught Sandy Koufax. "He was pretty easy to catch," Lachemann said.

The kids would work from mid-afternoon to 2:00 AM, cleaning the mud off the spikes, taking care of the baseballs, anything that a uniformed heart would desire. But on July 7, Lachemann got a good look at Drysdale's inning of 10,000 pennies. "Drysdale hated the Coliseum. Everybody knew that," he said. "That home run Robinson had hit a couple of nights before, that was just a little pop fly that got out. This time, Drysdale kept knocking him down, and Frank kept getting back up. They kicked out Drysdale, and the next time Frank came up, Turk Farrell was the pitcher. In deep left-center, there was a tunnel halfway up the seats. [It] must have been about 450 feet away. Frank hit one into that tunnel. That was how he dealt with it."

A major league umpire for 27 years, Tim Tschida saw plenty of Robinson. "Jim Maloney played with Frank in Cincinnati," Tschida said. "He said Frank got thrown at more than anyone he ever saw. Frank would basically stand right on top of the plate. They'd hit him, and he wouldn't even rub anything. He went to the mound just once."

Although Drysdale's missiles at Willie Mays' head became legendary, he only hit Mays twice, and Mays was one of the few right-handed hitters who could punish Drysdale to the tune of a .330 average and a .604 slugging percentage. When Joe Moeller asked Drysdale how to pitch Mays, Drysdale said, "Stick it in his ear."

Though Hank Aaron hit 17 home runs off Drysdale in 221 at-bats with a .267 average and never got hit once, he said: "When Drysdale is on his game," he told *True* magazine, "I'm outclassed,"

Drysdale plunked neither Aaron nor Dick Allen. It wasn't necessary for the latter. Allen was 3-for-46 against Drysdale. Cincinnati Hall of Famers Tony Perez (6-for-31, no home runs) and Johnny Bench (1-for-18, no homers) had no luck either. "Don knew how to brush people back," said Don Sutton, who joined the Dodgers in 1966 and huddled under Drysdale's wing. "It might be the way you swung. It might be your manner, the way you acted after you hit a home run, or you could be the guy who came up after the home run...But he told me he never wanted to hit anybody in the head. All he wanted to do was pop the buttons on their shirt, and that's what he did. I learned how to pitch inside, too, but it was a little different. I wasn't 6'6" and 235."

"Guys, who were on the on-deck circle and got a little too close to the plate during his warmup pitches, they would get it, too," Vin Scully said. "He'd get mad and try to put one 'between a guy's cap and his head,' as they used to say. It was like he was saying, 'If you want to time something, time that.'"

Beanballs, though, once had more dire consequences.

Ray Chapman was a 29-year-old shortstop for Cleveland in 1920 from Beaver Dam, Kentucky. He was a respected fielder, a prolific bunter, and he had led the American League in runs and walks two years earlier. He had just gotten married and told people around the team he would probably retire after the season. Carl Mays was also 29, also Kentucky-born and raised, and was in the midst of a 26-win season for the New York Yankees. On August 16, 1920, they met at the Polo Grounds. Mays, who pitched underhand and was known for throwing inside, came up and in with a fifth-inning fastball that bored in on Chapman's head as if it were a magnet.

The impact was so great that the ball bounced out to Mays, who assumed Chapman had somehow hit it with a bat and threw it to first baseman Wally Pipp. But Chapman was down with a fractured skull. He rose and was almost able to walk to the Cleveland dugout with assistance, but his legs quit functioning before he got there. After doctors removed a piece of his skull the next morning in hopes of relieving the pressure, Chapman died.

Tris Speaker, the Indians' player/manager, collapsed when he heard the outcome, and neither Speaker nor outfielder Jack Graney felt emotionally strong enough to attend the funeral, which packed Cleveland's St. John's Cathedral. What was described as an "immense floral banquet" lay front and center, thanks to the contribution of 2,063 fans. Mays was disconsolate, too. When he learned of Chapman's death, he volunteered to come to the District Attorney's office and met with assistant DA John Joyce. He did not accompany the Yankees on their next trip to Cleveland. Even as the Detroit Tigers and Boston Red Sox threatened to boycott any game Mays pitched, he disavowed bad intent. He said, "It was a straight fastball

I threw, such as I had delivered hundreds of times and I can't understand how it happened. I followed Chapman into the players' clubhouse, and he looked up at me, and said, 'It's all right, Carl. Everything will be all right.' I never threw a ball with the intention of hurting any ballplayer, much less Ray."

League president Ban Johnson dismissed the boycott and said he would take no action against Mays, but he doubted Mays would pitch again in 1920. Mays did, but the Indians won the American League pennant and then defeated the Brooklyn Robins in the World Series.

No major league player has been killed by a pitched ball since. But the knockdown was endemic to the game. Cy Young himself struck 161 batters in his 22 seasons. Pink Hawley needed only 10 to hit 210. Tony Mullane had 185 HBPs in his 13 seasons and regularly bragged, "Watch me polish his buttons."

The base on balls was an antidote to the frequent HBPs of the mid-1800s, and in 1884 the American Association voted to award first base to those who had been plunked, a decision as controversial and reviled as the extra-innings ghost runner in 2020. Gradually, baseball people accepted it because it took the assumption of premeditation away from the umpire. Then it became cut and dried. The recipient would get on base, no matter the intent.

The curveball came along and was harder to control, which brought on more contact. Pitchers began to throw higher in the strike zone because hitters were becoming expert at hitting low pitches. And there were several slow moves toward bringing the batting helmet into the game, though the National League did not make it mandatory until 1956, and the American League did not follow until 1958, and those who weren't already wearing one did not have to get one. But for most of the years, the knockdown was considered a necessary, even colorful, aspect of the game.

Hockey players do not pick up pucks and throw them at offenders, though they did use their sticks. Football players, who swing their helmets at each other, are not tolerated. But pitchers could always take projectiles and use them as preemptive weaponry. The responsibility of avoiding them fell to the hitters. "The pitcher has to find out if the hitter is timid," Drysdale said. "And if the hitter is timid, the pitcher has to remind him he's timid."

When Drysdale went nine innings in his first big league start and won at Philadelphia, he was 19 years old. Roy Campanella was the catcher. He called Drysdale "the closest thing to Ewell Blackwell I've seen."

Phillips, the Dodgers' scouting director, had Drysdale pitch American Legion baseball in Van Nuys, California, in 1954. Blackwell was the name that came to his mind, too. It was high praise. Campanella thought Blackwell was the best pitcher he'd ever faced. "He was definitely the meanest," Campanella said. "But there's a difference: this kid doesn't throw anything straight."

Blackwell was 6'5 ½" and 190 pounds and he also threw hostile pitches from approximately 10 o'clock. In 1947 he won 22 games for a woebegone Reds team, was second in MVP voting, and pitched 19 consecutive hitless innings. Only Eddie Stanky of the Dodgers kept Blackwell from throwing back-to-back no-hitters, delivering a hard smash underneath Blackwell's glove. The only man to throw consecutive no-hitters before or since was Johnny Van Der Meer, Blackwell's teammate. In winning 16 consecutive decisions, Blackwell compiled an ERA of 1.61. "He's a right-handed Carl Hubbell," said Bing Crosby, the singer who was a minority owner of the Pittsburgh Pirates.

The Reds had been ready to unleash Blackwell, but then Pearl Harbor happened, and Blackwell spent the next five years in Germany. He returned home like a conquering hero. As his wins mounted, his hometown of San Dimas, California, actually considered renaming itself "Blackwell." The Cincinnati papers sponsored a contest to nickname him, though he was already known as "The Whip."

Blackwell led the league in strikeouts in 1947 but only hit four batters. Many were ready to bail before they left the on-deck circle. "When I had to dig in on him," Ralph Kiner said, "I couldn't feel my legs."

After Kiner's Hall of Fame career ended, he became a broadcaster and was often asked in the postgame press rooms to recreate the day that he watched teammate Dino Restelli find out firsthand about The Whip. Restelli wore glasses that would get fogged on occasion. He called for time and backed out of the box, took out a red handkerchief, and wiped the lenses clean. And he took his time about it. He finally signaled to Blackwell that it was okay to pitch. Blackwell wasn't accustomed to needing permission. He responded with a hot fastball that sent Restelli down in a fogged-up heap. Many nights, after a couple of cocktails, Kiner would pantomime that moment as if it were "Casey at the Bat."

Blackwell then missed time because he had a kidney removed, hurt his shoulder, and then had his appendix removed. In 1950 and 1951, Blackwell returned to form, went 33–30, was named to his fifth and sixth consecutive All-Star teams but led the National League in hit batsmen both years. Fear had become his ammunition. "I was a mean pitcher," Blackwell said.

After Blackwell faded, Sal Magle upheld the standard for malevolence in the 1950s. So many of baseball's starkest moments ran through Maglie. In 1951 with the Giants, he started Game Three of a three-game playoff with the Dodgers, the one that ended with Bobby Thomson's "shot heard 'round the world." He was out of the game by then with Larry Jansen relieving and he was coming out of the shower in the clubhouse when he saw Horace Stoneham, the Giants' owner. Stoneman was telling Maglie how much he enjoyed having him on the club, and even though they would obviously lose this one, it had been a good season. Then they heard the roar outside.

Maglie was like baseball's Forrest Gump, having direct involvement in some of baseball's most historic moments. When Mays ran to the center-field wall and with his back to the plate caught Vic Wertz's drive in the 1954 World Series, the pitch came from Don Liddle, who had just relieved Maglie. When Don Larsen of the New York Yankees threw a perfect game in the 1956 World Series and beat the Dodgers 2–0, Maglie was on the mound for Brooklyn and pitched eight strong innings himself.

He had sunken cheeks and a 5 o'clock shadow and on the mound he resembled an avenging ghost. By the time he got to Brooklyn, a teenage Drysdale was waiting for him, an empty vessel eager to retain knowledge, and Maglie, then 39, periodically sat with him in the clubhouse and taught him the ropes or how to shove hitters through them. Although Maglie only hit 44 batters in his career, he was known as The Barber, the guy who turned the baseball into a razor blade. "When he was with the Giants, he used to knock down the whole Dodger team," Scully said.

"When he came over to us it was a little difficult," Carl Erskine said. "We hated him. He would throw at Campanella, Carl Furillo, and Jackie Robinson every game. He didn't throw at Gil Hodges, Duke Snider, or Pee Wee Reese. It all came from Leo Durocher, who was their manager. Our manager was Charlie Dressen, who was like a pup out of Durocher, and we'd play them 22 times, and it was very intense."

General manager Buzzie Bavasi learned he could get Maglie and did so for $100. But first he ran it past Erskine. "Maglie? You gotta be kidding," Erskine said. Then he thought for a second. "But first is he healthy?"

Slowly Maglie made the transition from Hatfield to McCoy, from hated Giant to beloved teammate. When Erskine saw Maglie put his arm around Campanella, he knew it would work out. "They started talking about how to get hitters out," Erskine said. "It was amazing. Sal turned out to be a really nice guy to be around."

But no two players despised each other the way Maglie and Furillo did. "And when Sal came to the Dodgers, guess who was his first roommate?" Scully said. "It was Furillo."

Maglie and Drysdale found common ground. Both had the same approach. Maglie had a breaking ball that landed outside. "It broke about as hard as anything I ever saw," Erskine said. Maglie needed something to keep hitters from reaching for that curve. Thus, he found the razor.

Eventually Drysdale learned to go inside twice. The first time, he said, could be interpreted as an accident. The second time was intended to dispel that interpretation. "That was something about Drysdale that I always enjoyed," said Clemens, who never was reluctant to menace the hitters. That essential and almost existential lesson came from Professor Maglie.

Mentorship can be a long thread. Maglie did not get to the big leagues as a regular starter until he was 33. He had jumped to the Mexican League, which was buying up major league players, and commissioner Happy Chandler banned all the defectors for five years. But while in Puebla, Mexico, Maglie listened to his manager, a Cuban named Dolf Luque, who was famous for his up-and-in game. By the time Maglie joined the Giants in 1950, he knew where his road to prominence would lead, usually off some hitter's cap. Maglie won 59 games the next three years and had a 45-inning scoreless streak.

Would Drysdale have earned the same reputation without Maglie? Maybe. But The Barber accelerated the process. Drysdale was a blank slate in those days. He hadn't pitched as a Little Leaguer, never really learned how to handle defeat, and wasn't really good at following unwritten rules.

He came to a Dodgers organization that already worshiped at the Church of Chin Music. Ralph Mauriello was a senior at North Hollywood High when Drysdale was a sophomore at Van Nuys. In 1954 Mauriello was pitching for the Dodgers' affiliate in Asheville, North Carolina. His pitching coach was Ray Hathaway, who had pitched 310 games in the minor leagues, and four for the Dodgers. Hathaway won 23 games in Zanesville, Ohio, one year. He had been through too much in his life to dabble in diplomacy. "He watched me pitch one day and said, 'Look, there are three things holding you back,'" Mauriello said. "'You have to learn the change-up, you have to follow through, and you have to knock hitters down. You have to; you must.' We would get into pissing contests about that. I didn't really want to do it. The Spartanburg club came to town one day and they had a guy [Joseph Fuller] who was leading the league in hitting. He got eight or nine hits in the first three games of the series. I'm pitching the fourth game. Ray says, '"Goddamnit, it's time to knock this guy on his ass. I want you to throw your best pitch as hard as you can about this far from the guy's nose.'"

Mauriello did. Fuller went down. "And we played the game, and he had the nicest, most polite 0-for-4 you ever saw," Mauriello said. "From then on I was a believer. It was standard practice. When you gave up a home run, you either threw at the next guy or you threw at him the next time he came up."

Ben Wade carried that torch, too. He was 16–6 for the Hollywood Stars, the popular Pacific Coast League team that preceded the Dodgers' westward move and he pitched five years for the varsity Dodgers, 16 years in the minors. "They called him The Policeman," Scully said. "He had no trouble coming inside. He's one of the guys who started the tradition."

Wade then became one of the most influential men in Dodgers history. He was the farm director for 16 years, and seven Dodgers that he drafted or acquired became National League Rookies of the Year.

*   *   *

Stan Williams would have been the Darth Vader of any pitching staff that did not include Don Drysdale. He was a 6'5" right-hander who prized velocity over accuracy, and his meanness was pure. He pitched for six teams over 14 years. In that frame he plunked 71 hitters. He came to the Dodgers in 1958. "I was with Boston and I faced Stan when he was with Cleveland," Ken Harrleson said, laughing at the thought. "The Steamer, yeah, he was something. He had been trying to hit me in the previous series, and they took him out before he could. This time, I knew it was coming. I backed out and tried to get out of the way, and the ball happened to hit my bat just right. It flew out of there, over the 351-foot sign. I'm running around the bases and yelling, 'Stan, I'm sorry. I didn't mean it!' It's got to be the only time I ever apologized for hitting a home run."

"It was kind of ironic that the Dodgers had that kind of pitching staff because of all the glamour in Hollywood," Tim McCarver said. "You'd expect them to be a little more prissy than they were. Every club had one or two guys who would knock you down, but nobody had as many as the

Dodgers. That's what nobody realized. They won because they played the game harder and tougher than anybody else."

Williams is given credit for the famous incident or series of them, in which Walter Alston came to the mound, told him to give the next hitter an intentional walk, ambled back to the dugout, and turned around at the sound of a full-blown brawl because Williams had beaned the batter. Williams said Drysdale actually did that first and also was the first to say, "Why waste four pitches when I can get the job with one?"

"Alston was waiting for Don with his arms folded," Williams said. "Don said, 'Hey, all you said was put him on.'"

Bill Bavasi, Buzzie's son, remembers that the Dodgers promised Williams a bonus if he would reduce his walks. No problem, Williams said. He went for the one-pitch solution instead. Williams also carried around a list of players that in his mind could be intimidated and would mark them off after he sent them flying. "Our whole pitching staff would get together," Williams said. "Our motto was: 'Two feet sticking up in the air.' We didn't feel we'd really knocked them down until we saw both feet up. Two things we wouldn't do: throw behind their heads or do anything that would jeopardize our chances of winning. We wouldn't hit somebody in the ninth inning of a close game. That wouldn't make any sense. But we definitely went 2-for-1. If you hit one of our guys, we would hit two of yours."

There was also an initiation. New hitters would routinely get dusted by the Dodgers. If they got up, brushed off the dirt, and stood in there, they earned a modicum of respect. "We'd say, 'This guy is here to play ball,'" Williams said. Others who squawked or shrank from the fight earned the privilege of hitting the ground again. "You had guys like Maloney in Cincinnati, Bob Veale in Pittsburgh," Joe Torre said. "They would test you.

My first week in the big leagues in 1961, I got knocked on my ass everywhere we went. They all wanted to see how you reacted to it."

Sandy Koufax rarely threw at people, but there was always the threat. Lou Brock of the Cardinals walked, stole second, stole third, and scored on a grounder one night. In the dugout Drysdale predicted Brock would have a problem. "Sandy doesn't like it when you score a run without a hit," he told Jim Lefebvre, who had graduated from clubhouse duty to the full-time second baseman's job.

Next time up, Koufax buried a fastball into Brock's ribs. Brock trotted about 70 feet and then collapsed and had to leave the field on a stretcher. "But you can't throw inside anymore," Harrelson said. "The umpires used to let us police the situation. But then baseball put the power in their hands. They didn't want it initially. Then as the years went by, they started to enjoy having that power. Their offseason speaking fees would go up from $200 to maybe a $1,000 or two. I remember a time with the White Sox, we hit 13 home runs in three days, and not one of our hitters had to pick himself up off the ground. If Drysdale had seen it, he would have gone crazy."

Drysdale and Harrelson broadcast a White Sox–Indians game, in which White Sox pitcher LaMarr Hoyt pitched high and tight to Tony Bernazard, who then ran to the mound. Hoyt came off the mound, and they began scrapping. Tim Tschida was the plate umpire. Afterward, the crew was watching the video, and Tschida laughed when he heard Drysdale on the air: "Oh, man, when you hit a guy, don't come off the mound! Stay on top of the rubber. Make them run uphill toward you!"

Despite all of that, during Drysdale's tenure from 1956 through 1969, the Dodgers led the National League in hit batsmen only twice, and the National League average for hit batsmen per game and per team ranged from 0.16 to 0.23 in the Drysdale years. Since 1900 the three most danger-ous years for hitters have been 2020 (0.47), 2021 (0.46), and 2022 (0.45). Yet there is almost no talk of beanball wars and very few incidents. One theory is that the brushback artists of the 1960s had superior command. As Drysdale often said, he could have busted up more hitters had he wanted to. "Everybody's throwing 98 mph now," Tschida said. "It's tougher to have command. When you had pitchers like Greg Maddux, Bret Saberhagen, and Bert Blyleven, you knew they could put the ball where they wanted to. Curt Schilling, too. And when one of those guys hit somebody, it was a red flag. You knew it wasn't an accident."

Another is that the hitters come to the plate dressed like actors from Medieval Times. The "armor," as pitchers derisively call it, sometimes runs from the shoulder to below the elbow. As pitchers have become less inter-ested in throwing inside, hitters often lunge to get the outside pitches, a habit known as "diving." That also can get you hit.

But the main reason is the warning instituted by Major League Baseball. When a pitcher knocks down a hitter, umpires are authorized to warn both benches. If the aggrieved team asks its pitcher to retaliate, then that pitcher and his manager are ejected. It removes the self-policing that players in the 1960s espoused. "Back then the priority was winning," said Joe Torre, who became Major League Baseball's executive vice president of baseball opera-tions after winning four World Series titles with the Yankees. That meant he was in charge of the umpires and player discipline, but Torre was also a former catcher who had worked for George Steinbrenner and Ted Turner as a manager. His ability to take punishment was unquestioned. "They did a good job with that," Torre said. "But then the priority became getting even. The game was no longer first and foremost. I would talk to the managers until I was blue in the face. I really think they started doing it because the players wanted them to. That became a concern of mine."

"Frank Robinson had that job before Joe did," Tschida said. "His thing was: eject them without a warning."

Eventually Tschida and the umpires learned to detect motivation. Some managers, like Dick Williams, Gene Mauch, and Ralph Houk, would hold their powder before retaliating, maybe for the next series. Back when pitchers still were hitters, some pitchers might take their pound of flesh after they had pitched five innings, knowing they could get the win even if they were ejected. "The way we used it was Texas justice," Tschida said. "But the pitchers have changed. I really do think it's taken away from the game."

But Tschida and other home-plate umpires will forget all those details long before they can erase the awful days, the ones in which hitters went down and couldn't rise again.

Tony Conigliaro hit his 100th big league home run when he was 22. No one in the American League had ever done that before. He was from suburban Boston, was playing for the Red Sox, was young and handsome and about to be rich, and deeply sampled everything that came with it. Dick Williams was one of several veterans who roomed with him because the Sox hoped someone could settle him down. No use, it turned out. "I never saw him," Williams said. "I was imparting veteran knowledge to a suitcase."

Yet Tony C had a way of bringing out the parent in everyone. Ted Williams told Conigliaro's business partner that the kid should quit crowding the plate so much because pitchers would eventually come inside. That was on August 17, 1967. The partner relayed the message, and Conigliaro said that if anything he would stand even closer. The next night, the Angels' Jack

Hamilton threw a fastball in the fourth inning that sailed in on Conigliaro. Players weren't wearing ear flaps on their helmets in those days. Conigliaro later said he tried to get out of the way "but it was like the ball was following me."

It blasted him in the cheek and knocked him nearly senseless. The Red Sox had to bring out a stretcher for him. Conigliaro was taken to Sancta Maria Hospital, and his left eye was completely shut. This was a civic trauma on several levels. The Red Sox were chasing a totally unforeseen pennant, one they eventually won on the final day of the season. And Conigliaro was a golden child. "That kid will hit 500 home runs," Angels coach Don Heffner predicted.

Two examples of Conigliaro's widespread fan appeal were Barbara Belkin and Lorraine DiLuzio, in their 20s. They were in the middle of their Friday night bowling league when they heard about the beaning. They didn't know Conigliaro personally, but they immediately left for the hospital, where they were told nobody was allowed in. "We'll send him some flowers tomorrow," Barbara vowed.

He needed more than flowers. Conigliaro missed the rest of 1967 and 1968. He did return in 1969 and hit 36 home runs in 1970. Strangely enough, the Red Sox traded him to the Angels, where he rented a place and realized things might be looking up when he learned Raquel Welch was his next door neighbor.

But Conigliaro was carrying a secret. He could no longer see out of the middle of his eye. On July 10 he retired, finishing that season with a .222 average and four home runs. He ended what turned out to be his final game with a couple of furious arguments with umpires. Lefty Phillips, the Angels' manager, thought Conigliaro belonged in an institution.

Conigliaro did make one false-start comeback with Boston in 1975, where he received a three-minute ovation before his first at-bat in Fenway Park. But he couldn't make it to the summer and retired for good. He suffered a heart attack in 1982, two days after the Red Sox had agreed to make him Harrelson's replacement in the broadcast booth, and he couldn't overcome the subsequent brain damage. At 45, he was dead.

Forty years prior, another vicious pitch curtailed another career. Mickey Cochrane was the third catcher elected to the Hall of Fame, a two-time Most Valuable Player who was a major axis of the great 1931 Philadelphia Athletics. When it was over, Cochrane had a .313 batting average for the Tigers, who had second baseman Charlie Gehringer and first baseman Hank Greenberg. Amid all the sports celebrities of the 1930s like Joe Louis, Jesse Owens, Babe Didrikson, and Lou Gehrig, Cochrane had a healthy following. Just after the Athletics won that World Series, Mutt and Lovell Mantle named their newborn son Mickey, in Spavinaw, Oklahoma, after him.

Cochrane was 34, serving as the Tigers' player/manager in 1937. On May 25 of that year, Cochrane launched a home run in Yankee Stadium off Irving "Bump" Hadley. He came up again in the fifth inning, and Hadley's 3–1 pitch came up and in and never changed course until it took a frightening bounce off Cochrane's head. Cochrane's skull was cracked in three places. He was whisked to St. Elizabeth's Hospital in New York and did not return to Detroit until June 8, where newspaper readers were warned not to gather outside Cochrane's home or take photos. With the possibility of infection, it was no sure thing that Cochrane would survive. In the hospital Hadley had tried to pay his respects but was told no visitors were allowed.

Hadley insisted the pitch was an accident. When Cochrane could speak publicly, he exonerated Hadley. "He's not the type of man who would throw at somebody and, besides, why would he throw a beanball on a 3–1 count?" he said. When Hadley next pitched in Detroit, the crowd remembered what Cochrane said and cheered him.

Another Hall of Fame player whose career was felled by the final fastball he saw was Kirby Puckett, perhaps the happiest warrior who ever played. There was no better scene on a typical baseball day than Puckett's arrival in the Minnesota Twins' clubhouse, as he walked to the lockers and either needled, encouraged, or celebrated every player he saw. Puckett was a square fellow, maybe 5'8" with an expanding midsection, but his bat was a merciless detonator, and he played the outfield and ran the bases with an epicurean glee. The Twins won two World Series with Puckett, and he led the American League in hits four times, recording 2,304 of them overall.

He had none after September 28, 1995. Cleveland's Dennis Martinez rode a fastball high and tight on Puckett, and it hit him straight on the upper jaw, breaking it. Puckett took one halting step backward and then collapsed. Cleveland catcher Tony Pena immediately knelt by his side, and Tschida, working the plate, beckoned the Twins' training staff to come out.

Puckett would spend the winter recuperating. But in spring training of 1996, he woke up with no vision in his right eye. He was diagnosed with glaucoma and never played baseball again. In 2006 he suffered the stroke that killed him. He was 45.

There is no direct, provable connection between the beanball and the loss of vision and the stroke, but the shame is that Puckett had several brilliant years left in him. Martinez was mortified when he saw Puckett writhing, saying later that he almost took himself out of the game. "I called the first two strikes," Tschida said. "The second one could have been outside. Kirby always set up right on top of the plate. Then Martinez came inside, but it was almost on the plate. He had such good control. For a split-second sometimes, you get that feeling. This guy's not moving, and you just scream. That's what Tony Pena and I both did together. 'Look out!' Kirby did not see that ball. He got hit with no protection. It's a sound I can still hear…It sounded like a cat fell out of a 10-story window and landed on the sidewalk."

Baseball is indeed played on a minefield. Cleveland pitcher Herb Score, the 1956 American League Rookie of the Year, never was the same after the Yankees' Gil McDougald sent a line drive off his eye on May 7, 1957. Catcher Ray Fosse absorbed Pete Rose's shoulder block at home plate in the deciding play in the 1970 All-Star Game. He was hitting .312 with 16 home runs at the time for Cleveland. He had two home runs in the 42 games he played after that and he never approached those offensive numbers again.

There's a difference between coincidence and recklessness. Drysdale and his peers tried to live within the margins of that difference, and there were days when Drysdale didn't mind crossing the line. It's a grim distinction. Not everyone in baseball bought it. "If a guy hit a home run off me, it was my fault," said Larry Dierker, the Houston right-hander of the 1960s and 1970s. "I don't think the whole thing about knocking down guys made the game better."

Perhaps the final word should go to Christy Mathewson, one of the most virtuous and accomplished pitchers who ever lived. Mathewson was a Bucknell graduate and serious about religion. He refused to pitch in Sunday games in the three ballparks that allowed them. He teamed with baseball writer Hugh Fullerton to uncover the Black Sox scandal of 1919, in which the White Sox took money to lose a World Series to Cincinnati.

When Fred Merkle, Mathewson's teammate on the Giants, neglected to step on second base during what appeared to be a game-winning rally in 1908, the umpires noticed that the Cubs retrieved the ball and stepped on second, forcing Merkle. They disallowed the run, fans at New York's Polo Grounds rioted, the umpires called it a tie and halted it on account of darkness, and it took 13 days to clear it up. Mathewson told the league president that Merkle, his teammate, had indeed failed to touch second. The tie became a New York loss. That enabled a one-game playoff for the National League pennant that the Giants lost to the Cubs. If there was a moral compass in baseball, Mathewson held it in his hands.

So when Mathewson wrote a book about pitching, he addressed the beanball. Because he was a man of his times, he approved of it. "When a new player breaks into the League, he is put to the most severe test by the other team to see if he is 'yellow.' If he is found wanting, he is hopeless in the Big League, for the news will spread and he will receive no quarter," Mathewson wrote. "It is the cardinal sin in a ball player. A favorite trick of a catcher is to say to a new batter: 'Look out for this fellow. He's got a mean 'bean' ball and he hasn't any influence over it. There's a poor 'boob' in the hospital that stopped one with his head. Then the catcher signs for a pitcher to throw the next one at the young batter's head. If he pulls away, an unpardonable sin in baseball, the dose is repeated. [You] almost had your foot in the water-pail over by the bench that time,' says the catcher. Bing! Up comes another 'beaner.' Then, after the catcher has sized the new man up, he makes his report. 'He won't do. He's yellow.' And the players keep mercilessly after this shortcoming, this ingrained fault which, unlike a mechanical error, cannot be corrected until the new player is driven out of the league."

In other words, most successful pitchers started their whole careers mad. It's part of the job description. Drysdale, more than any of them, was just extremely loud and incredibly close.

3

I'm Beginning to
See the Light

Of all the noises that rose toward Vin Scully's booth at the Los Angeles Coliseum, one was unique and personal. Whenever Scully heard a particular piercing whistle, he knew Scotty Drysdale was there. "You could hear it all over the place," Scully said.

Scotty had played a little baseball in his time. While the Dodgers were serving in their "bridge" ballpark between Ebbets Field and Dodger Stadium, Scotty was working for them as a part-time scout.

His day job was at the Pacific Telephone and Telegraph company as a foreman and an installer. When his son, Don, was pitching—and many times when he wasn't—Scotty was just behind the dugout. But baseball was no longer the means to anything. He was with the Los Angeles Angels organization in the Pacific Coast League at the time. The Angels were a farm club of the Chicago Cubs and they also had a lower affiliate in Oklahoma. That's where Scotty went—to the Ponca City Angels in 1935. Their manager was Mike Gazella, who had been a bit player on the legendary 1927 Yankees. None of that currency was good in Ponca City. These Angels were in the Western Association, where the Great Depression was embossed on the land and everyone who lived there. Beaten by the one-two punch of an epochal drought and the nonexistent economy, 18 percent of Oklahomans left the state during the 1930s. There were 40 major dust storms there in 1935 alone.

Scotty started the first game of a doubleheader against Hutchinson on May 30. He got the win 9–4, giving up four runs and five hits in six innings. Overall, he was 1–3 with a 6.69 ERA. There was no money in baseball, especially there. His mother, Myrtle, said in 1962, the year Don won 25 games, that Scotty had picked up the measles in Oklahoma, and the sandstorms were out of control. She suggested he come home and try something else, even though she was convinced he could have been a major league star. Scotty disputed her evaluation. All moms feel that way, he said.

There were semi-pro teams all over Southern California, and Scotty kept playing. The most famed of those were the Rosabell Plumbers based in Pasadena. Future major leaguers like Hank Sauer and Lou "The Mad Russian" Novikoff played for Rosabell. In 1936 the Plumbers won 51 games and lost two. Their owner was Charlie Pedrotti, who founded the Rosabell Plumbing Company near Chavez Ravine. In the 1940s Pedrotti would occasionally turn over the team to the mighty USC program, including coach Raoul "Rod" Dedeaux and Bill Sharman, who became a Boston Celtics star, a Los Angeles Lakers championship coach, and even played his way into the Dodgers dugout at the end of the 1951 season.

Scotty found other teams, too. Don, born in 1936, would spend weekend afternoons in the 1940s riding to games with his dad. He began playing, and when Scotty wasn't available to play catch, Don's mother, Verna, was. "He wore out the carpet in the car with his spikes," Scotty said. Don would take his bat and whack tennis balls against the side of the house—in the midst of so many other houses in the sudden city of Van Nuys and so many American Dreams.

*   *   *

Isaac Van Nuys acted on the California dream in 1865. He moved west from Kentucky and opened a general store. He and Isaac Lankershim became partners in a property company and by 1911 they were quite the entrepreneurs, shipping grain to Europe and buying a hotel in downtown Los Angeles. Mostly, they were in the business of envisioning. When William Mulholland began building the aqueduct that would bring water from Owens Valley, Van Nuys and Lankershim were ready. They bought 47,500 acres worth of land from what was an old ranch northwest of Los Angeles. On February 22, 1911, they held an auction, and a line of Pierce-Arrows and Packards formed quickly. Two trains lined up to bring more people, and the crowd was estimated at 15,000.

As the auctioneer took deep breaths, a lot was sold every three minutes. There were 150 plots sold that day for a total of $75,000, but officials from the land company owned by Van Nuys and Lankershim promised $1 million worth of further development. In April the electric train line, which was considered the most sophisticated of its kind in the world, would connect this new town with L.A. and, presumably, the world.

Colonel Tom Fitch, a renowned trial lawyer, spoke to the crowd on February 22 and spoke and spoke. Those, who could bear to listen to the whole spiel, could hear the blueprint for the next half-century. "There is but one Southern California in all the world, and nowhere else in all the world does the material exist in any country for the making of another," Fitch told the *Los Angeles Times*. "God broke the die with which he stamped beauty and fruitfulness upon this valley, which surrounds us on every side. Los Angeles is the Aurora, the eternal morning of American cities. Time will never write a wrinkle on her fair brow or cause decrepitude to lessen the speed of her advance in population, in wealth, and in program."

Fitch went on to predict that L.A. "will develop into a great manufacturing city without smoke and without smell…The trolley line will run through the center of the most beautiful boulevard in the world. I do not need to describe it for you. It is at your feet. Van Nuys is to be a city of itself as well as part of the great city to which it will be married. Orchards and vineyards will surround it in the near—yes, immediate—future, and it will make no difference what prices you may pay now for lots and acreage tracts. They will increase in value every day."

Some of Fitch's visions came to life, particularly the steepening of real estate prices. Otherwise, he was somewhat grandiose. But, if anything, he underestimated the tidal wave of humanity that was coming to the San Fernando Valley in general. The population of the Valley in 1920 was 21,000. Twenty years later it was 112,000. Twenty years after that, it was 800,000, and then it nearly doubled by the dawn of the 21st century, which will surprise no one who has attempted to go north on U.S. 101 from downtown Los Angeles.

Van Nuys lured a General Motors assembly plant to town in 1947. The Valley became the nation's aerospace capital. Motion picture and television studios moved in. Van Nuys' airport became the third busiest in the nation and still is the busiest for private flights. The "most beautiful boulevard" that Col. Fitch cited was actually Van Nuys Boulevard, which became famous for kids cruising in their convertibles on weekend nights. It was widely assumed that George Lucas' *American Graffiti*, which was filmed in 1973 and instantly became a cultural touchstone, was based on that boulevard, but that was modeled on Modesto, California, Lucas' hometown.

Nostalgia works in mysterious ways. Those who grew up in the San Fernando Valley, Orange County, and most parts of Los Angeles remember the orange trees, the endless summers, the innocent facade of high school life, and the other illusions of the 1960s and 1970s. If you ask them if it really was paradise, most of them will confirm it. The symbol of the Valley, at least until it developed a thriving pornography industry, was the situation comedy, the kind on which Drysdale sometimes appeared. *Leave It to Beaver* was typical. There were no drugs or thoughts of suicide or fears of school shootings on the street where the Cleavers lived. In fact, Tony Dow, the actor who played Wally Cleaver, Beaver's older brother, was a graduate of Van Nuys High as Drysdale was.

Every week, the *Van Nuys High Mirror* would run a gossip column that shined a light on the real stories of the hallways and the lockers. "Cynthia Newell has a crush on Jay Strong," it reported. And: "Marsha Connelly thinks Dari Rossi ought to give the other girls a chance." And: "Peggy Rose doesn't seem to be making much progress with Chuck Randall. How about it, Chuck?" Apparently, Drysdale's relationships weren't interesting enough to mention, except when he was once seen with Darlene Bateman at a party. As for his classmate Robert Redford, who briefly played first base for the Wolves, the columnist spotted him with Wanda Shannon, but there was no follow-up activity.

Drysdale said he was friendly with but not terribly close to Redford, who was known as "Bob" back then. "But mostly we were both trying to get to first base with Diane Baker," he said, referring to a classmate who became a TV actor of note and starred in *The Diary of Anne Frank* in 1959.

Underneath the carefree veneer, the kindling was building in the other Los Angeles, the flip side that would bubble with toil and trouble. The neighborhoods in the Valley and in other suburbs were almost uniformly white. As chronicled by Mike Davis and Jon Wiener in the book *Set the Night on Fire: L.A. In The Sixties*, a Federal Housing Association survey showed that between 1950 and 1954 there were 125,000 housing units built in greater Los Angeles. Only 3,000 of those were open to persons of color.

That's just a statistic. What resonated more was the purchase of a home in Pacoima by Emory Holmes, a Black psychologist. In the first month of his family's residency, Holmes observed a raft of hostile incidents, including tacks in the driveway, two visits by a mortician offering to pick up the dead body in the house, several unsolicited service calls such as the one from a TV repairman at 11:00 PM, and a painted message on the side of the house: "Black cancer here. Don't let it spread."

The White man, who sold Holmes the house, moved to Northridge and was fired from his job. A demonstration in front of his house turned loud and nearly violent. Los Angeles police chief William H. Parker was legendary for his surveillance methods and his aggressive hassling of Blacks and Latinos. Many Americans associated Los Angeles with the hit police drama *Dragnet*, starring Jack Webb and featuring the profile of City Hall as a lead-in. Parker's public information department went over the scripts with Webb and the producers each week, stripping away the racism for the most part but generally portraying the police as efficient, formidable, and as taciturn as Webb was when he said, "Just the facts, ma'am." Webb felt police officers were slandered by the media and some showbiz productions.

He died of a heart attack in 1982, and L.A. police chief Daryl Gates, a notable hard-liner who was once Parker's driver, decreed that Badge No. 714, worn by Webb's character Sgt. Joe Friday, would be permanently retired.

*   *   *

Scotty and Verna Drysdale lived immaculately. That filtered down to the kids. Bob Uecker, the catcher-turned-comic actor, would call Don "Felix Unger." By all accounts, Don and his sister Nancy were close to their parents, and it wasn't hard to see where Don got his humor and needling ability. "If Verna thought you were saying something that wasn't true, she'd say, 'Your butt is full of blue mud,'" said Scott Fieux, Nancy's son. "That was a Verna original."

"She had the Drysdale nose," said Ann Meyers Drysdale, who married Don in 1986. "She was quite a personality, and Donnie got a lot of his personality from her. She was tough. And I always loved the relationship Donnie had with Scotty. There was just a comfortableness about them when they were together, watching games, hanging out. Donnie always kissed our three children every night. He said if you kissed your children every night, they would kiss theirs, too. That's what Scotty did with him."

"But if you think I have a temper," Drysdale said one night, when his latest tantrum was being analyzed, "you should see my dad."

The Drysdales often spent the holidays at the ranch owned by Nancy and her husband Ed. It was on Bonsall, near Temecula, California, northeast of San Diego. She was an American Airlines flight attendant. He was a pilot. There were times when Nancy arranged to work the Dodgers flights before Peter O'Malley arranged for the *Kay-O'*, the team plane he named after his wife. Poker and bridge were involved, and Nancy was right in the middle of it. "My mom had a really wicked, sharp sense of humor," Scott Fieux said. "She had a very good personality for the job she had. Eventually, my dad got tired of the hustle and bustle. He wanted to retire and be a farmer. He bought the ranch, and there was absolutely nothing there at the time. We thought it was great."

The ranch was eight-and-a-half acres with avocados and oranges. The family raised cows and chickens and pigs. Scott and his brother, Kelly, were in the 4-H club. Whenever Don could get there, he got there, and Ann, who grew up with 10 siblings, reveled in it, too. "I remember standing up on the hearth so I could be close enough to talk to my uncle," Scott Fieux said. "We didn't really have much of a sense of how famous he was. He was just my uncle. Then I'd hear stories about how he used to throw high and tight to people and I remember the Hall of Fame ceremonies and what a big deal it was to people that he and Ann were married because she was such a great athlete in her own right. I'd start thinking, *Wow, he's not just my uncle. He's had an impact on the national pastime.*"

It was a sudden impact. The only athletic trait Drysdale didn't possess in abundance was agility. "Small feet," Jeff Torborg, his Dodgers catcher, said.

For a few strange weeks, Drysdale's career twisted in the wind. His arm began hurting during his junior year to the point that he couldn't remove his T-shirt without gritting his teeth. Doctors showed him the X-rays, which were spooky. His hipbone might have been connected to his thigh bone, as the song said, but his humerus wasn't connected to his ulna. In other words, there was a big space in the place where his right arm was supposed to be joined. If a model train had run down the tracks of his arm, it would have derailed.

The doctors quickly added that when a kid had grown in a hurry and had begun pitching suddenly and in high volume, such a thing could happen, and it wasn't unheard of. In a few months, Drysdale's arm was intact and working again. He gave up quarterbacking in the interim, which was just as well.

In the 10th grade Don was only 5'4", which is not what Scotty and Verna had anticipated. He had been so big during Verna's pregnancy that doctors wanted the Drysdales about the possibility of triage. "Then save my wife," Scotty said.

It never came to that, but Scotty was well over six feet, and his son's growth spurt was behind schedule. At least it was behind schedule *vertically.* Don's teammates called him "Porky."

North Hollywood was Van Nuys' most traditional rival. The star pitcher for North Hollywood was Ralph Mauriello. He was a senior when Drysdale was a sophomore. He remembered little about Drysdale except for the time Don, as a second baseman, somehow convinced the umpire to call catcher's interference. Mauriello might have forgotten about it, but the next hitter homered, and Van Nuys won, 3–2. That was one of two games Mauriello lost in his high school career.

Perhaps the most underrated name in Drysdale's story is Roger Grabenstein's. He was supposed to pitch for Scotty's American Legion Post 193 team one day, but he didn't show up. Scotty told his second baseman, Don, to get ready. "Just throw strikes. Don't try to do too much," he said. Don did and pitched all seven innings.

Goldie Holt, the Dodgers' area scout, was there. A few days later, Holt then brought Drysdale to a nearby field, told him to throw 100 pitches, and tracked the number of strikes. Drysdale threw 85. Again, there were no radar guns in those days. Jesse Flores was a renowned area scout for decades, and his son, Steve, followed his lead. One day Steve brought a radar gun to the ballpark, and Jesse asked him what it was for. Steve said it measured how hard the pitcher throws. Jesse said, "Steve, the hitters tell you that."

Mauriello had already signed with the Dodgers as a bonus baby when he next saw Drysdale in February of 1954. Drysdale was a senior at Van Nuys, already coming off a solid pitching year. Mauriello showed up to throw batting practice. He asked Holt who the big guy was, throwing on the side. When Holt told him it was Drysdale, Mauriello assumed it was an older brother he hadn't met yet. He had no idea it was Don.

Drysdale made second-team All-City as a senior in 1954. The best pitcher in town was Barry Latman of Hollywood. He signed with the Chicago White Sox and would win 59 games over 11 major league years with four different teams. The most established pitcher for Van Nuys was Jim Heffer, who won 22-of-27 decisions in his three years with the Wolves. Heffer was way ahead of everyone on the growth chart. "He had a beard like Sal Maglie even at that age," Drysdale said.

Van Nuys didn't need any other pitchers. In 1954 Drysdale threw a no-hitter against Hollywood and beat Fairfax on a three-hitter in the city semifinal game. However, Dorsey High won the final when future USC and Baltimore Oriole star Don Buford started a first-inning rally off Heffer. That pitcher and Drysdale befriended and pushed each other, sometimes literally. When Heffer spilled some ink on one of Drysdale's class projects, the two went to Fist City, and Drysdale's punch left a scar on Heffer's forehead.

Drysdale ran into trouble against North Hollywood one day, and Heffer had to relieve him. "I'll save your butt," Heffer told him when they crossed paths. Then San Fernando roughed up Heffer the next week, and Drysdale came in. "Now it's my turn, smart ass," Drysdale told him.

Major league scouts followed both. There was no draft in those days. The best prospects were known as "bonus babies," and if they signed for more than $4,000, they had to spend their first seasons with the big league club. Back at Lafayette High in New York, Sandy Koufax was in that category. Drysdale was not, but the local scouts began to gather. Rosey Gilhousen, who would later sign George Brett for the Kansas City Royals, said Drysdale was the best pitching prospect in the city.

Drysdale even got to meet Branch Rickey, the Mahatma, the man who brought Jackie Robinson to the big leagues and had supervised the building of the Boys of Summer. Rickey was now running the Pittsburgh Pirates, but he wanted to see the prospects for himself.

On June 15, 1954, after Drysdale's high school graduation, Rickey filed this scouting report:

"6'4," 185 pounds, 18 years of age. A lot of artistry about this boy. Way above average fast ball. It is really good. Direction of the spin and the speed of rotation are the same on all fast ball pitches. Angle of delivery the same, stride is wide, and placement on fast and curve ball needs no coaching. Let him alone on all his fingering. He is good. I don't know about his agility or whether or not he has body control or can field his position, but his work on the hill itself has an unusual amount of stamina. Intelligent face and manner, shows good breeding.

"This boy's curve is fairly good and he shows control if it also. He has a change-up on his curve that is usable.

Change-up on the fast ball is too fast and he lets up on his delivery. This will take considerable work but I am very sure that this particular chap will acquire an effective change on his fast ball.

"It is my judgment that his aptitude would be far above average. He is a definite prospect. With proper handling, I could see this boy on the Pittsburgh club in two years. It is probable that this chap is worth whatever it takes except that Pittsburgh is in no position to make him a bonus player.

"This boy has a high scholastic record—almost a straight-A."

Drysdale was considering Stanford, in fact, and could have joined the cast of thousands who were dominating college baseball at USC. But the Dodgers offered $4,000, right up to the bonus baby limit. He signed at Otto's Pink Pig, a restaurant on Van Nuys Boulevard that Bob Hope and Dorothy Lamour sometimes visited. Sometimes it's good to be Porky.

Still 17, Drysdale would begin his pro journey with the Bakersfield Indians, the Dodgers' Class C team. The Indians played in Sam Lynn Park, which was laid out so that home plate faced west, and hitters dealt with the sunset for the first few innings of summertime games. It was apparent that the kid didn't need such help. He had pitched an exhibition inning with the Hollywood Stars against the Channel Cities minor league team and in succession struck out Al Gionfriddo, Don Demeter, and Dave Melton. All would become major leaguers, and Demeter would play alongside Drysdale in Brooklyn and Los Angeles.

Drysdale's first game was an 8–4 win against the Salinas Packers. Later he was matched up against Bob Thorpe of the Stockton Ports. Thorpe went 28–4 that season, pitched 300 innings, and completed 32 of his 33 starts. The Cubs jumped him all the way to the big league club. Thorpe suffered a sore arm, retired at 24, and, while working as an electrician's apprentice in San Diego, was electrocuted on a power line and died. On this night, Drysdale beat Thorpe 7–5 and went to finish his first pro season with an 8–5 record and a 3.48 ERA for a team that was 20 games over .500.

The 60', 6" path to the plate was not a problem. The long bus rides were. "Sitting on these buses is killing my knees," he told Scotty.

"Then pitch your way out of the bus league," Scotty replied.

That process began when Drysdale came to Vero Beach, Florida, the next spring. It took him all day to get there with several connecting flights, but he walked into the quaint complex amid the palm trees and realized the gravity of his destination. The pictures in his newspaper were now alive and walking all around him—from Gil Hodges to Roy Campanella to Don Newcombe. At one point Drysdale asked Campanella what he had to do to become worthy of the majors. "You don't have to change anything," Campanella told him. "Just keep doing what you're doing."

On March 8 the Dodgers held an intrasquad game: the Pitlers vs. the Hermans. Jackie Robinson pinch hit for the pitchers on both sides. When Drysdale came to the mound and delivered some warmup pitches that appeared to come from the Florida Panhandle, Robinson handed his bat to Charley Thompson. "I'm not ready to hit against that sort of stuff just yet," Robinson said.

Drysdale didn't think anybody was. "If I can win in Bakersfield, I can win here," he said. "I can make it up here right now. Why should I be sent out to Montreal?"

But he was. And he was the youngest player in his league for the second consecutive year. On the other hand, he was one step from the majors. Manager Greg Mulleavy, who became the Dodgers' first-base coach during their championship days of the 1960s, specifically asked for Drysdale. "We'll give him to you," said Fresco Thompson, the farm director. "But the first time you skip him in the rotation, you're losing him."

"He's only spent one year in organized baseball," Mulleavy told *The Montreal Gazette*. "You wouldn't think a kid like that would be ready for Triple A. But every once in a while, it happens. You get a Johnny Podres."

Podres had won the clinching game of the Dodgers' first successful World Series the year before. He had won 21 games for the Dodgers' Class D team in Hazard, Kentucky, as a rookie, then spent a year in Montreal on the way to Brooklyn.

Drysdale kept getting the older players out in his early starts in Montreal. His fiery side also began to show. He was kicked out of a game against Toronto for disputing balls and strikes. During a sweltering doubleheader in Havana, Cuba, Drysdale took a dim view of the way teammate Chico Fernandez declined to take out the second baseman in the midst of a double play. He lost 1–0 and he picked up a chair in the clubhouse.

"Don't throw it," Mulleavy said.

Across the room left-hander Tom Lasorda was getting ready to pitch the second game. "Go ahead and throw it," he told Drysdale, who did. It left a sizeable hole in the clubhouse wall.

A couple of hours later, Lasorda came back in, steaming in more ways than one. He, too, had lost 1–0. "Throw the chair," Drysdale yelled. "Throw it."

Lasorda did, widening the hole in the wall by a chair's length.

Lasorda was already a celebrity in Montreal. He pitched nine seasons there, won 107 games, and, in a three-season stretch beginning in 1952, won 45 games and lost 18. The Dodgers only called him up on two occasions, and his major league record was 0–4. In 1955 he was sent down because the Dodgers kept Koufax, the bonus baby. He managed to stay miffed about that until the day he died in 2021. In between, Lasorda became the most famous manager in the game with two World Series championships, a gold medal with the U.S. Olympic team in 2000, and, eventually, a place in Cooperstown.

Lasorda showed Drysdale how to take the game seriously and, if necessary, personally. And Drysdale surely noticed the way Lasorda made hitters sprawl. "Tommy would knock guys down just for fun," Mauriello said.

Along the way, Drysdale took on a soft-drink machine and lost. The official story was that he was upset with the way his game had gone, and he tried a right cross and paid for it with a broken metacarpal. He attempted to freeze it with ethyl chloride on gamedays and he kept pitching, and when it healed, it was positioned at a different angle. Some thought it actually helped the movement on his breaking ball.

Mauriello said he had heard another version of this from Glenn Mickens, Drysdale's Montreal teammate. Drysdale was having a beer when a stranger asked him where he was from. When Drysdale answered, "California," the fellow said, "Oh, the land of fruits and nuts." Drysdale thereupon knocked the fellow off his barstool, and his hand took the brunt.

In any event, Drysdale's record was 11–11 with a 3.33 ERA. He also hit eight batters. A pitcher like Drysdale in the modern era would be given more time to refine himself. The two biggest walks-per-nine-innings rates of his career were in those minor league seasons. As he improved his slider, he also got more strikeouts. But even then Drysdale gave up few home runs: just 20 in 43 minor league games. "He's the best right-handed pitcher in the league right now," said Reggie Otero, the Havana manager.

The Royals won the International League regular season pennant by a half-game over Toronto. They were eliminated in the semifinals of the playoffs by Rochester. Drysdale was not involved in the games. The innings had mounted in his lightly used shoulder, and he went to New York for a consultation. Buzzie Bavasi, the Dodgers' general manager, said doctors thought it was bursitis. Drysdale went home and avoided throwing for most of the winter.

He felt fine when he resumed and prepared for another flight—or several—to get to Vero Beach in the spring. He figured he would prepare for another season in Triple A and then maybe Brooklyn would call him up sometime during the season. After all, this was a world championship club. But 1955 didn't immunize the Dodgers from 1956. Billy Loes hurt his arm. Karl Spooner, once considered their next great pitcher, hurt his arm. Don Bessent hurt his arm in a very Florida way by throwing a golf club at a snake that had invaded the fairway. And Podres had been drafted by the Army. For Drysdale there was daylight.

Five of Drysdale's six starts in exhibition season were major league quality, including six strong innings in an exhibition against Milwaukee in Jacksonville, Florida. He pitched 23 spring training innings and gave up 21 hits and eight runs. "That kid," manager Walter Alston said, shaking his head, "Every day he comes to pitch."

Umpire Augie Donatelli would cause a stir 12 years later by running his hands through Drysdale's hair in search of performance-enhancing fluids. In the spring of 1956, he worked the game in Jacksonville. "He's the best-looking pitcher I've seen all spring," Donatelli said. "And I've seen some good ones. You don't find kids like him every day. It's really something the way he can hit that outside corner with his fastball. He hits it like Sal Maglie. Only he's a lot faster than Maglie."

"I'd keep him on the team just based on what he showed today," general manager Buzzie Bavasi said. "Wouldn't you?

The weeks went by, the cards kept falling, and Drysdale found himself with the team, going north to Milwaukee. When they got to Brooklyn, Bavasi called him in and said he was Dodgers-certified and on the varsity. "Perhaps no kid in history has pitched fewer baseballs to become a major leaguer," Dick Young wrote in the *New York Daily News*. "Exclusive of exhibitions, he has worked in 53 ball games. That includes 10 high school games in his senior year at Van Nuys, Calif."

Drysdale's only problem was his lust to throw the ball as soon as catcher Campanella threw it back to him. Campanella fixed that with frequent visits to the mound and with the way he knocked the mud off his spikes, using one foot against the other. "I've got the cleanest pair of spikes in the game," he said, laughing.

And every now and then, Drysdale would give away how much of a greenhorn he was. Drysdale still had some finer points to digest. He and Maglie were scheduled to pitch a doubleheader, and he asked Maglie, "Are you going to pitch the long one or the short one?" In the minors one game of a twin bill would be nine innings, and the other was seven. Maglie informed Drysdale that in this league everything goes nine.

Drysdale ordered subscriptions to the New York newspapers and had them sent to Van Nuys. Then he got ready for his first major league start on April 23 in Philadelphia. The fans in Connie Mack Stadium had whiled away the late innings of the previous game by throwing bottles at the New York Giants' fielders to the point that some of the Giants found batting helmets and wore them at their positions. It was also cold the night of Drysdale's starting debut—so cold that every other game in Major League Baseball was postponed.

Drysdale, by then known as "Airedale" by his teammates, was antsy in the hotel lobby in the middle of the afternoon, checking out the gray sky and waiting for the bus. Teammate Jim Hughes laughed when he saw him. "Hey, Airedale, stop worrying," he said. "They'll call the game."

Or they won't. When they didn't, Drysdale got on the mound, and suddenly it was sunny and warm and very Van Nuys in his mind. As 12,690 fans took their blankets and jackets to Connie Mack Stadium, the first Phillies batter that Drysdale faced was Richie Ashburn, an eventual Hall of Famer who handled the bat like a composer's baton.

Long before announcers talked about batters "spoiling" pitches with foul balls, Ashburn was the main supplier of souvenirs to folks in foul territory. In 1957 he fouled a ball off the nose of Alice Roth, whose husband was the sports editor of *The Evening Bulletin*. The paramedics gathered quickly and began to cart off the bloodied Mrs. Roth…just as Ashburn fouled off another pitch that hit her in the knee. Legend has it that one of Alice's sons later asked her if she could take him to a Philadelphia Eagles game so he could get hit with a football.

The point is that Ashburn, a .308 lifetime hitter with 2,574 hits, struck out 571 times in his 15-year career and walked 1,198 times. He never struck out more than 50 times in a season and struck out only 45 times in 1956. The first time he faced Drysdale, he struck out swinging. Bobby Morgan was behind him and he struck out. Granny Hamner was behind Morgan and he struck out, too. Three up, three down, no fair balls.

Could the game be this easy? The Dodgers got three runs off Murry Dickson, who had made his major league debut when Drysdale was two years old. Drysdale, in fact, got a one-out single at the beginning of that rally and scored when Pee Wee Reese singled. Four of the Phillies' nine hits came in the eighth and ninth innings, and a sacrifice fly by Hamner ruined the shutout. Drysdale won 5–1 with nine hits, nine strikeouts, and a walk. "Here," Campanella declared, "is your next Rookie of the Year."

After the game Drysdale used the clubhouse phone and called Scotty in Van Nuys.

Six days later the Pirates would beat up Drysdale in a 10–1 win. He would spend the whole of 1956 with the Dodgers, turn 20 on July 23, start occasionally, relieve occasionally, and generally was a peripheral contributor to another National League pennant. He was 5–5 with a 2.64 ERA and, yes, he hit three batters in those 99 innings, all in losses, two of them the final batters he would face.

In October Drysdale sat in the dugout and watched the Yankees' Don Larsen throw a perfect game in the World Series. Not a bad year. Now the only buses in his life were the ones he would ride from the hotel to the ballpark and back. He assumed the long rides were in his past and that Brooklyn would fill up his foreseeable future.

4

THERE USED TO BE A BALLPARK

When the Brooklyn Dodgers moved to Los Angeles in 1958, everything in baseball tilted. It was probably the starkest, most significant relocation by any sports franchise before or since. Only the Cleveland Browns' move to Baltimore approaches it.

For one thing, the Dodgers took the Giants with them, depositing them in San Francisco, and the Giants had (and still have) a more successful tradition than did (and do) the Dodgers. For another, it reduced New York's Major League Baseball membership by two-thirds, and for most of the country, New York was the planet around which baseball had revolved. Nineteen times between 1932 and 1957, at least one New York team had played in the World Series.

But the Dodgers did not sneak out of Brooklyn in disguise or take a moving van west in the middle of the night. Walter O'Malley, the Dodgers' owner, had made his intentions known. He badly wanted a new ballpark near the train station on Flatbush and Atlantic Avenues. Robert Moses, the legendary planning director of New York City and a man with more influence than any mayor or team owner, was just as publicly opposed. In 1956 and 1957, the Dodgers scheduled 15 "home" games in Jersey City, a way of pressuring Brooklyn officials to approve the stadium plan. Dick Young, who covered the Dodgers for the *New York Daily News*, began one game story with the phrase, "Inching their way westward…"

Finally, O'Malley, with significant help from L.A. City Council member Roz Wyman, convinced Giants owner Horace Stoneham to bathe in California's milk and honey. So the final game in Ebbets Field was on September 24. There was no ceremony, no field-storming at game's end to literally steal the bases, and not really any kind of last good-bye. Danny McDevitt pitched a five-hitter, and the Dodgers beat Pittsburgh 2–0. Only 6,702 attended, following an attendance pattern that had cost the Dodgers 800,000 fans since 1947. Chris Kieran of the *New York Daily News* called it "one of the most poorly attended wakes in the history of baseball."

Ebbets Field organist Gladys Goodding found every maudlin melody she could find, concluding with "Auld Lang Syne" when the usual walk-out song, "Follow The Dodgers," was started and interrupted. Before that she had played "Que Sera Sera," "Am I Blue?", "Thanks For The Memories," "Say It Isn't So," and "When The Blue Of The Night Meets The Gold Of The Day."

Oddly, the ground crew covered home plate and the mound, raked the field, and generally went about its duties after the game as if it expected another game to be played there. Emmett Kelly, the famed clown, sat in the dugout with catcher Roy Campanella before the game and wiped away ersatz tears. A few spectators hung around to express regrets. But by then it was fait accompli and hardly a civic cataclysm, though hundreds of thousands of folks, who claimed to be on hand, have tried to make it so.

Among the saddest people on hand were the Dodgers themselves. Perhaps the saddest of that group was Don Drysdale, who had turned 20 in July but still led the pitching staff in strikeouts. His new workplace would be the Los Angeles Coliseum, only 23 miles from Drysdale's birthplace in Van

Nuys. But Brooklyn was his new home geographically and culturally. The players did not just come to life when the Ebbets Field lights came on. They were neighbors, customers, parishioners, pedestrians. The guy at the cleaners, the butcher, the cop on the street were all familiar. They were in a place where everybody knew their names. Rarely did anyone abuse that privilege.

Their loudest critic was their best loyalist. Hilda Chester, the famous fan known as Howlin' Hilda, had a voice envied by foghorns. "I love you, Vin Scully," she once boomed, as the young Fordham grad continued his narration in the press box. Chester cleared her throat. "Look at me when I tell you that!" she commanded.

Drysdale loved the place, the ballpark, the town, all of it. As he mentioned in his book, *Once a Bum, Always a Dodger*, he and his teammates ingested many thousands of calories at Armando's Italian Restaurant on Montague Street down the way from the Dodgers' offices. Drysdale was broadcasting Dodgers games in 1988, so when the club went to play the Mets, he decided to revisit the neighborhood, which is something Scully, a native New Yorker, never did.

Big D was crestfallen to see all the changes and how faint the Dodgers' footprint had become, especially when he realized that the site of Ebbets Field now contained apartments with no commemoration of the home of the Boys of Summer. The death of Ebbets Field inspired Joe Raposo to write "There Used To Be A Ballpark" in 1973. Frank Sinatra, Drysdale's friend and Raposo's biggest fan, made it a hit:

"Now the children try to find it
And they can't believe their eyes
'Cause the old team just isn't playing
And the new team hardly tries

And the sky has got so cloudy

When it used to be so clear

And the summer went so quickly this year.

Yes, there used to be a ballpark right here."

But on the day of Drysdale's homecoming, he got out of the car in front of Armando's and someone on the sidewalk saw him and yelled, "Hey, Drysdale!" Big D hadn't thrown a pitch in Brooklyn in 30 years. Armando's was the Dodgers' hangout. Arthur Miller and Marilyn Monroe were frequent diners, too. It finally gave up the economic ghost in 2018 after 82 years. It is closed, and so for a while was the Bossert Hotel, where Dodgers callups would stay and where the 1955 champions had their victory party attended by Scully and his date Joan Ganz, the eventual creator of *Sesame Street*. Ian Schrager's hotel group is planning to redo the Bossert.

All around the Bossert, Brooklyn has become prosperous and hip and it built Barclays Center, where the NBA's Nets play. Barclays Center's address is Flatbush and Atlantic, literally an escalator ride above the Long Island Railroad and several subway lines. It is exactly where O'Malley wanted to build the new Ebbets Field.

Even Shea Stadium, which opened in 1964 for the Mets, is long gone. So, presumably, are the holdover fans from the 1950s who used to seek out Scully when the Dodgers would play the Mets. "So, Vinnie," one would invariably ask, "when do you think they're going to come back?"

Diplomatically, Scully would tell them that, no, the Dodgers probably aren't coming back.

*   *   *

From 1950 to 1960, the population of Los Angeles County rose from 4.15 million to 6.04 million. The state zoomed from 10.5 million to 15.7 million and would almost double itself between 1950 and 1970. So the Dodgers were only doing what the rest of America was doing, what Oklahomans had done to escape the Dust Bowl, what New Yorkers were increasingly considering.

In 1940 representatives of six other states outnumbered New York natives among residents of California, but by 1990 more California residents had come from New York than from any other state. Ralph Mauriello's family made the jump in the late 1940s from the Williamsburg section of Brooklyn. His father, Salvatore, had come to New York from Italy. He was a barber, reluctant to take vacations because he would miss out on customers.

One day Salvatore looked up and saw a plane. It made him decide to visit California. He and his wife went to the airline office, peeled off two $100 bills, and flew to Los Angeles on a Friday night. "We didn't have a phone in our house," Mauriello said. "I was at my sister's. She was three years older. She gets a telegram: 'Send Ralph out here. He's a big boy. You can meet us later. We're moving to L.A.' So here I am, 14 years old, getting on a plane for California. It was September 1, 1949, and when I landed, it was 100 degrees. But there was a tree and there was a park. Everything around me in Williamsburg was buildings and concrete. And now we had a real refrigerator, not just an icebox."

The first place they lived was near Echo Park, close to Chavez Ravine. Salvatore eventually decided the San Fernando Valley would be better. The family settled next to a Red Car station, where Ralph could board a streetcar. The Red and Yellow Cars were part of what was the Pacific Electric Railway System. In the 1920s it was the largest of its kind in the world. It operated well beyond the city limits into Riverside, Orange, and San Bernardino counties. By the time the Mauriellos came, the system was doomed, thanks to freeway construction and the onset of the automobile. For a kid like Ralph, already accustomed to the New York subways, it was somewhere in the neighborhood of paradise. "The Red Cars went from Long Beach to Glendale," Mauriello said, describing a 32-mile line, as he sat in a restaurant booth near his home in Simi Valley. "The stop was a half-block from where we lived in Echo Park. I could take the Red Car to school in the Los Feliz district. The Green Car operated on a narrow gauge track. If you wanted to go to the Coliseum to see the Rams, back then you'd take the Green Car, and it would go down Figueroa and then Vermont. My dad needed a license to operate out here. I had to help him with the tests. He had trouble with the English part of it. He was a whiz in math, but he had spent all his life figuring it out with his fingers. I had to teach him long division. I started baseball, and he was very much into it. I remember hitting a baseball and breaking a window across the street. He was so proud."

Mauriello would eventually play for USC and pitch for the Dodgers.

Rene Lachemann remembers riding his bike to the Los Angeles Coliseum when he was serving as an attendant in the visiting clubhouse. He'd ride all the way from his home in southwest L.A. He would also ride to Rancho playground and sometimes leave the bike there. Somehow it never rode away before Lachemann got back. "Or you could hitchhike if you wanted," Lachemann said. "We didn't have Little League like it's organized today. Benny Lefebvre, Jim's dad, was in charge, but basically you threw a bat up in the air, and somebody caught it, and you grabbed it, and somebody grabbed it above your hand, and that's how you picked teams. If you went to school and had a problem with somebody and you had a fight, well, you'd have the fight, and that was the end of it. I always say, 'There's nothing better than the place I grew up.'"

Larry Dierker would become an All-Star pitcher for the Houston Astros. He lived in Woodland Hills. He watched the first Dodgers teams, but mostly he was busy. "It was idyllic," he said. "Just like heaven. There weren't that many freeways. There was the 101 basically, but a lot of times, I would just ride my bike. The Little League field was three or four miles away, and the Pony League field was in the same complex. I'd just stick my glove in the handlebars and go. I was big into bodysurfing back then. I'd spend three or four hours down at Zuma Beach. After that I'd find some summer basketball games at different schools. On weekends we'd play American Legion baseball on Saturdays and Sundays. I'd pitch both days. I mean, what a way to live."

Wes Parker would be the Dodgers' first baseman on World Series teams in 1965 and 1966. He grew up comfortably in Brentwood. His dad moved west from Boston to establish a steel business. "Then when the Communists threatened to strike, he decided he'd just lease the land to tenants," Parker said. "He got pretty wealthy that way."

It wasn't unusual for West Side parents to become concerned about spoiling their kids. Wes wound up attending Harvard School, now Harvard Westlake, a sports and academic powerhouse today but a military school back then, 14 miles from Brentwood. "We wore full uniforms to school with ties, and our shoes were shined," Parker said. "We'd have formations and parades. Sometimes we'd stop traffic on Cahuenga Avenue. It was such a great place to grow up. I never had a key to the front door, didn't need one. The smog hadn't come to the West Side yet. They had just built the Santa Monica Freeway. I never noticed the city changing that much until I was playing for the Dodgers. At first I would leave at 4:00 in the afternoon and I'd still get to the ballpark in plenty of time. Then, as the years went on, I had to leave a little earlier. At the end it was 2:30."

It's possible that no one outside the Dodgers' hierarchy heard Vin Scully broadcast more innings than Al Michaels did. His family grew up in Brooklyn. He could walk to Ebbets Field. Sometimes his mom, Lila, would tell the teachers Al had to miss school for family reasons, and he'd gratefully spend the afternoon watching the Dodgers. The Michaels family moved to L.A. in 1958, just as the Dodgers did. Al followed Vin's voice as if it were a north star. Sports were the throbbing heart of the family because his dad, Jay, came to L.A. to begin the sports division of the MCA talent agency. Along the way Jay helped broker the deal that put the American Football League on ABC. Al remembers seeing the league's master schedule around the house.

Al would win the same Frick Award that Scully did and find the same place inside the walls of Cooperstown after he'd broadcast the Cincinnati Reds and San Francisco Giants games and then, of course, branched out into network sportscasting of all kinds. Without baseball he would still be known for his epic call—"Do you believe in miracles? Yes!"—when the American hockey team beat the Soviets in the 1980 Olympics or his 35-plus years as the play-by-play voice of primetime NFL games on Sunday, Monday, and Thursday nights.

Michaels has been the lead presence in the most popular primetime show in the history of television. ABC's *Monday Night Football* has had the best ratings of any telecast for 12 consecutive years, which is an all-time record. Michaels was the voice for 11 of those years and 16 on *Sunday Night Football* overall. But baseball and Scully and the Dodgers gave him the foundation to do that, and he wound up at the Coliseum and Dodger Stadium quite a bit, though Lila also spirited him out of school for afternoons at Santa Anita and Hollywood Park.

The family lived in Cheviot Hills, near what is now the Santa Monica Freeway, or "the 10," as the locals call it. It's a handsome but tranquil neighborhood that borders Rancho Park Golf Course, where Charlie Sifford once won the Los Angeles Open. The first part of it opened in 1961. Eventually, the 10 made it easier for Michaels to get to the Coliseum and see the Dodgers and Drysdale. Michaels lives in Los Angeles today. There is nothing ambivalent to him about the California promise. "Sometimes you hear this BS about how Los Angeles isn't a good sports town," Michaels said. "I always like to remind people that on November 2, 1958, the Rams played the Bears in the Coliseum and beat them 41–35, and the crowd was 100,470. And on December 2, 1958, they beat the Colts in the Coliseum 30–28 in a year when the Colts would go on to win the NFL championship, and that game drew 100,202. And all three games of the 1959 World Series drew more than 92,000. For a kid like me, it was about as exciting as you could get."

But for many outsiders Los Angeles was—and is—an indecipherable puzzle. For the Dodgers, who came from Brooklyn, it was like being removed from a sardine can and getting thrown into an ocean. Walking was complicated. Neighborhoods were indefinable. Freeways could be confounding. Where else did the Harbor Freeway go, and which harbor are they talking about? Where did all these roads start, where did they end, and if you ever took a mistaken exit, could you correct it? The players had only a few months to figure it out, along with homes for their families and schools for their children. Only then would they turn their attention to baseball.

Eventually, Gil Hodges, Duke Snider, Pee Wee Reese, Rube Walker, and Carl Erskine found places in Long Beach near Virginia Country Club but 45 minutes away from the ballpark. Carl Furillo needed a two-bedroom furnished apartment somewhere near Manhattan Beach, and the sportswriters put it in their notebook stories and listed the Dodgers' main switchboard number. "If you'd asked the players on the Dodgers to take a vote, it might have been 25–0 to stay in Brooklyn," Don Drysdale said.

"It was a big adjustment for the front-office people," Peter O'Malley said. "I'm 21 years old. My sister Terry is a year or two older. Where are we going to live? What's it all about? We didn't know anyone. Furillo was shook up by it. I think Hodges was. Deep down, I always suspected Don thought it was cool. The city was flat as you flew in. Then, all of a sudden, you saw the high rises. I did not have the impression this was a big city. Quite the contrary. I realized this is not New York or Philadelphia, where I'd gone to college [at the University of Pennsylvania]. It'll take a while to get to know it. It would take time to appreciate it."

Walter O'Malley hunkered down. He had a stadium to oversee in Chavez Ravine with all the complications. He set up shop at the Statler-Hilton hotel. "The tallest building in town outside city hall," Peter said.

Walter gathered the front-office hierarchy of Buzzie Bavasi, Al Campanis, and Fresco Thompson. "Hollywood is going to embrace us," he told them. "But don't go Hollywood."

Some of that was inevitable. Kay O'Malley's best friends became Mervyn LeRoy, the producer, and his wife, Kitty. Kay had suffered cancer of the larynx in 1927 just before she married Walter and she could only whisper, but Kitty could understand her. On weekends the O'Malleys retreated to their mile-high second home at Lake Arrowhead, where Walter would make blueberry pancakes.

But Walter often spent weeknights at the office at the hotel. Mondays through Fridays were full of tumult. Walter was one of the few who could see the promise behind it. "We had studied what happened in Milwaukee," Peter O'Malley said. "We saw how the town had taken in the Braves when they came from Boston. We figured that would happen here."

It was already building. In late October the Dodgers held an introductory luncheon at the Statler-Hilton. There were 1,100 there at $6 a pop. Umpire Beans Reardon announced: "Play ball!" And the officials on the dais threw rubber baseballs into the crowd. Harold Parrott, the business manager, thanked the locals for sending in so much cash for ticket applications "that we can already pay for Snider and Reese this year."

In some ways the Dodgers and Giants were missionaries. They were bringing their game to a place that was unrelatable to many Americans. Even though the state had swelled in population and influence, there were only 19 California natives in the starting lineups of the 16 major league clubs in 1958. Drysdale was one. He got the ball for Opening Day at San Francisco's Seals Stadium on April 15. He gave it up in the fourth inning while down 4–0, as the Giants won 8–0.

The Dodgers came home and rode convertibles to the Coliseum for their first game. Each convertible had the player's name on the passenger door. Fifty-seven city buses were reserved by various organizations, and 190 extra policemen and sheriff's deputies were assigned to the Coliseum. After the home opener, United Press International commissioned the oft-married Zsa Zsa Gabor to write about the phenomenon. "Of course, I'm delighted about Major League Baseball coming to Los Angeles," she wrote. "With all those men and that enormous diamond, what woman wouldn't be?"

Finally, on the day after the U.S. Senate approved President Eisenhower's interstate-highway bill by a margin of 84–4 and ensured that more freeways were coming, Los Angeles joined the major leagues. The Dodgers outlasted the Giants 6–5 before a crowd of 78,472.

Problems were immediate and obvious. The Coliseum best suited Olympic ceremonies, track and field, and football. The left-field fence was 251 feet from the plate. O'Malley ordered a screen on top of the fence, but that didn't comfort the pitchers or most left-handed hitters like Snider, who were staring at a vast wasteland in right-center. It took a 440-foot drive to clear the fence at its deepest point. Was this the right way to treat a walking Brooklyn institution, usually found in the same sentence with Willie Mays and Mickey Mantle? Mays laughed at Snider during batting practice. "What did they do to you, Duke?" he yelped.

Out of curiosity, Snider and Don Zimmer attempted to throw a ball over the rim of the Coliseum, which was 106 feet high. Wagers were made. Snider figured to get $200 out of it. But on his third throw, he dislocated his elbow. Bavasi found out and headed for the clubhouse. Zimmer hid inside a locker. Bavasi fined them each $273, but near the end of the season with the Dodgers headed for seventh place in an eight-team league, Snider finally threw one over the wall and got at least the $200 back.

Drysdale sympathized with Snider, but he mainly feared for himself. Before the opener a group of media types were taking batting practice. "Even they were hitting it over the fence," Drysdale said. "How am I supposed to get Mays and Hank Aaron out? This is nothing but a sideshow."

His first home start on April 20 was the third game of the opening three-day series against the Giants. Two omens were established. Drysdale exchanged knockdown pitches with the Giants' Ramon Monzant, who had decked Charlie

Neal and Gino Cimoli before he was sent to the dirt by Drysdale. "You've got better control than that," umpire Frank Secory told Drysdale.

And the Giants won 11–2, ridding themselves of Big D after five innings. Danny O'Connell lofted two home runs. One of them sailed over the left-field fence that Drysdale had taken to calling "the Thing." There were 12 home runs in the opening series, and the press box consensus was that four of them were cheap or "Chinese" in the unfortunate vernacular of the day. The phrase, sometimes altered to "an Oriental lob," had come from the Polo Grounds, where the Giants had played in New York. "If you were accustomed to pitching there, the Coliseum didn't bother you that much," Erskine said.

But Drysdale had spent only two years of road games in the Polo Grounds and then he had home run possibilities staring over his right shoulder on every pitch. And he was also 21. "How many home runs did O'Connell hit last year, eight?" Drysdale snapped afterward. "I'd be out there yet in any other park. With the fence the way it is, you have to pitch everybody like Mays."

Fielders were nervous, too. Because the seats were set high, they were looking into a wall of white shirts, and baseballs were hard to discern. But there were no alternatives. National League president Warren Giles said the Dodgers had to play inside the city limits, which ruled out the Rose Bowl, another incompatible site. And Wrigley Field, where the Angels would begin play in 1961 and which was the home of the *Home Run Derby* TV show, didn't have enough seats.

Drysdale lost his first five decisions of the year, four at home. He walked 13 batters in his first four starts. In his fifth he delivered three walks, two wild pitches, and a hit batter. On August 8 Drysdale won his second start at the Coliseum. He went eight and two-thirds innings to beat the Giants 6–3. "I came out mad and I stayed mad," he said. At that point his ERA was 5.02, and his record was 6–11.

However, Drysdale learned that the left-field wall taketh away and giveth, too. He hit seven home runs in 1958, five to left. Snider wound up hitting .312 but had only 15 home runs. He had hit 40 or more in each of the five previous seasons. And, eventually, Drysdale salvaged a 12–13 season with a 4.17 ERA and led the club in innings with 211 and two-thirds. Sandy Koufax, still trying to refine his gifts, went 11–11 with a 4.48 ERA. Left-hander Johnny Podres was tagged for 27 home runs and went 13–15, and the Dodgers finished 71–83, their worst record since 1944.

Upon looking back, Drysdale identified several bumps in the road. He had a tender elbow when the season started. His spring training was truncated by his duties in the Army Reserve, where Koufax accompanied him. He was, after all, expected to function like a staff ace for a curious new audience, even though he was still just 21. And he missed the leadership and the tough love of Campanella, whose auto accident on January 28 and subsequent paralysis removed a three-time MVP from the franchise. Campanella would not let Drysdale work himself into a stew. "You get hot on me today, boy, and I'll boot you right in the pants," Campanella told *True* magazine. "Do you want to get your butt kicked or do you want to pitch?"

Drysdale's temper was as exaggerated as everything else about him, and at times it could spark laughter. When Walter Alston asked the pitchers to step up their running program in spring training, he groused, "Tell me how many games Jesse Owens won last year." There was also the day when Drysdale, in perhaps the most unintentionally funny observation he ever made, said, "Nothing makes me madder than to have someone say getting mad hurts my pitching."

"He was a lot like those German shepherds in the K-9 unit, the ones in the police department," Parker said. "I was around those dogs. They were so sweet and cuddly until it was time to swing into action. That was Don. Put him on the field and he was as mean as he had to be. But it wasn't his desire to be mean. It was his desire to win. Same reason he threw at people. He was protecting us, that's all."

After one Coliseum-bred home run, Drysdale went to first base to take a throw for the third out and then heaved the baseball into the stands. That could have been a problem. So could the load of helmets that he slammed against the dugout wall during another one of his fits. There was the night the Dodgers got him five runs, he gave up three, and Alston removed him. Driven over the edge, Drysdale emptied his locker and began laying waste to everything he saw. With all of his belongings and clothes on the floor, he still didn't feel any better. So he tried to punt a bag full of bats. All that did was hurt his foot. So he grabbed the bag to throw it against the wall. But he slipped on the concrete floor, took a header, and watched the bats fall out of the bag and clang against the floor. At that point there was little Drysdale could do but laugh. So he did. "I was certain this was the most stupid thing I had ever done," he said. "So I took a shower and felt fine again."

"We want to be careful not to kill Don's competitive spirit," Bavasi said. "He really is a very fine fellow who means right. Besides, we don't feel a man should be fined for getting mad at himself."

"I'm the one that has the temper," Don's wife, Ginger, said when she had read one too many stories about her towering inferno. "He'll say, 'Aw, honey, why don't you make a record when you get mad. That way you can play it instead of saying the same things over and over again.'"

Note: don't try that at home.

The feeling was that 1959 would be different, and that it had better be different. No one knew how long L.A.'s grace period would last. As Drysdale went nine innings to beat Philadelphia in a mid-March exhibition (yes, that type of thing happened back then), the Dodgers welcomed a chance to start 0–0.

And the Coliseum? It was still there, as was the intrusive left-field wall and its inadequate screen. Its familiarity bred even more contempt from Drysdale. "Trade me to Cucamonga," he said.

But as often happens, the perceptions dissipate once they run into a hard shelf of numbers. In the four Coliseum years, Drysdale won 36 at home and lost 25. On the road, he won 21 and lost 25. His ERA in the Coliseum was 3.14. His ERA on the road was 3.91. The opponents' batting average against Drysdale was .231 in the Coliseum and it was .250 on the road. Some torture chambers are more comfortable than others.

*   *   *

Surviving 1958 and cleansing the palate for 1959 was essential for Don Drysdale. He began a personal six-game win streak on August 8, and five of those wins came at the Los Angeles Coliseum. The sixth was the best. He squelched the Giants 4–0 on a five-hitter on September 2 and he became the first pitcher of the season to pick off Willie Mays at first.

There were other forces working. The next day, Drysdale and Ginger Dubberly filed for a marriage license. Dubberly was working on her own career. She was a model employed by the Adrien Company and she had just been crowned Miss Torrance. In January she was a princess in the Rose Parade. A few months before he knew who she was, audience member Peter O'Malley took a snapshot of her float. Dubberly served as queen of the Sportsman's Show and appeared at automobile fairs. She was doing fine and she was only 18 in April of 1958. Don was 21. When they met the combustion was spontaneous.

Dubberly came to the Coliseum as part of a promotion by the *Los Angeles Mirror News*, which occasionally did photo shoots of celebrities spending "a day with the Dodgers." Dubberly took a few hacks in the batting cage and was generally in the dugout area while the Dodgers and Drysdale loosened up. Photographer Bill Knight made the formal introduction. "Don looked at me, and I looked at him," Ginger told Groucho Marx when she and Don were guests on *You Bet Your Life*. "And then they took some more pictures. I did a little investigating of his marital status. Then he asked for my phone number. Seventeen days later, I talked him into getting engaged."

They reserved the First Methodist Church of San Gabriel for Saturday night on September 27. That was also the next-to-last day of the season. On September 26 Drysdale finished his official duties with a 6–3 win against the Cubs. After the day game, he and Dubberly were married before a crowd of 400. Dick Yoxall, a baseball teammate of Drysdale's at Van Nuys High, served as the best man.

In November the Drysdales served a rite of passage when they appeared on *You Bet Your Life*, the classic quiz show in which Marx pushed all guests' buttons before giving them questions. When Marx asked Don if Ginger was a good cook, he frowned and reluctantly said, "No."

"That's Drysdale for you," Marx said. "Another wild pitch."

"Well, I have to admit I'm not very good," Ginger said, indignantly. "But I've only been doing it for three-and-a-half months."

They honeymooned in Hawaii, where Don eventually opened a restaurant and where Ginger and daughter, Kelly, still live today. When a reporter asked them about the coming season and the potential clash of careers, Don said Ginger was welcome to keep working "as long as it doesn't interfere with baseball."

"It won't," Ginger said. "I'm going to be right down there at Virile Beach with you this spring."

"That's 'Vero,' honey," Drysdale said.

Apparently, Ginger's cooking improved greatly through the winter. Drysdale came to Vero Beach and showed uncommon mastery. Presumably his virility was acceptable, too. He pitched 28 innings and gave up two runs.

Buzzie Bavasi also traded Gino Cimoli for Wally Moon, an outfielder swap that seemed inconsequential at the time. That happened as the Dodgers were bringing in the right-center wall to a more manageable 370 feet. Some still wondered why Bavasi would trade a right-handed bat for a left-handed bat. But Moon was dexterous enough to find another way. He showed everyone else how to send soft fly balls over the nearby left-field screen, and soon L.A. was celebrating the "Moonshots." Moon hit 19 homers with 74 RBIs and also 11 triples, which led the league.

Beyond that, the Dodgers began to figure out this strange, sprawling land. Walter O'Malley had wanted the first Dodgers team to bring as much Brooklyn as it could because the fans knew all the Brooklyn players. That was a mistake, he said later. The Dodgers were aging, and with age comes an unwillingness to adjust.

The '59 Dodgers would be different. They still had Gil Hodges, Duke Snider, Jim Gilliam, and Clem Labine, and Drysdale remained the featured starting pitcher. But there were younger Dodgers like Norm Larker, Ron Fairly, and a right-hander who started walking normally at age 12, thanks to operations to correct clubfeet. Larry Sherry came from Fairfax High in Los Angeles. His brother, Norm, was a catcher who would eventually find the key to unleashing Koufax. Before long Sherry would be associated with champagne.

The 22-year-old Drysdale worked 270 and two-thirds innings, won 17, lost 13, and had a 3.46 ERA. Sherry and Sandy Koufax were 23; Johnny Podres and Danny McDevitt were 26. Maury Wills, fighting his way from what seemed like a life sentence in the minors, came up to bring speed at shortstop. The Dodgers turned a promising start into a true pennant race.

Drysdale was still dealing with his aggressions—or making hitters deal with them. He hit Mays in the shoulder, and it was ruled that Drysdale had done it deliberately. The National League fined him $50, which caused major squawking from Drysdale and Walter Alston. "Is that boy rough? You joking or something?" Mays said. "That ball looks like it's coming in from third base. You better be ready to get out of there."

"They can think what they want," Drysdale said. "I'm not changing."

On May 22 Mays went 0-for-5 against Drysdale, and the rest of the Giants struggled, too. Drysdale went 13 innings that night, outlasting Johnny Antonelli. He threw 173 pitches. He walked two and got 27 swings and misses and he gave up six hits. He kept chopping away until Hodges singled with two out in the bottom of the 13th, and the Dodgers won 2–1. It might have been the best regular-season game Drysdale ever pitched and it was one of several bread crumbs that kept leading the Dodgers toward October.

In mid-July Drysdale and Antonelli matched up again—this time in San Francisco's cozy Seals Stadium. Drysdale won again 3–2, as Hodges and Charlie Neal lofted wind-blown home runs. "I should be paid double for pitching here," Antonelli fumed. "I got beat by a couple of lousy fly balls."

Welcome to Drysdale's world. "I don't pitch to ballparks anymore," Drysdale announced. "Last year I tried to adjust to the Coliseum and I failed. Now it's just another ballpark to me. Usually, I can tell if a batter's going to swing based on the position of his feet. If I think he's swinging, I'll pitch him tight, and he'll hit it off the handle."

With all their improvement, the Dodgers were two games behind with 11 games to go, scrumming with the Giants and the Braves, who had won the past two National League titles. On September 19 Drysdale beat Antonelli again to keep the Dodgers tied for the lead. The Dodgers went ahead by one game with two to go when Hodges cracked an 11th-inning home run off Bill Henry to beat the Cubs. Sherry struck out Dale Long to seal it. Hodges was playing with a swollen elbow after getting hit two days prior and he was still playing with a torn tendon in his ankle. On the final day, Roger Craig beat the Cubs 7–1, as his wife Carolyn spent hours at the ironing board back in Long Beach, trying to keep herself occupied.

Los Angeles was getting its first case of pennant fever. Clammy hands turned radio knobs in order to get all the scores, and smudged hands picked up every newspaper available. KTTV showed the game in L.A., which began at 10:00 AM on a Sunday morning and claimed three million viewers and 95 percent of the viewing audience. A priest told Hank Hollingworth of the *Long Beach Independent* that the crowd for his 9:00 AM mass that morning was the largest he'd ever seen. The 11:00 AM? Not so much.

St. Louis was sweeping a doubleheader over San Francisco, and the Braves were beating Philadelphia. That left the Dodgers and Braves in a best-of-three playoff. The Dodgers won Game One in Milwaukee, landed in L.A. at thirty minutes past midnight, and were amazed to see 5,000 fans at the airport.

It was up to Drysdale to put the city in its first World Series, but all those innings began sitting heavily on his arm. Eddie Mathews' fifth-inning home run put the Braves up 4–2, and Podres relieved Drysdale to begin the sixth. It would be 5–2 before the Dodgers got some help from their Boys of Late Autumn. Moon, Hodges, and Snider began the rally that Carl Furillo ended with a sacrifice fly off Warren Spahn, who was relieving. In the 12th inning, Hodges walked, and Joe Pignatano singled with two out, and Furillo grounded to shortstop Felix Mantilla, whose throw sailed past Frank Torre at first and bounced off the shoulder of Greg Mulleavy, the first-base coach.

The Dodgers had won 6–5 and flew off to Chicago to meet the pitching-rich, speedy White Sox for a World Series that not even O'Malley and Bavasi had foreseen. Upstairs, Bavasi's wife, Evit, had spent the game working her knitting needles, putting together a sweater that had preoccupied and inspired her. Over the previous week, the Dodgers had won every time she had tended to her knitting. In the two days she didn't get around to it, they lost. Now she had finished her sweater and there was a World Series to win. "I guess I can make it bigger," she said.

After the Dodgers split the first two in Comiskey Park, Drysdale would start the first home World Series in Los Angeles history. A World Series record crowd of 92,394 showed up, and Western Union cranked out 260,000 words from reporters who showed up from all points. The Dodgers responded with a show-and-tell explanation of how they got to this point with only 88 regular-season wins. Drysdale ducked and dodged his way through 11 Chicago hits and four walks while giving up only one run.

He had to pass another composure test during that game, thanks to Don Gutteridge and Tony Cuccinello, the White Sox first- and third-base coaches. They picked up something in his delivery that messaged what pitch was coming. Gutteridge whistled, and Cuccinello kept yelling code phrases like "Be ready" or "Come on." At one point Drysdale glared at Ted Kluszewski, the hitter whose massive biceps forced him to cut off his uniform sleeves when he was in Cincinnati. "Don't listen to them," Drysdale yelled. "They've got it all wrong. They'll get you killed."

Catcher John Roseboro defanged the Sox running game by throwing out Nellie Fox; Luis Aparicio, who would enter the Hall of Fame in 1984 with Drysdale; and Jim Rivera. The Dodgers won 3–1 on another hit by the 37-year-old Furillo. By now Evit Bavasi's sweater could have warmed an elephant. The attendance record lasted one day. The Game Four crowd was 92,650, which might have frustrated those who sought to attend the circus next door at the L.A. Sports Arena.

Hodges, 35, stroked the home run that won it 5–4 amid frenzied toots from miniature trumpets sold by the Dodgers souvenir department. Game Five went to the White Sox 1–0 in front of 92,706, though Koufax was brilliant and portentous with a five-hitter through seven innings. It ended two days later in Chicago. Snider reached back into his Brooklyn scrapbook for the go-ahead home run, and Sherry got the last 17 outs to boost his World Series record to two wins and two saves, for which he received a Corvette for becoming World Series MVP. The Dodgers won 9–3, a victory that eventually would reward each player with a $11,000 bonus.

When the team landed in Los Angeles the next day on Walter O'Malley's 56th birthday, there was an estimated crowd of 5,000, and Desi Arnaz of *I Love Lucy* was the master of ceremonies for the program. He explained that Cubans, such as himself, were huge baseball fans. "It's our favorite sport," he said, "between revolutions."

The *Los Angeles Times* editorial page could not be accused of understating the event: "The opponents of the Chavez Ravine field argued that there was not enough enthusiasm for Major League Baseball in Southern California to justify the city's encouragement of it as a civic enterprise. Their noses have been rubbed in their propaganda…The team has made the people for a couple of 100 miles around aware that they have a common interest. The Dodgers are not just a Major League Baseball team. They are supernatural. Partially as a result of the Dodgers, Los Angeles may become Los Angeles again—a city again, not an incident in a bright cloud of satellites that refuses even to follow the decent Newtonian laws of gravitation."

Said Ginger: "It's the biggest thrill of my life, and this town deserves it."

*   *   *

Eventually the Dodgers would find friends in L.A., though few of them were exactly neighbors. Showbiz people regularly visited the Los Angeles Coliseum. Some were from New York and had always been Dodgers fans. Some just had a knack for knowing where the action was—like the front row of Lakers games in The Forum during the Showtime days. Some just had smart press agents who knew how to position them. "Walter O'Malley had seen some of the Japanese stadiums, where they had seats on dugout level," Vin Scully said. "He thought that would be a great idea. Doris Day would get there early, make cookies and snacks for the players. Cary Grant and Jeff Chandler were there quite often. Nat King Cole and his wife were there for every game. I became pretty good friends with them. They'd sit there and bet nickels and dimes on everything: fair or foul, fly ball or grounder. During the 1959 Series, he had an engagement at Chez Paris in Chicago, and we were there playing the White Sox. It was an awful game, worst one you ever saw. Nat came out to perform that night but with no voice. He really couldn't sing at all." Scully went backstage afterward and asked Cole what was wrong. Cole said he was too hoarse from cheering even at a game with no suspense.

"We'd peer through the back of the dugout to see who was there," Stan Williams said. "We'd see Humphrey Bogart, Lauren Bacall, always Nat. Stan Jr. was the first Dodgers baby born in L.A., and Jeff Chandler carried him up to the clubhouse. My wife loved that. Ransom Jackson was with us, and he was looking up in the stands and said, 'Look, there's Lana.' We all ran over to see Lana Turner, and he said, 'There she is: Lana Schwartz.'"

Erskine pitched the first game at the Coliseum. In the fifth inning, he noticed teammates craning their heads out of the dugout, looking up to gaze upon stars in the seats. "Bing Crosby, Lana Turner, Sammy Davis Jr.," Erskine said. "Chandler was a big Giants fan, so he'd take batting practice with them when they were in town. Jerry Lewis would take batting practice with us. They made a movie called *Geisha Boy*, and part of it was being filmed at Hollywood Park. They took us over there and they filmed a bunch of stuff, mostly of us cutting up."

But eventually Scully became the star of the Dodgers and then really of L.A. itself. He did 67 years of Dodgers games on radio and TV. His precise and grammatically pristine baritone became the soundtrack of every summer.

The first commercial transistor radio came along in 1954, and Sony's version hit the marketplace in 1957. It was small and portable with an earphone jack, and if it hadn't already existed, the Dodgers might have invented it. With all those fans flooding the Coliseum, someone had to explain who the players were, what was going on, why one batted ball became an error and another became a hit. That fell to Scully, and soon his voice could be heard throughout the Coliseum, row by endless row. "Vin deserves extraordinary credit," Peter O'Malley said. "He introduced us to Los Angeles. He was the link, the first impression and the lasting impression. Sitting there and hearing him was new. It didn't happen at Ebbets Field or anywhere else. If you didn't bring a radio, it didn't matter. You could hear somebody else's radio."

Scully obviously knew the power of the reverberation. Frank Secory was an umpire who occasionally antagonized Don Drysdale. During one disagreement Drysdale yelled, "A potato has better eyes than you."

On August 24, 1960, Scully mentioned that Secory was celebrating a birthday. "Now when I count to three, let's wish him a happy birthday," Scully said on the air. He got to three, and most of the Coliseum crowd of 27,626 bellowed, "Happy birthday, Frank!" Secory, working third base, nearly jumped out of his skin.

Meanwhile, Hollywood was always looking for tall, swaggering young men who had specific appeals to both genders. The executives found Drysdale, who began rolling up credits. Chuck Connors had grown up in Brooklyn, played one game for the Dodgers in 1949, and played 66 more for the Cubs in 1951. In 1966 he helped settle the contract holdout that Drysdale and Sandy Koufax staged in spring training. Then he played Lucas McCain in *The Rifleman*, and Drysdale made several appearances—once as a member of the notorious Skull Gang who hit Connors with a gun barrel and knocked him out.

He made another appearance as Roy Grant, son of a trail boss, in *Lawman,* an ABC series that lasted four years. Drysdale took Beth, played by Dodie Heath, to the local saloon in exchange for allowing her to keep her injured heifer. Well, one thing leads to another, as often happens in the Wild West, and Drysdale punched out a patron who he thought was acting untoward, Beth fell while fending off another suitor, and then Drysdale was jailed by mistake. Eventually, Drysdale is freed, fortunately for the Dodgers.

To Tell the Truth was a game show that featured a four-celebrity panel. Three people were marched out to face them, each claiming to be a person of some accomplishment, two of whom were imposters. It was late 1959 after the Dodgers had won a World Series, and the real Drysdale was standing there in a Dodgers uniform. Not surprisingly, Monique van Vooren, Kitty Carlisle, and Tom Poston correctly identified Drysdale after some pointed questioning such as "What is a change of pace?" and "What is a southpaw?" Only Don Ameche actually knew who Drysdale was and recused himself.

In 1963 Drysdale recorded "Give Her Love" with "One Love" on the flip side for Reprise Records, the place where Frank Sinatra recorded his classics. After the Dodgers swept the Yankees in the 1963 World Series, Joey Bishop's variety show welcomed Drysdale and teammates Frank Howard, Tommy Davis, Ron Perranoski, Jim Gilliam, and Moose Skowron for a chorus. Drysdale was the lead singer and was the only one who wasn't in uniform, coming out in a tuxedo instead. They sang "High Hopes," one of Sinatra's hits and also the theme song for John F. Kennedy's presidential campaign in 1960. The Dodgers substituted: "We've got Koufax" and "We've got Drysdale" instead of "We've Got High Hopes" to begin the choruses.

In all these endeavors, Drysdale showed the no-sweat assurance that showbiz people still hold dear. It's a style that suits Los Angeles, too. The fact that L.A. could be as seething and violent as Drysdale was in his workplace? That also made sense, too. When Williams looked back at those glittery days, he mostly remembered 1962, when the Dodgers let the National League pennant get away and lost a three-game playoff to San Francisco. "We still got invited to a party after the season was over," Williams said, "because they never considered us losers."

Dean Martin's house was the site, and Sinatra and Davis Jr. showed along with a good cross-section of people whose names would eventually be on sidewalk stars at Hollywood and Vine. Diane McBain was there. She was a member in good standing of Hollywood's parade of blondes and she played roles opposite Elvis Presley and Richard Burton. "I was dancing with her," Williams said. "It seemed like she was putting the moves on me. And if that didn't make my wife mad enough, here comes Donna Reed. My wife went up to her and told her how much her husband had been in love with her. Yeah, the scene was very different for all of us."

They had inched their way westward all the way from Brooklyn, and 2,795 miles had never seemed so far.

5

All or Nothing at All

The stadium was ready for its close-up. The next day, the Dodgers would play Cincinnati in the first game of the 1962 season. Every seat would be prime. The hills surrounding Chavez Ravine would wear the sunshine just right. The seats would be clean, the hot dogs would be fragrant, and there would be parking, glorious parking, as far as the eye could see.

For Walter O'Malley, there was one last flourish before he opened the gates to Dodger Stadium. He invited Roz Wyman, 31-year-old member of the Los Angeles City Council, to his box that overlooked home plate. He also made sure Bob Mitchell, the organist, was there. It was right about the time that the evening games would start. Mitchell played "Take Me Out to the Ballgame." O'Malley and Wyman took it all in. No one else was there.

"Without you," he told her, "this does not happen."

Twenty-six years later, on a Saturday night in October, Nancy Bea Hefley would be playing "Happy Days Are Here Again," mostly to herself because no one else could hear the tune as Kirk Gibson circled the bases with the miracle home run that won World Series Game One.

Wyman was there that night, too, and most days and nights when the Dodgers played. O'Malley let her select eight permanent seats each year. Wyman was the youngest Los Angeles City Council member in history.

She had started her political career at USC. When she was elected, the *Los Angeles Times* ran a headline that read, "It's A Girl!"

She was Rosalind Wiener then, daughter of pharmacists in the Koreatown neighborhood. She married Eugene Wyman in 1954. Wyman died of a heart attack when he was 47, and his law firm assumed control of the tickets. Roz sued the firm and recovered the tickets. Aside from the advancement of Democratic party causes, Wyman prized the Dodgers like family. She cold-called Walter O'Malley in Brooklyn and floated the idea that he should move the Dodgers west. That hadn't occurred to O'Malley, but a new stadium in Brooklyn had. "You won't have any rainouts here," Wyman told O'Malley. He still dismissed the idea, but Wyman had a hearing problem when it came to the word "No."

When New York planning executives began their opposition to O'Malley's plans, L.A. was still sitting there. By then Wyman had already been working on Horace Stoneham, the owner of the Giants, who wasn't happy with the Polo Grounds. Stoneham was considering Minneapolis, home of the Giants' Triple A team, but warmed to California when he heard O'Malley might move.

The Dodgers came west in 1958, but that was only the first step. O'Malley had taken helicopter tours over Chavez Ravine. He knew he needed his own stadium, so he persuaded L.A. officials to donate those 315 acres in exchange for "stadium considerations" and Wrigley Field, then a minor league ballpark on the south side of town that O'Malley had quietly purchased in the fall of 1957. L.A. voters had to approve Proposition B to authorize stadium construction, and the vote was hastily scheduled for June 3, 1958. It would be the first time they would be asked to accommodate a pro sports team and the plans of its owner. When the details came down, opponents sprouted up everywhere.

Chavez Ravine was just north of downtown. The value of its location was unquestionable. It also was believed to be sitting on top of oil reserves, and the city would retain its rights to the assumed revenue. But the ravine was unused at the moment. More than 1,800 families, most of Mexican descent, had lived there. Under housing development policy, the city announced plans for a complex called "Elysian Park Heights" and used eminent domain to acquire the land and relocate the families. They were moved out, and the neighborhoods were razed in 1951 and 1952. There were only a few families left when the Dodgers arrived in 1958. Then Norris Paulson became the mayor, came out against the project, and supported a referendum that would stop it, which passed. The families were taken away long before the Dodgers moved in.

However, the evictions did not help the Dodgers' cause on Proposition B even as O'Malley kept pointing to the estimated $345,000 in property taxes they would pay. Opponents insisted they should pay twice that. At the time the tax revenue from Chavez Ravine was only $6,000. Proposition B passed by nearly 24,000 votes, far too close for O'Malley's digestive system. "If anyone, even the Good Lord himself, had told me nine months ago of what the Dodgers went through in this move to California, I would not have believed it," O'Malley said softly. "I can't believe I'm not dreaming. This is the most confusing move West since someone opened the Oregon Trail."

And the Oregon Trail didn't cost $12 million to build. Meanwhile, Roz Wyman had planted a similar seed in the head of Bob Short, who owned the Minneapolis Lakers. Short saw how the Dodgers were doing and didn't need to be persuaded. The Lakers, who had the NBA's dominant team before the Boston Celtics began stringing championships, began playing at the L.A. Sports Arena in 1960. Then O'Malley and Wyman looked upon their own baseball city of hope.

If anyone else was humming "Happy Days Are Here Again," it was Don Drysdale. No longer would he feel that he was pitching in an elevator, even though the numbers showed that he had been more successful within the Los Angeles Coliseum than without. Instead, he would win the fourth game of the new season in Dodger Stadium, beating Milwaukee's Lew Burdette, pitching nine innings, striking out 11, and picking up an RBI double with his bat.

Dodger Stadium is the third oldest ballpark in today's major leagues. It has had some work done, just as Wrigley Field and Fenway Park have, but fans have the same view, they walk the same corridors, and they park in the same lots. It was designed for pitching—and a lot of it—with a center-field fence 410 feet from the plate, a "power alley" that was 380 feet away, and with heavy air in the spring and early summer. Six L.A. pitchers have won Cy Young Awards in its lifetime.

The first five years of Dodger Stadium made up the most successful chunk of time in franchise history. In that frame the Dodgers went to three World Series, won two, and tied for another National League pennant after 162 games before losing a three-game playoff. Tommy Davis drove in 153 runs, and Maury Wills stole 104 bases. In those seasons Drysdale won 98 games, lost 70, led the National League in innings pitched once, strikeouts once, and number of starts four times.

It is easy to argue that Sandy Koufax recorded the best five years in the history of pitching. He won 111 and lost 34, won the National League ERA title all five years, was the leader in WHIP four times and strikeouts three times, won three Cy Young Awards, and won a Most

Valuable Player award and finished second twice. He threw 54 complete games in 82 starts in 1965 and 1966 and threw a no-hitter in each of the first four years of Dodger Stadium, including a perfect game in 1965. In the process the Dodgers refined a stick-and-move style of winning that was unique to them and their habitat. With home runs at a premium and with a hard, fast infield, they fell back on speed and execution, a process later known as "little ball." It was rendered obsolete by the analysts that took over baseball in the early 2000s, but it worked when it was applied correctly. "In 1965 we were probably the fifth best team in the league," said Wes Parker, the first baseman. "You looked at San Francisco, Milwaukee, Pittsburgh, Cincinnati. They had monster teams. They had so much more offensive talent, but we beat them all with pitching and defense and not making mistakes. We never gave anybody an edge or a run or an opening. We were just so solid defensively."

In four of those five years, the Dodgers led the league in steals—and by embarrassing margins. In 1962 they stole 198 bases, 112 more than anyone else. The 1965 Cardinals were the only other National League club to steal 100 bases even once in those years. And in 1962 L.A. had a fairly conventional approach, ranking second in runs and fifth in home runs. But in the next four years, the Dodgers were sixth, eighth, eighth, and eighth in a 10-team league when it came to runs. In '65 they were dead last in home runs with 78. That was 19 fewer than anyone else in the league. Milwaukee led with 196. "Tommy Davis broke his ankle that year," Parker said. They also traded Frank Howard, their power source, as part of a five-man flotilla to Washington in exchange for lefty Claude Osteen.

Of the 1965 Dodgers, who had more than 15 plate appearances, only one hit .300. That was Drysdale, who clubbed seven homers and whose

OPS (on-base percentage plus slugging percentage) of .839 was easily the best on the team.

A typical uprising for the Dodgers would begin with Wills getting a single or a walk. He'd steal second. Parker, batting second, would bunt Wills over to third. (Parker had 19 sacrifices that season as a first baseman. That was repeated to an extent that baseball might never see again.) Then Willie Davis, Ron Fairly, Lou Johnson, or Jim Lefebvre would bring home Wills with a sacrifice fly or a base hit. Time after time, day after day, they did that. It was a gnat attack that wound up producing 97 wins, "It was the most exciting type of baseball I'd ever seen," Osteen said. "Every single night it seemed like we'd win the game in the ninth inning. And a different way each time."

Never has a pitching staff borne such a high percentage of the responsibility for the fortunes of a team that won for that long. In four of those five years, the Dodgers led the N.L. in ERA. Four times they had the only staff under 3.00. They were either first or second in strikeouts in each of those years. The 1965 team played six 1–0 games and won five. It also scored one or zero runs in 17 percent of their games.

Maybe it was because they had to fight with slingshots and sticks or maybe it was because they knew they'd never score if they didn't pool their resources and work together, but the Dodgers were uncommonly connected even in an era when most teams stayed together year after year. "They were great," Howard said. "They created a family-type atmosphere. And they taught you how to act like a professional. If you're in the clubhouse, your jersey top goes here, your sweatshirt goes here. If the shoes need to be cleaned, put them in front of your locker, and the next time you see them, they'll be clean. It was a great way to grow and develop."

Joe Moeller gained appreciation for the Dodgers after the Houston Astros selected him the 1967 Rule 5 Draft. "I never knew how good it was until I got traded to Houston," Moeller said. "Nobody there knew what was going on. The coaches and the manager weren't on the same page. You could go to a Class D team in the Dodger organization, and they would be completely organized. Everybody was doing the same thing. I couldn't wait to get back there."

A kid from Morningside High who worked those visiting locker rooms with Rene Lachemann, Lefebvre was the Rookie of the Year in 1965. On August 24 he was in the home stretch of a season, in which he would tie for the club lead in home runs (alas, with only 12), and the Dodgers led the league by a half-game as they played in New York. Ron Swoboda led off the bottom of the ninth in Shea Stadium. His ground ball darted through the legs of Lefebvre, the second baseman. The Dodgers would not get another out. John Stephenson's three-run double off Bob Miller erased their 3–1 lead, and the Mets won 4–3.

Lefebvre didn't even look around to find a bag to put over his head. He sprinted off the field and never looked up. "I didn't want to see anybody," Lefebvre said. "I went to the back of the bus. I went to my room at the hotel. I didn't want anybody to call me, didn't want to go out to eat."

Lefebvre was still there at 10:00 AM on the 25th when the phone rang. He had recuperated just well enough to answer it. A voice that Lefebvre vaguely recognized told him this: "I saw the way you played last night. I saw you with your head down. Listen: it happens. A lot of times, it happened to me. You're one of the reasons we're doing so well this year. So don't let it bother you. Go out there and do something about it tonight. We need you. Get your chin up. So a play like that happened? Big deal."

Lefebvre hung up the phone and stared at the ceiling. He had just had his self-esteem cleaned, ironed, and pressed by none other than Jackie Robinson. And Robinson had retired after the 1956 season. "Can you imagine that?" Lefebvre said 48 years later. "I thought, *That's Jackie Robinson, watching me. I better get my ass in gear.* That day right there changed my life. And that's why I always felt special when I played there. I was a Dodger. That's a hell of a thing to say."

Lefebvre wasn't the only one. In 1956 Bob Aspromonte was up for the proverbial cup of coffee. He was 18; Robinson was 37. "We were in spring training, and they moved me from the outfield to third base," Aspromonte said. "I was fielding some grounders and Jackie said, 'That's an outfielder's glove. You need an infielder's glove.' He gave me his glove. At the end of the day he said, 'Keep it.' I had it for two years. That's just the kind of guy he was; they all were."

The year before, Roger Craig was pitching for the Dodgers' Triple A team in Montreal, Canada. When the Dodgers called him up to the majors, Montreal was playing in Havana, Cuba. Craig got to Brooklyn, and Walter Alston said, "Go up and get your wife in Montreal and bring her down here." When Robinson overheard Craig say he didn't know which airport to go to or where any of them were, he said, "I'll take you." In the car, through the traffic, Robinson told the kid about major league life.

Don Zimmer was from Cincinnati. When the Dodgers would come to Cincinnati one day early to start a series, Zimmer would invite them all to Western Hills Country Club. By "all" Zimmer meant the players, the newspaper writers, the trainers, the broadcasters, the equipment men, everybody. They'd play golf all morning and half of the afternoon and then they'd eat and drink until sundown.

Drysdale also was giving. "I didn't think I was going to make the big club in '65," Lefebvre said. "I came to Vero Beach thinking about Triple A. I had a good spring, and they took me with them, and the first time we had an off night, Drysdale said, 'Hey, rook. Guess what? You're going out with me tonight.' You sensed it very quickly. He was the guy we all wanted to be like. He was our leader."

In his Coliseum days, when Drysdale's shoulders weren't strong enough to shrug off almost anything, he could get hot and bothered over the unequal division of leadership. He would often say, "I wish we'd score more runs" and he would yell at Zimmer, catcher John Roseboro, or others when bad breaks came. And, of course, he might hold an innocent, weak-kneed hitter accountable, too.

But as Koufax began to board his own personal rocket ship, as Osteen became a stabilizer, and as some of the hard shots to left began falling short of the warning track in the new park, Drysdale got more comfortable. "He wouldn't blame us when we didn't make plays," Lefebvre said. "Sandy and Don would get together with the infielders. They'd say, 'Look, when this guy comes up, I want you playing at a certain spot. If I don't get him to get it in the right place, that's my fault, not yours.' We'd get to the seventh or eighth inning and I'm in these meetings on the mound as an infielder, and Don is telling me that he's going to get the guy to hit me a double-play ball. I'm a rookie. I'm thinking, *Can you believe this?* But then the guy would hit me a double-play ball. That was the formula back then." Lefebvre laughed. "All I know is that when Don was pitching, the other team would have problems all of a sudden. I'd hear guys say, 'You know, my back doesn't feel good today. My arm is sore all of a sudden.' Amazing."

There was no free agency when Drysdale pitched, so he could not have left the Dodgers under any circumstances short of retirement. But in a sport where managers were and are so disposable that the Cubs tried to get through an entire season without one, Alston lasted from 1954 through 1976 on a series of one-year contracts. When Drysdale worked with Dick Enberg on the Angels broadcasts, they presented a trivia question each night. One night Enberg asked, "Name the player who had the longest major league career playing for one manager."

Drysdale thought for a minute and said, "Well, you know I played a long time for Walter Alston."

Bingo.

*   *   *

Before spring training in 1962, the baseball writers held their banquet at the Beverly Hilton, and Don Drysdale, Maury Wills, and Willie Davis sang "Diamonds Are a Girl's Best Friend." Some diamonds were friendlier than others in Drysdale's mind. It was time for him to put his pitching where his complaints had been. The opening of Dodger Stadium needed to be his moment.

The previous two seasons were unfulfilling for the club that had sneaked away with the 1959 World Series title. The Dodgers were 82–72 in 1960, as Koufax walked 100 batters, and they were 89–65 in 1961 as they finished four games behind the pennant-winning Reds. Remnants of Brooklyn like Roger Craig, Duke Snider, and Gil Hodges were still there. Drysdale was 15–14 in 1960 with a 2.84 ERA in 1960, and in 13 of his 36 starts, the Dodgers gave him zero, one, or two runs. The next season he was 13–10 with a 3.69 ERA. It was time to start winning again.

Drysdale responded by losing 12 pounds and posting a 1.07 ERA in the Grapefruit League. He also chose a new approach. "I'm convinced now that a pitcher can't consistently throw the ball past major league hitters," he said. "Instead of throwing as hard as I can, I'm going to throw to spots and pace myself. That way I'll have something left for the late innings."

Roy Campanella followed Drysdale from station to station in Vero Beach, Florida, and told catcher John Roseboro to tighten the reins. He said Drysdale was throwing too many curveballs. "He's doing the hitters a favor," Campanella said. "He throws sidearm, and his curve is too late. I told him in 1957 to waste the curve. I made him put it low and outside."

Campanella also told Roseboro to leave the umpires alone, that any arguments just raised Drysdale's blood pressure. "I've thought for years that Don should be the best pitcher in the major leagues," Campanella said. "But I'm disappointed in his won-loss record the last four years."

That record was seven games over .500. But Dodger Stadium was supposed to change all that, particularly with a mound built high enough to make Drysdale resemble Godzilla in a blue cap. On April 10, home-plate umpire Al Barlick yelled, "Play ball," and a crowd of 52,564 watched Johnny Podres begin the season with a pitch to Eddie Kasko, who took it for ball one, then doubled and scored. Over the next six months, the new ballpark would open every baseball emotion and pour it over an accumulated crowd of 2,775 million fans, exhausting every one.

Drysdale began with a 6–3 win against Milwaukee, pitching nine, striking out 11. By May 5 he was 4–1. The Dodgers had provided him 40 runs in six starts. But he still hadn't forgotten about the haunted house from which he'd escaped. He kept dumping on the venerable building, headquarters of the 1932 and 1984 Olympics, as if it were an ex-girlfriend. "I threw more change-ups today than I have in a long time," he said on April 27, when he beat Pittsburgh 7–2. "That's because of the ballpark. When you gave up a hit in the Coliseum, you immediately began thinking about one going over the screen. Now you don't."

On May 23 Drysdale beat the Mets 3–1. It was the Mets' first season, a misadventure so bizarre that it somehow won the hearts of New Yorkers who weren't supposed to possess one. Ed Kranepool and Rod Kanehl became celebrities amid the rubble of a 40–120 record. Left hanging in the expansion draft, Craig was one of the original Mets and he was the losing pitcher that day.

Two days later Drysdale opened up Drysdale's Dugout on Hayvenhurst and Oxnard in Van Nuys, California. He had signed up to appear in an Alcoa Theatre production of *Flashing Spikes*, starring Jimmy Stewart and with Vin Scully appearing, too. "The way to get opportunities like that is to do well in your own field," Drysdale said. "If I wasn't doing well, they wouldn't ask me."

Life was good. Baseball gods were now showering Drysdale with runs and allowing fly balls to stay well within the fences. Within a nine-day period, the Dodgers scored 25 runs in three of his starts. "Now I can pitch the same way at home as I do on the road," Drysdale said. "I couldn't get into a groove at the Coliseum. I always tried to compensate for that screen."

There was the usual mischief. On May 10 Drysdale spun Bob Aspromonte, an old Dodger and Drysdale's friend. Bob Bruce sent down Drysdale next time up, so Drysdale decked Roman Mejias in the next inning.

On May 27 Drysdale threw 153 pitches in a 2–1 win against Art Mahaffey and Philadelphia. Roseboro sent a foul ball into the Dodger Stadium seats and hit Scott Drysdale, who left briefly with a bloody nose. On that same day in San Francisco, Craig started a brawl by low-bridging Orlando Cepeda, and Willie Mays body-slammed the Mets' Elio Chacon.

On June 19 Drysdale slid hard into second, knocking down the Cardinals' Julian Javier. That brought some howls, so when Javier came to bat, Drysdale dusted him. "He's a dirty pitcher," said Johnny Keane, the St. Louis manager. On June 23 Drysdale plunked Wally Post of the Reds in the ninth inning. The Dodgers were leading 14–2 at the time.

All this good clean fun was accompanied by Koufax, who had led the league in strikeouts the year before. Had he found a way to turn the protons and neutrons in his left arm into true energy? On June 13 he began an eight-game stretch in which he gave up four earned runs and went 6–2. When he beat New York on July 12, he was 14–4 with a 2.06 ERA. But he had to leave the game after seven innings because he could no longer pitch through the numbness between his left thumb and index finger, as diagnosed by Dr. Robert Kerlan. Raynaud's Phenomenon, they called it, and it was crazy to think it could happen to such a phenom. "It made everything you touch feel like ice," Vin Scully said.

It also became the prevailing theme for a season that was now absorbing shadows. Koufax pitched only five more times, a total of nine and two-thirds innings, and would go 0–3.

Drysdale pushed on. When he won his 13th game on June 27, he heard general manager Buzzie Bavasi mention that long-awaited 20-win season once too often. "What are they going to do if I don't win 20, get rid of me?" Drysdale barked. "It bugs me that I always seem to be carrying the ball in this 20-win business. Nobody's saying Sandy or Podres have to do it. How long did it take Whitey Ford to win 20? If I'd been pitching for the Yankees, the Giants, or Milwaukee exactly the same way I've pitched, I'd have won a lot more games."

The All-Star Game was a far less convivial event than it is now. There were actually two of them in 1962, and the first was in Washington, and

President Kennedy attended. National League president Warren Giles held a pep talk before each Midsummer Classic, and the players generally believed their high-speed, black-hearted style was more compelling than the A.L.'s. Drysdale knocked down the Twins' Rich Rollins, then got knocked down by Detroit's Jim Bunning. The National League won.

Drysdale got back on the horse and went 5–0 in his next six starts. The sixth one was at home against the Cubs, and he threw a nine-hitter with no walks and beat the Cubs 8–3. That gave Drysdale a 20–4 record on August 3. "Sammy Cahn writes a lot of songs," Drysdale said, philosophically. "I pitch a lot of ballgames. He told me not all his songs are hits. Neither are all my games."

On August 7 Drysdale beat the Mets again, and when Stan Williams won the next night, the Dodgers led by five-and-a-half games, and people began to wonder if Drysdale could be the first man to win 30 since Dizzy Dean in 1934. "I think," said Ernie Banks of the Cubs, "that they are ogling the gonfalon."

But the Dodgers knew they had to wrest the National League from the cold, hard hands of the Giants, who had not been to a World Series in eight years. On August 11 they gave Drysdale his first loss since June 15, 5–4. The Dodgers were incensed by the soggy Candlestick Park surface. "It's like a rice paddy," Wills said. And Ron Fairly claimed if the field bore any more water, "I'd get pneumonia."

Billy Pierce laid down the rules of engagement when he hit Willie Davis in the first inning. Drysdale fulfilled his "one of ours, two of yours" promise by knocking down Mays, then drilling third baseman Jim Davenport in the hand, breaking it. It escalated at Dodger Stadium on September 6, when Frank Howard homered off Billy O'Dell, who then floored Fairly. Drysdale responded by knocking down Mays and Willie McCovey. When he came to the plate, O'Dell sent him sprawling. The Giants scored four off Ron Perranoski in the ninth and won it 9–6.

A seven-game win streak inflated the Dodgers' lead to four games on September 15. They also led by four games with eight to go. Then they led by two games with three to go. Bobby Thomson and, for that matter, Ralph Branca had long since retired. What could stop the Dodgers now?

Baseball, and its endless possibilities, could.

Drysdale won his 25th game of the season on September 19 with a 4–0 win in Milwaukee. He would not win another. The Cardinals shelled him on September 23, driving him out in the fourth inning, and won 12–2. Houston outlasted him two days later, winning 3–2 in the 10th when Al Spangler homered off Ed Roebuck.

St. Louis came to Los Angeles for the final weekend. San Francisco was playing host to Houston. Drysdale went eight innings and gave up five hits and two runs (neither earned) on September 27. Howard dropped a fly ball, and pitcher Ernie Broglio, whom the Cardinals would later trade for all-time basestealer and Hall of Famer Lou Brock, not only followed with a RBI single, but also beat the Dodgers 2–0.

The Dodgers' lead was down to only one game. Podres, hero of 1955, pitched against Curt Simmons, a former Philadelphia "Whiz Kid" from 1950. They reeled back the years and found 14 zeroes to put on the board in the first seven innings. "Best game I ever pitched in my life," Podres said.

But in the eighth inning, catcher Gene Oliver slammed Podres' 1-2 pitch over the left-field wall. The Cardinals won 1–0. A half hour before that, the Giants had beaten Houston 2–1, when Mays homered off Turk Farrell. As the Giants and their fans waited, play-by-play man Russ Hodges did a re-creation of the last two innings in Los Angeles. Seat cushions flew triumphantly when Hodges declared it over. *Los Angeles Times* columnist Jim Murray made up his own classified ad: "Wanted: One nearly-new 1962 National League pennant, slightly soiled with tear stain in the corner. Warning: If you return pennant to Dodgers direct, please be sure to tape it to their hands."

Game One of the three-game playoff, the same kind that the Dodgers had won at Milwaukee's expense in 1959, was in San Francisco. The Dodgers' heads were still living in yesterday.

Once they got to the hotel, Fairly turned to Snider and said, "Duke, what are we doing here?"

No one seemed to know. Mays slammed two home runs, Koufax lasted one inning, Howard had an errant throw that broke Wills' sunglasses; the motorcycle cop, who was leading the Dodgers' team bus, got caught on a dead-end street…just the type of 8–0 day that you deserve when you misplace a pennant.

The Dodgers now had to decide whether to use Drysdale on two days' rest. "I don't see why they'd be saving me for the first exhibition game," Drysdale thundered. Decision over.

But the doubters had a point. Drysdale was out in the sixth inning, when a base hit by Davenport, his HBP victim, put San Francisco ahead 4–0 in Dodger Stadium. The Dodgers then scored seven, the Giants tied it again, and Fairly's sacrifice fly scored Wills in the ninth to win it 8–7.

It ratified the decision of Leo Durocher to wear the same T-shirt he wore when he managed Thomson and the Giants in the 1951 playoff. "A lot of us didn't like Leo," Joe Moeller said in 2023. "He would sit at the end of the dugout and get the writers around him and then he would second-guess things that Walter did. He was trying to get his job."

Game Three of the playoff and Game No. 165 of the season arrived on Wednesday. Podres faced Juan Marichal, and after seven innings, the Dodgers led 4–2. Then came a ninth inning that was as unforgiving as that street near Candlestick Park. When it was over, the Giants led 6–4, and they had hit two balls out of the infield. The series-winner was Davenport's walk off of Williams with the bases loaded.

Mitchell, the organist, played "Look for the Silver Lining." The Dodgers fortunately couldn't hear him. Their clubhouse was closed for 56 minutes. Snider was sitting in that clubhouse, just as he'd sat in mourning after the 1951 playoff. There was little to ask and nothing to offer. Alvin Dark, the winning manager, saw the big picture. "I'm sorry about what happened to Koufax," he said. "That was what made the difference."

Later that night, Durocher was at a Sunset Boulevard restaurant and was overheard saying, "I would have won it." It was a city's introduction to the collateral damage that can happen when a pennant explodes. Brooklyn fans could have provided a support group.

In November Drysdale won the Cy Young Award, then given to the best pitcher regardless of league. He was 25–9, and his 314 ⅓ innings and 232 strikeouts led the National League. He was fifth in MVP voting. The Dodgers were 31–10 when he started. Nobody had told them they'd have to be 32–9.

6

IT WAS A
VERY GOOD YEAR

After the Dodgers had drop-kicked their chances to win Game Three of the 1962 playoff, Walter O'Malley immediately gathered his front-office staff. "The 1963 season starts now," he said.

Actually, the 1963 season would either start—or stop—with Sandy Koufax. The Dodgers had no trouble putting their finger on the biggest upcoming issue. The question was whether Koufax could put his finger on a baseball. Raynaud's Phenomenon, which deadened Koufax's thumb and index finger, wasn't the worst of it. Dr. Robert Kerlan flatly said that Koufax had been facing amputation within a 48-hour period. Coming to his rescue was Dr. Travis Winsor, who took an arteriogram and discovered a blood clot deep within Koufax's left palm. Winsor suggested a new drug called filbriolysin, which dissolved the clot.

When Koufax got to Vero Beach, Florida, he assured everyone that the numbness in his pitching hand was largely gone except for some tingling in his fingertips. Each spring training performance by Koufax was better than the previous one. But the test came on April 10, the second game of the season, after Don Drysdale had won the opener in Chicago. It was 34 degrees that day. That gave Walter Alston 34 reasons to move Koufax back—perhaps to the home opener. But neither the Dodgers nor anyone else played the game that way, not back then. Koufax and the Dodgers won 2–1, and he threw 159 pitches, only five of which were hit safely by the Cubs. Ten were third strikes.

The silver lining, which seemed so hidden and vague when organist Bob Mitchell played that tune the previous October, was now shining like a beacon. There would be clouds, as there always are. Maury Wills and Tommy Davis were playing through injuries. Rumors kept circulating that the Dodgers weren't living in Camelot anymore, that there were problems in the clubhouse. Granted, Wills wasn't the most popular Dodger, but that hadn't mattered when he was stealing bases and pulling out runs like a card trick.

Since Alston was again operating on a one-year contract, there were rumors about him, too. Leo Durocher and Charlie Dressen, the former Dodger manager who was now in the front office, were circling. O'Malley finally had to come forth with the dreaded vote of confidence, announcing that Alston was in no danger of getting fired and that he didn't think Durocher really wanted to manage anymore anyway. O'Malley knew differently, of course, and Durocher would become the Cubs manager in 1966.

With everyone on edge, it's very possible that the Dodgers' 1963 season was saved on the shoulder of the Airport Parkway in Pittsburgh. On May 6 Drysdale pitched in Pittsburgh's Forbes Field and took a 4–2 lead into the sixth. Then Jim Gilliam at second base made a wild throw. Then the Pirates tied it. Then, with two out, Drysdale was confronted with pinch-hitter Johnny Logan—yes, his sparring partner at Ebbets Field six years prior. Logan bashed a two-run single, and the Pirates led 6–4 and would win 7–4.

The Dodgers were now 12–14. Drysdale, of course, carried a dark heart to the team bus. They were headed for St. Louis. The Pirates were headed for Chicago. Several Dodgers noticed that Pittsburgh's bus seemed nicer and more spacious than their own. Their seats were tight. Five Dodgers refused to sit at all. Once they got on the highway, the voices came from the back. "Why don't we get a bigger bus?" one player yelled.

"Why don't you win some ballgames?" replied Lee Scott, the traveling secretary.

The caterwauling got louder, and finally Alston, whose tranquil nature was never misinterpreted as softness by anyone who had noticed his meaty hands, told the bus driver to pull over. "Can everybody hear me?" Alston asked.

Silence.

"I've heard enough wrangling about the buses," Alston continued. "We're not going to ride in a better or worse bus than the other clubs do. But if any of you don't like the bus we get, you come to me, and we'll step outside right now and discuss it among ourselves."

More silence.

The bus started up again, and Alston beckoned Scott and said, "And don't you ever again tell my club to win some ballgames. I'll be the one to do that. No one else."

Got it.

The Dodgers went to St. Louis and won 11–1 the very next night. Then they won 47 of their next 66 games. On July 20 they led the National League by seven-and-a-half games.

*   *   *

The Dodgers were refining their minimalist style and, if anything, reducing it. Seven times they won 1–0 games in 1963. They scored zero runs or one in 20 percent of their games. They were 33–18 in games decided by one run. Errors or big innings by the opposition were difficult to overcome. But Sandy Koufax and Don Drysdale brought big erasers with them.

Drysdale pitched typically. His ERA and WHIP were better than in 1962, when he won the Cy Young Award, but he finished 19–17. He led the league in starts (42) as he did the year before and would do the next two years. His 251 strikeouts were a career high and so was his 4.40 strikeout-to-walk ratio. He only hit 10 batters and generally avoided confrontation. But this time the Dodgers gave him only 3.3 runs per 27 outs when he was in the game. Ten times he lost games when he put up a quality start (six or more innings, three or fewer earned runs).

His natural irritability could be excused this time. In September he came down with shingles. Every shingles victim has a novel way of expressing the pain—or the inability to escape it. Drysdale said it was like "going 3-and-2 to Willie Mays."

But few people outside the Dodgers clubhouse knew. On September 20 he threw a seven-hit shutout at Pittsburgh and pronounced that he "has got this shingles licked." It was his first win since August 30, but he had not missed a start. "When I went on this road trip, I spent more time packing my medicine bag than my suitcase," he said. "I had shots, pills, sprays, lotions, and ointments. I was a walking drugstore. But it worked. The only thing left from my shingles attack are these scars on my side."

Drysdale had become a given. His work was dimmed by Koufax's year of genius. Among other things, Koufax broke Carl Hubbell's National League record for shutouts by a left-hander in a season with 11, and his 25 wins, 1.88 ERA, and 306 strikeouts all led the league. It was a pitcher's Triple Crown that he would repeat in 1965 and 1966. The man, who once averaged six walks per nine innings, now averaged 1.7 and he went nine or more innings in 22 of his 40 starts.

There would be one more challenge. In early September St. Louis put together 19 wins in 20 games. The Cardinals were young and ambitious and inspired by Stan Musial, who had announced he would retire at the end of the season. When Drysdale lost 6–1 to Dallas Green and the Phillies, the Cardinals were within a game of the lead and had the opportunity to kill off the Dodgers with a three-game series in Busch Stadium.

Walter O'Malley successfully petitioned KTTV Channel 11 to show it live in prime time. The first live road broadcast outside San Francisco was in 1959. In the first hour of the first game, the game drew a 35 rating and a 65 share. Johnny Podres won the first game 3–1, as Musial hit what would be his final home run in the majors. The Dodgers were ready to finish the fight. "Lew Burdette was in their dugout calling us chokers," Drysdale said. "He was giving us the business, clutching his throat. Now we'll see what happens. The shoe is on the other foot."

He spoke with the knowledge that Koufax's shoes were next on the rubber. This time Koufax anesthetized the Cardinals early. He threw a four-hitter with no walks for that 11th shutout of the season, and the Dodgers won 4–0 in an hour, 54 minutes. "Not my best game, but my biggest," Koufax said.

The Dodgers would lead by four games if they won the series finale and two games if they didn't. They trailed Bob Gibson 5–1 but were within 5–4 in the eighth when Walter Alston sent Dick Nen to pinch-hit for reliever Bob Miller. Nen was from Banning High in the South Bay. He had been busy with the Pacific Coast League playoffs when the Dodgers summoned him. Nen got there in time to catch the team bus for the first game of the series and sat around the other two days until Alston picked that time and place for Nen's major league debut. Nen turned on Ron Taylor's 0–1 pitch and sent it over the right-field roof at Busch Stadium, tying the game, and the Dodgers won it in the 13th.

Nen was a September call-up, so he wasn't eligible for the World Series. That didn't matter to Drysdale. "That home run is going to cost us money," Drysdale proclaimed. "You know why? Because I'm going to propose a full share for this kid when we get our World Series split. And I'm not kidding." In the end Nen got a $1,000 cash award, which nicely augmented his $7,000 salary.

On September 25 the Cubs beat the Cardinals in the afternoon, which gave L.A. the pennant. Koufax went ahead and beat the Mets anyway, and after some bubble gum and cake in the clubhouse and some champagne at a party in the Stadium Club, the Dodgers began to contemplate the World Series, which would begin in Yankee Stadium.

The Yankees had played in five of the six previous World Series and had won three. Beyond that, you had to go back to 1945–46 to find two consecutive World Series that didn't involve the Yankees. They were baseball's defining force. The comedian Joe E. Lewis said, "Rooting for the Yankees is like rooting for U.S. Steel." But the stalwarts like Mickey

Mantle, Roger Maris, Whitey Ford, and Yogi Berra were now on the back nine of their careers.

In Game One Koufax reduced them to victimhood. He struck out 15, breaking a 10-year-old World Series record set by ex-teammate Carl Erskine. "No, he doesn't pitch like anybody in our league," Ralph Houk, the Yankees' manager, told the *Long Beach Independent*.

In Game Two Willie Davis doubled home two runs in the first inning, and Podres took it from there, winning 4–1. Alston used Ron Perranoski to get the final two outs. That was a nice touch since Perranoski would finish fourth in the league MVP voting for winning 16 games in relief and putting up a 1.67 ERA in 69 appearances, a National League high. It also was the only relief appearance by any Dodgers player in the World Series.

The clubs flew west to greet a bubbling city. The Dodgers put 12,300 tickets on sale for Games Three through Five. Some fans showed up five days in advance and camped out. There were only seven security guards and three operative ticket windows, and when the gates opened at 5:00 AM of the morning of Game Three, 5,000 extra fans showed up. They walked over the early birds and their sleeping bags, and scalpers were selling game tickets for $500. There were fistfights, and there was a woman named Olivia Greene from Compton, California, who picked up her tickets and then fainted. Police made sure the goods were in her hand as they put her into an ambulance.

It was time to lighten the mood. For Drysdale it was the biggest game in his career. He dealt with it by throwing the best game of his career—up until then or maybe ever. The Dodgers won 1–0, getting their run off Jim Bouton when Tommy Davis bounced an RBI single off the shin of second baseman Bobby Richardson. Drysdale gave up three hits and one walk and struck out nine. The Yankees did not hit a ball out of the infield until the sixth inning, and Mantle resorted to bunting, successfully popping one over the charging infielders. Mantle knew very well what Drysdale might do. They had become friends, but Mantle remembered a Grapefruit League game in 1956. Drysdale popped Mantle in the ribs, and whenever he would see Mantle during batting practice, he would chirp, "Where do you want it today, big boy?"

The 27th out was the most difficult, but that drive by Joe Pepitone died in Ron Fairly's glove on the warning track. "As far as stuff and command, he had everything," Alston told the *New York Daily News*.

"I was able to put everything where I wanted to," Drysdale said. "Those Yankees are tough. This must be my biggest thrill."

Behind him in the clubhouse, someone said, "Good job, Bambino." Don turned and smiled at his dad, Scott.

"He was never in trouble," said shortstop Dick Tracewski. "He picked apart the outside corner with great fastballs all day long."

Then the Yankees were confronted with Koufax again, though Koufax was still reveling in what Drysdale had done. "God," Koufax exclaimed. "How am I supposed to follow that?"

Rhetorical question. Koufax won Game Four 2–1 and pushed his strikeout total to 23. That surpassed Detroit's Hal Newhouser World Series record—except that Newhouser had gotten his Ks in a seven-game series.

After Mantle and Frank Howard exchanged home runs, the Dodgers won it when Pepitone couldn't pick up a throw by third baseman Clete Boyer. When the ball got by Pepitone, Gilliam scurried to third. Then

Gilliam scored on Willie Davis' sacrifice fly. Four minutes after the final pitch, Linda Warshauer of Van Nuys, California, had a baby girl. She named her Sandy.

The numbers looked like fractions. The Yankees hit .171 for the World Series, scored four runs in four games, struck out 37 times, and walked five times. For the Dodgers the three starters worked 35 and one-third of the 36 innings. The longest game of the four lasted 2:13. The total time of the Series was 8:17. In 2018 the Dodgers and Red Sox would play an 18-inning World Series Game Three that lasted 7:20.

It was a different story in 1963. "We've never seen pitching like that," Mantle said. Others wondered if the Yankees had seen it at all.

*   *   *

The Yankees would win the American League again in 1964 but lose the World Series and would not visit another one until 1976. The Dodgers basically cleared their throats in 1964. They finished 80–82, even though Sandy Koufax was 19–5 with a 1.74 ERA, and Don Drysdale put up 40 more starts and finished 18–16 with a 2.18 ERA.

In some ways it was the best year of Drysdale's career. He led the National League in innings and had a career-low WHIP of 0.965. He came extremely close to winning 20 games for a sub-.500 team, standing at 18–13 with four starts left. He gave up zero, one, zero, and four earned runs in those starts and went 0–3, as the Dodgers scored six runs total. Six times that season, they failed to score when he started, and he had four 1–0 losses. Bill James, the modern-day champion of statistical analysis, said Drysdale deserved the Cy Young Award in '64. Instead it went to the Angels' Dean Chance, who won 20, lost nine, and had a 1.65 ERA.

The other problem, as 1965 dawned, was Johnny Podres' elbow surgery. Koufax and Drysdale were the only starters to win more than seven games in 1964. Buzzie Bavasi tried to fix that by trading Frank Howard, Dick Nen, third baseman Ken McMullen, and pitchers Pete Richert and Phil Ortega for Claude Osteen and third baseman John Kennedy. Osteen became an essential Dodger with a 147–126 record, two 20-win seasons, and a 3.09 ERA in nine seasons. "Our team has to have 90 to 95 percent effort out of everybody in every game, 162 games a year to win," Drysdale said before the Dodgers broke camp.

Left unsaid, among the tooth-grinding, was the fact that 90 to 95 percent of Koufax and Drysdale would still be unmatchable. But the season would be a tightrope walk through high winds and above a frayed net. On May 1 Tommy Davis, the two-time N.L. batting champ, lay helpless one stride short of second base against the Giants. He had fractured his ankle during his slide and would not return until the final game that season. Drysdale was pitching to his standards, going deep into games, hoping to pick up stray runs here and there. He lost five consecutive games when the Dodgers scored nine runs. Then he won four consecutive games when they scored 32. In those nine starts, he pitched eight or more innings six times. But what the fans couldn't see was the training room, in which Drysdale spent most of his pregame and postgame hours tending to his left knee. "It went out on me a few times today," he said casually after a win in July.

The mound in Dodger Stadium was a lot like Drysdale's fastball: high and hard. All those innings, all those pitches, all those landings had jarred something loose in there. Wayne Anderson, the trainer, said he had to use ammonia to get Drysdale out of a stupor at one point. "He'd win a lot more games if he wasn't so tough," Anderson said. "He's like a bricklayer."

On August 11 Drysdale beat the Mets 1–0, when Maury Wills singled, went to second on a passed ball, and scored on Jim Gilliam's single.

In other news: a young man named Marquette Frye was given a field test for drunk driving that evening in South Central Los Angeles, near the intersection of 116th and Avalon. As Frye and his brother, Ronald, and his mother, Rena, began to argue with police, a battalion of what became 26 police vehicles arrived. That was the launching pad for six days of what the police and most of White Los Angeles called a riot and what residents of the Watts neighborhood called rebellion, and it spread throughout the L.A. Basin. By week's end there were 34 deaths, 1,032 injuries, and 16,000 police deployed in the area.

The unemployment rate among Blacks in South Central was 30 percent at the time. Mayor Sam Yorty blocked federal programs that would have provided jobs and 20,000 recreational opportunities in the city. Watts became a national catchphrase for the rage of the 1960s, a widespread brew of despair, fear, and resentment that triggered more and more violent, urban warfare in Newark, New Jersey, and Detroit in 1967.

The Dodgers went to work as usual, though smoke from the Watts fires drifted north to Dodger Stadium, and an NFL exhibition game between the Rams and Cowboys at the Coliseum, not far from Watts, was postponed. Did those subliminal tensions ever reach the diamond? No one can say, but what happened on August 22 almost seemed like a macabre pantomime, a perversion of that old saying about sports imitating life.

John Roseboro, the Dodgers catcher, lived in South Central Los Angeles. During the disturbance he heard a rumor that marchers would be coming to his house. So he took a gun and sat on the porch, though nothing ended up happening.

The Dodgers and Giants were headed down the stretch in yet another pennant race when the two got together in the afternoon at Candlestick Park in San Francisco. Juan Marichal, the Giants pitcher, was brilliantly pursuing his trade far away from his home in the Dominican Republic, where he was a hero. In 1965 there was a civil war going on, and the U.S. had sent 20,000 troops there. Additional pins and needles weren't usually required when the Dodgers played the Giants. Marichal was already incensed that Drysdale had knocked down Willie Mays earlier in the season.

Marichal began the game by knocking down Wills and then knocking down Ron Fairly. Koufax sent a fastball over Mays' head. Marichal was due to bat in the third. Roseboro wanted him to go down, too, but Koufax threw a breaking ball inside. When Roseboro threw the ball back to Koufax, he wanted to shake up Marichal. The ball barely tipped Marichal's ear. The Giants pitcher still had the bat in his hand and suddenly, horrifyingly, hit Roseboro in the head with it. Everyone met between the plate and the mound. Everyone but Drysdale, who had already been sent ahead to his next start in New York. Mays approached Roseboro and noticed there was blood in the catcher's eye socket. "Your eye is out, man," he said. Mays took him into the dugout and tried to stop the bleeding with a towel.

Meanwhile, Dodgers pitcher Howie Reed tried to charge Marichal, who kicked both Reed and Willie Crawford. Giants infielder Tito Fuentes also brought a bat to the scene before the Dodgers collared him. Roseboro needed 14 stitches. "He had a knot in the middle of his skull that it would take your whole hand to cover," Bill Buhler, the Dodgers' trainer, told the *Los Angeles Times*.

Marichal was only suspended for eight days, which meant he missed two starts and was fined $1,750, a record at the time. It is inconceivable that a pitcher could have done such a thing today and played any more baseball that season—or maybe even the next one. "If it hadn't been for Mays, I don't know what would have happened," said Lou Johnson, the Dodgers' outfielder.

Roseboro sued Marichal for assault and got a $7,500 settlement. Somehow, the two forged a reconciliation. Roseboro visited Marichal in the Dominican Republic, and Marichal spoke at Roseboro's funeral in 2002.

On September 9 Drysdale and Osteen were in the training room during the game, listening to Vin Scully on the radio, and Koufax was pitching. Anderson was there and so was his assistant, Jack Homel, a guy with iron fingers who would work out the knots. "He could raise you off the table," Osteen said. "You'd jump and he'd say, 'Oh, did that hurt?'"

As they groaned and moaned and listened, Koufax got to the fifth inning, and the Cubs still didn't have a base runner. "Get your uniform on," Drysdale told Osteen. "We've got to watch this."

They found their uniforms and went to the dugout and witnessed the last four innings of Koufax's fourth no-hitter and his first perfect game. And, yes, Koufax won. He did so in the most Dodgers way imaginable. Lou Johnson led off the fifth inning with a walk, got sacrificed to second by Jim Lefebvre, stole third, and scored when catcher Chris Krug threw the ball into left field. The Dodgers did not get a hit until the seventh, when Johnson doubled, and did not get another. The one-hitter was the best game Bob Hendley ever pitched—topped by the best game that anyone could. Koufax retired all 27 Cubs and struck out 14 of them. The whole thing was over in an hour and 43 minutes—quicker than most movies, or in some cases, a Dodgers fan's drive home.

At that point of the season, the Dodgers needed every out. Koufax's masterpiece kept the Dodgers a half game out of first place. Five days later when Hendley beat Koufax 2–1 in Wrigley Field and then when Ernie Banks sent a second-inning liner off Drysdale's ankle and knocked him out of what would become an 8–6 Dodgers loss, they were four-and-a-half games behind San Francisco and a game behind Cincinnati.

What happened next was an illustration of how a starting pitcher can become a Goliath and how there are never enough slingshots or stones to conquer two. Much less three. Drysdale was back on the mound two nights later in St. Louis. More importantly, he was back at bat. He drilled a two-run single and lasted five innings in a 3–2 win for his 20th victory.

Koufax shut out St. Louis the next night. Osteen and Ron Perranoski shut them out the next afternoon. Drysdale won at Milwaukee 3–1 on September 21. Koufax and Drysdale shut out the Cardinals on September 25 and 26. Drysdale unfurled another shutout in September 30—this one 4–0 against Milwaukee. All told, the Dodgers won 13 consecutive games and gave up five total runs in the last seven of them, and Drysdale was 4–0 during the streak with one earned run.

On September 28 Johnson's 12th-inning home run put the Dodgers a game ahead of the Giants. The next day Koufax shut out Cincinnati, while the Giants were losing 8–6 on Bob Gibson's grand slam. Yes, Goliaths were pretty good with wooden weaponry; Drysdale was hitting .296 at the time, the best average on the club. "Give me 400 at-bats," Drysdale said with a grin, "and I might be back on the bench where I belong."

Don Drysdale signs an autograph for a fan from Japan during the Dodgers' Goodwill Tour in 1956. (Peter O'Malley)

Don Drysdale stands in Ebbets Field during his rookie year in 1956. (Peter O'Malley)

Don Drysdale poses during his breakthrough season in 1957 when he went 17–9 for the Brooklyn Dodgers. (AP Images)

Big D casts an intimidating presence in 1959, a year he led the National League in strikeouts (242) and hit batsmen (18). (AP Images)

From left to right: Tokyo Yomiuri Giants manager Tetsuharu Kawakami, Don Drysdale, Dodgers president Walter O'Malley, and National League president Warren Giles appear at spring training in Vero Beach, Florida, in 1961. (Peter O'Malley)

Don Drysdale gets some side work done under the watchful eye of pitching coach Harold "Lefty" Phillips (foreground left) during spring training in 1967. (Nobuhisa Ikuhara)

Don Drysdale, who was a fixture in Hollywood, stars as Roy Grant in ABC's *Lawman* in 1960. (AP Images)

Jim Bouton of the New York Yankees and Don Drysdale of the Los Angeles Dodgers hang out in Dodger Stadium before the start of Game Three of the 1963 World Series, in which Drysdale threw a three-hit shutout. (AP Images)

From left to right: Don Drysdale, Tommy Davis, and Sandy Koufax perform on Bob Hope's show in 1963. (AP Images)

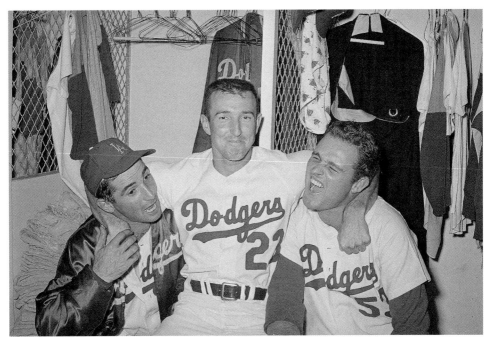

Claude Osteen, who won Game Three of the 1965 World Series, clowns around with Sandy Koufax (left) and Don Drysdale (right) of the eventual World Series champions. (AP Images)

Los Angeles Dodgers general manager Buzzie Bavasi poses with Don Drysdale (left) and Sandy Koufax (right) after settling their contentious contract negotiation in 1966. (AP Images)

Los Angeles Dodgers pitcher Don Drysdale holds up a ball marked "58 ⅔" to indicate the number of scoreless innings he pitched before the Philadelphia Phillies snapped his streak in June of 1968. (AP Images)

Ronald Reagan, the California governor at the time before going on to become president, presents Don Drysdale on Don Drysdale Day in September of 1969. (Peter O'Malley)

On March 22, 1984, Dodgers president Peter O'Malley (left) and Vin Scully (middle) unveil Don Drysdale Drive in Dodgertown at Vero Beach, Florida. (Peter O'Malley)

Fellow Dodgers join Don Drysdale for his 1984 Hall of Fame induction at Cooperstown, New York. In front is Roy Campanella, and behind Campanella (from left to right) are Peter O'Malley, Carl Erskine, Duke Snider, Pee Wee Reese, Sandy Koufax, and Drysdale. (Peter O'Malley)

Ann Meyers Drysdale acknowledges the Dodger Stadium crowd after throwing out the first pitch on Don Drysdale Bobblehead Night on May 14, 2022. (AP Images)

Drysdale finished with a chef's kiss on the final day of September, blanking the Braves 4–0 and reducing the magic number to two. That was his 23rd victory, and he also raised his batting average to .302. With his knee still throbbing, Drysdale got through the game in 89 pitches and later said he felt "strong as a bull." "Sandy Koufax and Don Drysdale are probably the greatest pair of pitchers any ballclub ever had," said Bob Scheffing, the Cubs' manager.

Koufax was 26–8 with a 2.04 ERA. Drysdale was 23–12 with a 2.77 ERA. Koufax started 41 games; Drysdale started 42. That's 83 starts for two pitchers in a 162-game season. Koufax completed 27 games; Drysdale completed 20. Koufax threw eight shutouts; Drysdale threw seven. Koufax threw 335 ⅔ innings; Drysdale threw 308 ⅓. Koufax struck out 382 batters, a record for post-1900 baseball; Drysdale struck out 210. The Dodgers were 30–11 when Koufax started and 26–16 when Drysdale did. Koufax lost six games in which he produced a quality start. Drysdale lost eight, and Osteen, who was 15–15 overall, lost 10.

Then the Dodgers eyed the Minnesota Twins, who had American League MVP Zoilo Versalles at shortstop, deluxe pitchers like Mudcat Grant and Jim Kaat, and a thunderous lineup with Harmon Killebrew, Bob Allison, and Don Mincher. The Twins scored 774 runs. No other American League team had scored more than 680. The Dodgers had scouted them, but their best scout was Osteen, who had faced them often when he was pitching for Washington. It was time for Bavasi to weigh in. "We can sweep them if we play the way we can," he said.

"We've heard that talk," Killebrew said. "The boys have been talking about that."

Game One at Metropolitan Stadium in Bloomington, Minnesota, happened to fall on Yom Kippur. Koufax would not pitch. Since Drysdale would take the hill, that didn't seem like a drop-off at all. But Mincher homered in the second inning. Drysdale's bad knee buckled as he bent to field Grant's bunt in the third, and the throw skipped past Lefebvre, covering first. Versalles then homered. Drysdale gave up two doubles. The Dodgers were down 7–1 with two out, and Walter Alston made the slow walk to the mound.

The situation was so absurd that Drysdale could only look at Alston and laugh. "Right now," he said, "I bet you wish I was Jewish."

Drysdale's equanimity lasted to the end of the Twins' 8–2 win and beyond. "If I have to get beat, I'd rather it happen this way," he said. "It was a case of bad command. I couldn't get the ball anywhere near the plate, and when that happens, you don't deserve to win. There were just a lot of bad pitches."

The Twins also cited Drysdale's spitball, which he laughed off. "The ball Mincher hit was a high slider," he said. "If it was a spitter, it must have been a bad one. Maybe somebody should teach me how to throw a good one."

Minnesota manager Sam Mele called Koufax "the only pitcher that I would pay to see warm up." But Kaat would become a Hall of Famer and in some eyes the best fielder who ever pitched. "It was actually a great situation with no pressure," Kaat said. "Nobody thought I was going to beat Koufax anyway."

The two were in a tight duel when Lefebvre slammed what appeared to be at least a run-scoring double to left. Allison dove, slid, and backhanded the ball like a snow cone before he landed headlong. It was one of the great catches in World Series history. Lefebvre didn't see the catch but did see Fairly, the base runner, running back across second and toward him. *Why is he running the wrong way?* Lefebvre thought.

Alston called upon his most reliable pinch-hitter for Koufax in the seventh. That was Drysdale, whom Kaat retired. A couple of errors by Gilliam came into play, and the Twins won 5–1 to take a 2–0 series lead. Maybe there would be a sweep after all. "I thought we were going to lose four straight," Wes Parker said. "The Twins just pummeled us. What people don't remember is how Claude Osteen saved us. He was always overlooked, but he shouldn't have been."

Osteen pitched a five-hit shutout in Game Three and then handed the ball to Drysdale for Game Four. Big D was better this time, going nine innings and giving up only five hits, but it was the Dodgers' guerrilla offense that flummoxed the Twins. It included six hits that never left the infield. L.A. won 7–2, which brought Koufax back into the World Series. He threw a four-hit shutout in Game Five, but the Twins were already dazed and confused by Wills' four hits and Willie Davis' three steals. The 7–0 win took the World Series back to Minnesota. "Remember: I said we'd win four straight," Bavasi reminded the writers. "I didn't say which four."

That disclaimer went out the door when the Twins won Game Six 5–1, as Grant launched a three-run homer. "Now we're at Game Seven, and the home team has won every game," Parker said. "I'm thinking, *How are we going to manage this?*"

"Manage" was the correct word. The night of Game Six and the events of Game Seven were a definitive time for Alston, Drysdale, and Koufax. The options were clear. Drysdale had three days' rest. Koufax had two. Drysdale had given up four home runs to the Twins, however, and Koufax was Koufax. "This is the kind of terrible problem every manager would like to have," Jim Murray wrote in the *Los Angeles Times*. "It's like trying to decide whether to date Elizabeth Taylor or Jane Fonda."

Drysdale knew what Alston was thinking and also knew Alston wasn't afraid to manage without a parachute. If Koufax started and flamed out, Drysdale was better suited to warm up quickly, and then the left-handed Perranoski would be available at the end. The left-right-left aspect was appealing to Alston. But the Dodgers knew they'd be getting 100 percent of whatever Drysdale had. They couldn't be as sure about Koufax. Alston, Bavasi, and the coaches kept pondering and theorizing. Finally, Drysdale himself opened the door to their office on the morning of the game. "Smokey," he said, addressing Alston, "I'll be in the bullpen if you need me."

"That summarized Don about as well as anything," said Bill Bavasi, Buzzie's son. "He made it easier for everybody."

Drysdale began warming up in the first inning but stopped when it appeared Koufax was himself. Rarely did he watch games from the bullpen. "I could hear Sandy's pitches and the catcher's mitt popping," he said. "That's pretty good from 400 feet away."

Drysdale also did not mention his role as facilitator. He depicted it as the manager's call. "I have absolutely no complaints," he said. "Whatever Alston's reasons were, they were good enough for me."

"Don is one of the finest team players I've ever had," Alston said.

Johnson homered off Kaat in the fourth. Parker followed with an RBI single. Fire up the *Kay-O'*, the Dodgers' plane. Koufax gave up three hits and no runs and won 2–0. The Dodgers had been champions before. But this time they were legends. "You are talking about the greatest pitcher alive and maybe dead," Grant said. "The only thing I can do better than Koufax is sing and dance. As far as pitching goes, I'll wait until he is through."

Koufax came into the clubhouse and Drysdale immediately hugged him and kissed him on the cheek. "You beautiful, beautiful fellow," Drysdale exclaimed.

7

Me and My Shadow

Bill Bavasi was eight years old, sitting in the back seat of the car, when he heard his dad, Buzzie, tell his mom, Evit: "This is going to be a problem."

Bill understood perfectly. The defending world champion Dodgers were addicted to Sandy Koufax and Don Drysdale. No other controlled substance would do. The withdrawal symptoms were severe bouts of shivering on the part of Buzzie, the general manager. As the Dodgers began to gather themselves for another trip to Vero Beach, Florida, Buzzie was developing hypothermia.

The 1962 National League pennant floated away when Koufax developed a mysterious lack of circulation in the fingers of his left hand. The Dodgers had swept the Yankees in the 1963 World Series because Koufax, Drysdale, and Johnny Podres were untouchable. They had just edged the Minnesota Twins in the 1965 Series because Koufax had dominated Game Seven on two days' rest. That year Koufax won 26 games, and Drysdale won 23. Together they pitched 47 complete games. The Dodgers won 97. They were 56–27 when Koufax or Drysdale started.

Bavasi, the general manager of the Dodgers, already had one salary problem. Maury Wills, the 1962 Most Valuable Player and the matchstick of the Dodgers' brushfire offense, was already campaigning for $100,000 in 1966. That wasn't happening. Wills didn't help himself when he had been a no-show for a clinic in Pasadena, California, that accommodated 6,000 kids.

Instead Wills was on his way to a nightclub engagement in Minneapolis, where he would play the banjo. Bavasi was at a Lakers–Celtics game in the Sports Arena when someone asked his reaction. "I think he's somewhere over Omaha right now," he said, "and I hope he keeps on going."

Could the Dodgers win without Wills? Unlikely, but some of the Dodgers wanted to try. Wills had been polarizing, particularly when the Dodgers appointed him the captain of the team. He began devising club policies and then would sit out when manager Walter Alston superseded them.

Could they win without Koufax, Drysdale, or both? Unthinkable. Yet on February 20, the two pitchers announced they wanted a total of $1 million spread over three years. The news shook seismologists out of bed. A deal involving multiple years and a holdout staged by multiple players were both too audacious in the context of the mid-1960s. But there was a third last straw. Koufax brought in a negotiator. This was not man-to-man bargaining in the Montague Street office in Brooklyn, not anymore. This was the way the showbiz folk did it. J. William Hayes was an entertainment lawyer who had represented Vincent Edwards, the star of *Ben Casey*, a popular drama on ABC. He also represented producers Aaron Spelling and David Wolper and actors Robert Stack and Lloyd Bridges. "I know they want a bundle," Bavasi said. "But I am prepared to make each of them an offer and I want them signed, sealed, and delivered so they can begin spring training. It is not our policy to give contracts of more than one year's duration, and that includes Walter Alston."

Bavasi felt his bonds with Koufax and Drysdale were tight enough to make this work. He had known them both since they signed. Like most people, he respected and admired Koufax and adored Drysdale, whom he called "Donald." He, though, also feuded with Drysdale throughout their years together as intensely as a father and son would. Bavasi never shrank from rebuking Drysdale in the newspapers. Drysdale preferred to hear those criticisms in person and shot back in kind. But Bavasi knew Drysdale's buttons were eminently pushable, particularly in the daily tempest of his early years.

One night Bavasi called the Drysdale home, where Don's wife, Ginger, was attending to Kelly, the Drysdales' 18-month-old daughter. "What are you doing?" Bavasi asked.

"Putting the baby to sleep," Ginger replied.

"Which one?" Bavasi asked.

Bavasi primarily objected to the assumption that Koufax and Drysdale were equals. Everyone was familiar with the Western TV show *Gunsmoke* back then. Drysdale was Chester to Koufax's Matt Dillon. Bavasi said that if Koufax wanted to peel off a few bills and compensate Drysdale, that would be fine with him. But he swore he wouldn't succumb to such a leverage play. "We were in the Army reserve together," Koufax said on a visit to Dodger Stadium in late March of 2023. "Don had a restaurant and bar. After a reserve meeting, we were sitting around at his place, and Don's wife, Ginger, was the one who suggested it. She brought it up and said it'll be like a small union. So that's what we did."

Drysdale and Koufax also compared notes. Koufax told Drysdale that he had gone to see Bavasi about his contract and came away disappointed. "You try to be fair," Koufax said, "and they try to pull something like this."

"When did you talk to him?" Drysdale asked.

"Today."

"Today?" Drysdale asked. "I talked to him yesterday. He told me the same thing he told you."

At the time Willie Mays was the highest-paid player in baseball with a two-year contract that paid him $125,000 per. Hayes' first proposal would have paid Koufax and Drysdale $166,000 each per season through 1968. Koufax had just turned 30 on December 30. (Tiger Woods and LeBron James also have December 30 birthdays.) Drysdale would turn 30 on July 23. The average salary in Major League Baseball was $19,000. The reserve clause was steadfastly in place, keeping players bound to the teams with whom they had originally signed. A holdout was the only weapon that players had, but it was becoming more popular. San Francisco's Juan Marichal, Minnesota's Mudcat Grant, and Cincinnati's Jim Maloney were all pitchers who were planning holdouts. "I'm looking for security and I think I'm entitled to it," Koufax said. "If you hurt yourself in baseball, you're looking for a job. For too long, people have been comparing [Drysdale and me] to each other."

As players prepared for camp, they applauded the men whom the newspapers were calling the Gold Dust Twins, or simply K&D, which sounded more like a cafeteria. Angels shortstop Jim Fregosi signed for $41,000. "That's slightly short of a million," he said.

Claude Osteen, the underestimated third starter who had saved the Dodgers in the 1965 World Series, announced that he was on the hunt for Koufax's "arthritis" from the previous year, so he could transplant it into his own elbow. Asked where the Dodgers would finish without K&D, Philadelphia manager Gene Mauch said, "Two games south of Spokane."

At Vero Beach teammates pasted a photo of Koufax and Drysdale over an exit sign in the clubhouse. Bavasi enlisted a photographer, then knelt in front of the door with hands clasped in prayer. "We loved the holdout," pitcher Joe Moeller said. "It gave me a chance to pitch for one thing. I was going to send them a telegram to say, 'Hang in there, guys.' But it stunned everybody. The fact that they did it together, I mean. Now that we know how much the owners were making at the time, it makes a lot more sense. But $100,000…that was a lot. There's no question they deserved it. You never heard anybody say, 'What are they thinking?'"

It was not quite March. Laughter was still possible. So was patience. Walter O'Malley, for his part, issued statements that could have come from the United Nations. "It's that time of year," O'Malley said. "It might be spring fever. They are entitled to good money, and I am sure they will get it. They are fine boys. I have studied the approach of the boys and I must say it's pretty good. By going as an entry, they figure, well, maybe the old man can do without one of us. That is a logical outlook. They are entitled to get anything they can out of Buzzie Bavasi. The only question is what Buzzie will get out of me."

Bavasi himself was not quite as calm. He had an ironclad budget on a sheet that was now soaked with coffee, courtesy of K&D. Control had escaped him. It was replaced by a ticking clock. "I was in the room when Buzzie was talking to Dad," said Peter O'Malley, who succeeded Walter and ran the Dodgers until 1998.

Peter still had an office near the top of an office building on Figueroa Street, five minutes south of Dodger Stadium, early in 2023. It is a window to an unhurried past. When he needed to find the date of Drysdale's funeral service, he opened a large cabinet that revealed dozens of red, bound address books, ones that went back to Walter's days, recording everything on the O'Malleys' agenda. When he needed to write a letter, he summoned an assistant to take dictation via shorthand. Everything O'Malley has said or done almost without exception has been deeply calculated.

Many things Bavasi said or did were conceived the second before he said or did them. "I'll try to be diplomatic here," Peter said. "I hate to criticize someone when they're no longer here. But I think Buzzie could have handled things a little better."

*   *   *

Emil Bavasi was nicknamed "Buzzie" by his sister Iola because he was always buzzing around the house in Larchmont, New York. As a grown-up he was just as hard to ignore. The Dodgers won four World Series and lost four others when he was running the show and he kept a hard thumb on the clubhouse and the ledger, too. Walter O'Malley's budget was ample for the times but not infinite. It was geared toward scouting and talent development. However, Bavasi held the high cards in any player negotiation and he played them with a Snidely Whiplash glint in his eye. Sometimes he would startle a player by asking, "How much do you think you're worth?"

The player would invariably mention a figure lower than what Bavasi had prepared. Many other times Bavasi would ask the player if he was up for a game of chance and then write salary figures on three different slips of paper and ask the player to pick one. The Dodger would be pleasantly surprised when he picked the highest number. He left the office smiling, not yet knowing that all three of Bavasi's slips had borne the same number. "That's what he did to me," Moeller said. "You'd walk in there and he'd start yelling at you: 'What the hell do you want? Tell me why you think you deserve this money.' But when it was all over, he might give you 20 bucks out of his pocket. Or if you got sent down to Spokane, he might pay for your family to be with you. That was nice. But he would do things that made you feel guilty."

"You'd think I'd be miserable," Bavasi told *Sports Illustrated*, "arguing and cajoling and disagreeing with the people I like best in the world. But I like arguing and cajoling and disagreeing and so do the ballplayers. The competitive spirit comes out."

Tommy Davis, who drove in 153 runs in 1962 and won the National League batting titles in 1962 and 1963, wanted $25,000. Bavasi found that unfeasible. Davis came to the office, and Bavasi set a proposed contract on his desk that paid Davis $9,000. Then his assistant, Edna Ward, called and said O'Malley needed to see Bavasi, who excused himself.

Davis peered at this dummy contract, as Bavasi knew he would. Bavasi had walked out of the room, knowing Davis couldn't resist looking at the contract. When Bavasi came back, Davis admitted that on second thought maybe he was a bit over his skis. He had come to the conclusion that he should ask for something more fair like $12,000. Bavasi congratulated Davis on his epiphany and as a goodwill gesture said he could offer $18,000. That was one of Bavasi's goals all along. The other was to make sure Davis thought he'd won, which Davis did.

Those players who knew Bavasi's story could see past the bluster. They knew he had been the general manager for the Dodgers' farm club in Nashua, New Hampshire, and that he welcomed Don Newcombe and Roy Campanella to play there in 1946, just as Jackie Robinson was making his debut in Montreal, home of the Triple A affiliate. When the Lynn Red Sox began taunting the Black members of the Dodgers, Bavasi challenged them all to a fight, though he first made sure that his manager, the formidable Walter Alston, was on hand.

Bavasi's unwavering defense of his players was noticed. Newcombe and his wife named their daughter Evit after Mrs. Bavasi. There were days when Bavasi was one of the boys. At spring training he noticed Norm Larker, affectionately known as Dumbo, jogging in labored fashion. "Dumbo, you're so slow I could beat you in the 100-yard dash," Bavasi told him.

"I've got $250 that says you can't," Larker said.

"You're on," Bavasi said.

The next day, Bavasi showed up with spiked track shoes. Larker got a little nervous. "Oh yeah, I ran a 9.4 when I was in college," Bavasi told him.

By then Bavasi had recruited Don Drysdale to run interference. "Norm, I've seen the old man run," Drysdale told Larker. "He can fly. Are you sure you want to do this?"

Larker got cold feet without spikes and proposed a $100 settlement. Bavasi, who probably hadn't run a total of 100 meters in five years, accepted it, and then returned the track shoes to wherever he'd borrowed them. No word on whether any of the money filtered back to Drysdale. "Lots of clubs go out of their way to make one or two stars happy," said Roger Craig, the pitcher who came west from Brooklyn and wound up with the Mets in 1962. "The Dodgers take care of the players right down the line. You gotta pinpoint Bavasi for being responsible."

In 1959 the Dodgers sent Craig to Spokane, Washington, in Triple A. That meant a $1,500 pay cut. Craig asked Bavasi if he would get it back if he were called back up. Bavasi grudgingly promised he would. Craig returned in June and won a game against Cincinnati. He and Bavasi shook hands. When Craig pulled his hand away, there was a $50 bill in it. "Take your wife out and have a good time," Bavasi said. The next day he asked Craig if he wanted the $12,500 in a lump sum or spread out over time. "It's a happy club," Craig said. "A happy club that gets first-cabin treatment will play its heart out."

But the fencing match over salaries was no longer sport for Bavasi when Sandy Koufax and Drysdale brought out the long swords. It did not help that Bavasi tried to divide and conquer, upbraiding Koufax for thinking he was worth that much more than Drysdale, upbraiding Drysdale for thinking he should be in the same salary ballpark as Koufax. Bavasi still felt he could call their bluff before the Dodgers went to Vero Beach, Florida, for spring training. He called Drysdale, and the two pitchers met for breakfast with Bavasi at the Roosevelt Hotel. By the time the coffee got cold, the dimensions of the new frontier were clear. Bavasi offered Koufax $115,000 and Drysdale $100,000 but only for one year. "Believe me, it's no fun for me to tell Drysdale that he's not as good as Koufax, but I had to do it," Bavasi said.

No dice. Koufax and Drysdale weren't talking that day, but Bavasi filled the vacuum. "All I will say is that I offered more than any two players have ever been paid," he said. Well, that wasn't all he would say. "It was more than two players on the same club have ever been paid," he went on. "They were not impressed. We are too far apart for further discussion. I would have to tear up every contract among the other men and make them new contracts. They certainly see why I can't pay them five times as much as Ron Fairly, for example. I might be faced with an entire outfield or infield negotiating as a unit. Ninety-nine percent of the players in baseball would be happy to sign for what I offered each of them yesterday. They must readjust their thinking. They were not impressed by my figures, although I was."

The prospect of Koufax and Drysdale leaving on top was more than anyone could comprehend. A sign on the Hyatt House on the Santa Ana

Freeway near Anaheim, California, announced, "Dodgers Have Offered Koufax Orange County."

Meanwhile, J. William Hayes had advised Drysdale to lay low, though most reporters who covered the Dodgers had Drysdale's phone number and called him periodically. "If there's a picture of Drysdale riding a horse and lying in a hammock, there could be reactions," Hayes said. "We think it could only lead to trouble."

There were no such reins on Bavasi. When Koufax turned down $7,000 for a TV appearance with Bob Hope, Bavasi observed, "If he'd take a few of those jobs, I wouldn't have to pay as much."

On March 6 Bavasi said, "I don't think they're bluffing. But I know I'm not." On March 8 Bavasi said, "Three owners have told me not to give in."

A harsh light finally found Drysdale. The Hotel and Restaurant Workers Local 694 of the AFL-CIO announced plans to picket Drysdale's Dugout, the restaurant in Van Nuys, California, in hopes of getting a union contract and fringe benefits. Drysdale left the response up to his partner, Jack LaFaye, who said Drysdale was pro-union "all the way" and that the pitcher had asked the workers if they wanted to be organized, and "none of them did."

Drysdale did observe that he was pitching hay and grooming his horses as a way of staying fit. Presumably, he wasn't brushing back the horses with 90 mph bales.

On March 12 there was rumbling from the top of the mountain. O'Malley announced that his "final offer" would pay Koufax $100,000, Drysdale $90,000, and Wills $70,000. "And as far as I'm concerned the negotiations are off, and we'll play this season without all three of them," he said.

An enthused Bobby Bragan, manager of the Braves, told the *Los Angeles Times* that the Dodgers would be "no factor, like on the tip sheets at the dog track," without their 1-2 punch. "And if Wills doesn't show up, you can say they fell at the first turn."

Claude Osteen, beginning to sense the gravity, said, "It would be like driving a car without a steering wheel."

When the calendar turned to mid-March, Wills finally agreed to meet Bavasi in Dodgertown. And there was movement from Koufax and Drysdale. But it was taking them toward Hollywood, not Vero. Paramount announced Koufax and Drysdale would be appearing in a movie called *Warning Shot* directed by Buzz Kulik, who would later direct *Brian's Song* and had directed several episodes of *Playhouse 90* and *The Twilight Zone* for TV. David Janssen was the star, and Koufax would play a police sergeant and Drysdale a TV commentator. Shrewd casting, at least for Drysdale.

Publicist Bob Yeager said Koufax and Drysdale had signed with Bob Banner Associates. Banner was a TV heavyweight who had produced the Garry Moore and Dinah Shore variety shows and would create events that would raise money to save Carnegie Hall, starring Jack Benny, Carol Burnett, and Julie Andrews. These were not representatives of street theater. The TV world sensed there was a market for K&D and was eager to test it. Yeager also said shooting would begin on April 4. Drysdale denied that. Then Hayes also floated the idea of a 10 week tour of Japan that would produce at least $100,000.

Koufax said somewhat mournfully that he was fortunate to "have done what I did. But if this ends it, well, that's it. They said, 'Well, we will miss you, and that's the last I've heard.'"

When Bavasi heard about the movie contract, he said, "Well, I guess that settles that."

Resistance and contempt were growing. Wrote Jack Smith in the *Los Angeles Times*: "Anybody who has seen Drysdale in a Gillette razor blade commercial can guess at the torture of seeing him in a full-length movie."

Lefty Phillips, the Dodgers pitching coach and the supervising scout when the Dodgers signed Drysdale, said he doubted if either career would survive the empty spring. "Most pitchers have adhesion problems in their shoulders after just laying off for the winter," Phillips said. "To be inactive for an entire year would be a lot worse."

On March 22 Drysdale emerged from hibernation. He began working out at Pierce College. This seemed to confirm the report that Drysdale had told trainer Wayne "Doc" Anderson to "keep my stuff dusted off." He played host to 190 Little Leaguers at Pierce. He worked with Notre Dame High in Sherman Oaks and helped pitcher Mike Link with his curveball.

He revealed that he had spoken to O'Malley unilaterally, bypassing Bavasi, who proclaimed that his feelings were officially hurt. Bavasi explained that he had a "more personal" relationship with Drysdale than with Koufax. "I'm disappointed that he would do that," Bavasi said. "But unless I'm naive, I have to believe they won't sign. They can't act and pitch at the same time. If they can make more money in the movies and they tell me they're independently wealthy, I wish them the best of luck."

O'Malley was more soothing. "They are good boys, and I sincerely believe they want to play baseball. And I do hope that somewhere along the line, a rule of reason will apply," he said. "I was rather pleased that they called."

The dissonant messages were not helpful, Peter O'Malley said. After all, Walter O'Malley's call would be the only decisive one. Bavasi's emotions and opinions were stirring the waters. "I always thought the quickest way from point A to point B was a straight line," he said. "With Buzzie there always had to be a few curves in it."

There would be a few more sliders thrown. On March 23 the Drysdales gave a joint interview. "We're both terribly upset," Ginger said. "Every year Buzzie has played one against the other to get them to sign. How would you like to be in the position of fighting your best friend for a raise? One day, the boys sat down and said, 'Aren't you tired of all this?' What gets me is that we're neither needed or missed."

She claimed that Bavasi sent them a letter saying, "Haven't changed my offer one bit. Wish you were here. Miss you. The weather is fine."

"They're asking me to accept a $10,000 raise," Don said. "They have given me bigger raises in years when we didn't win the pennant or the World Series. They haven't given us an offer except for the first one, and that was an ultimatum as far as we're concerned. We told them we wouldn't accept another one."

Drysdale scheduled a meeting with Jeff Corey, a drama coach. Two days later he agreed to act in a TV series called *The Iron Horse*. Dale Robertson, a popular leading man at the time, was the star. "It's about a train or a fellow who inherits a train," Drysdale said. "I would have a running part week by week. It's not a pilot. It's already been sold to ABC. It would be a seven-year deal."

Opening Day was looming. Jim Maloney signed with the Reds for $46,000. Cincinnati general manager Phil Seghi explained that he'd told Bavasi he would hold out Maloney from Dodgers games if Bavasi would do the same to Koufax and Drysdale. "I didn't get an answer," he said, "so I figured I'd better go out and get Maloney."

The laughter had turned nervous and brittle. Los Angeles was anxiously drumming its fingers on a tabletop.

At the annual Western Bancorporation shareowners' meeting, J.A. "Foghorn" Murphy observed that the company should pay attention to the holdout. "If Koufax and Drysdale, working a couple of hours a day twice a week, think they should get $1 million for three years, then the full-time head of a $7 billion corporation ought to receive as much," Murphy said. He made a motion that would pay Frank L. King, the chairman, $1 million over three years. At the time King was paid $120,000.

The Dodgers' opener was April 12 at home against Houston. On March 25 Juan Marichal showed up at Giants camp. A couple of days after that, Bavasi finally called Drysdale. "I called Donald because you know how hard it is to get hold of Sandy," he explained.

"Fun is fun," Bavasi told Drysdale. "But this is getting serious." He offered to fly back to Los Angeles.

They met at Nikola's Restaurant. That in itself was a sign of progress. Nikola's was at 1449 W. Sunset, just down the street from Dodger Stadium. It was known as a hangout for USC Trojans fans and a likely place to spot John McKay, John Robinson, and O.J. Simpson. When it came time to negotiate the deal to build Dodger Stadium, Walter O'Malley used Nikola's as the setting while he fenced with city negotiators, generally ordering a White Label scotch with a splash. Nikola's was closed on this day, but the owners gave a back room to Bavasi and Drysdale. By then Chuck Connors, the former Dodgers first baseman who had become the star of *The Rifleman*, had become an intermediary. "These boys are ready to sign," Connors told Bavasi.

But Connors wasn't at Nikola's, and neither was Hayes. The meeting, like the famous tree in the novel by Betty Smith, had its roots in Brooklyn.

As Bavasi recalled it in 1967, he told Drysdale, "All right, Donald, what is it going to take?"

Drysdale suggested $125,000 for Koufax, $110,000 for himself, and one year only. He said Koufax knew about this and had blessed it. Bavasi said he could also vouch for O'Malley but said he'd have to wait until an exhibition game ended in Vero before he could tell him personally. The first pitch was just a few minutes away. They both went to the pay phones—Bavasi to call O'Malley and Drysdale to call Koufax. The news went out that afternoon.

The great holdout was over. Los Angeles could move back from the ledge. Baseball could avoid bankruptcy. Bill Bavasi has a more specific memory. "My understanding is that it originally came down to Sandy getting $125,000 and Don getting $100,000," he said. "Sandy said, 'No, Don should get the same thing I'm getting.' Buzzie said, 'No, we can't do that.'"

O'Malley had budgeted $225,000 for both. There was no room for Buzzie to wiggle. Koufax clearly deserved $125,000. "But Buzzie was pretty loyal to Don and he thought he should get more than that," Bill recalled. "So he told Edna Ward to draw up the contract and give Don $110,000. He'd figure it out later."

Back in Vero Beach, O'Malley beamed over the results of his patience. "Sometimes you stand pat," he said. "And sometimes you draw another card."

Koufax, according to Bavasi, was overjoyed. "Now I don't have to act in that movie," he said.

Screen Gems released Drysdale and Koufax from *Warning Shot*, though Koufax and Drysdale would still appear on ABC's *Hollywood Palace* on April 9. *Warning Shot* came out in 1967 with Keenan Wynn playing the part that Koufax forfeited and Steve Allen filling Drysdale's role. *The Iron Horse*, which was actually about a gambler who wins a train in a poker game and has to figure out how to get it on track, had a two-year run on ABC. "I told everyone I deserved the Oscar that year," Buzzie Bavasi said, "just to spare the movie industry from having those two guys on the screen."

The exhalations at Vero Beach threatened to blow down the palms. "I'd rather be part of the Big Three than the ace," Osteen said.

"Yeah, baby," outfielder Lou Johnson said. "My money was in danger."

Chub Feeney, the general manager of the Giants, skillfully disguised his regret. "It's wonderful that we have the stars of our league back," he said. "It would not seem fair beating the Dodgers this year without them. I hear Sandy is getting 15 percent of the club and Don 12.5 percent."

Drysdale said that even his goat was "getting sulky" at his home in Hidden Hills during the vigil, but he also made sure Hayes was not forgotten. "He gave us wonderfully good counsel," Drysdale said. "There's no telling what we would have done without him. We've got to thank him. From a business standpoint, he didn't need us at all. This was just a drop in the bucket compared to some of the business negotiations he has handled."

And that was the subtext to all of this. Off the field, the Dodgers were playing in a faster league. In Brooklyn they were part of the everyday furniture of the place. They became friends with the people in the streets mainly because they all walked the same streets. Their bankbooks and lifestyles were roughly the same. But in L.A. the Dodgers were embraced by the singers, the actors, and the show business community. Their idea of fair compensation was in a different realm.

Bavasi remembered a conversation at Ebbets Field with actress Joan Caulfield, as they both watched Joe Black pitch. The ballpark was at capacity that day with 32,000 on hand. Caulfield asked Bavasi how much Black was making. "He's making $12,000, and that's what he'll make next year, too," Bavasi replied.

Caulfield shook her head. After one year in Hollywood, she said her price per picture had risen to $100,000. "Yeah, but none of your pictures get rained out," Bavasi said.

Mark McCormack had already become famous for representing Arnold Palmer, Jack Nicklaus, and Gary Player. Soon Bob Woolf would become the groundbreaking agent in team sports, first handling the business affairs of Red Sox pitcher Earl Wilson and then representing Ken Harrelson and John Havlicek and eventually handling over $1 billion worth of player deals. Tom Reich and then Scott Boras would take the business to unforeseen orbits in baseball, as would Howard Slusher, Marvin Demoff, and Leigh Steinberg in football. Today the top athletes live behind gates and moats, just like the top entertainers.

Bavasi could have used an agent himself. After the 1966 season, Walter O'Malley left the salary line empty on Bavasi's contract. O'Malley told Bavasi that he'd done a good job and he should write in whatever he thought he was worth. Bavasi figured he should just write down what he'd made in '66 without a raise and that O'Malley would benevolently bump up the figure himself. When the deal came down, Bavasi was making no more and no less than he was before. "So much for my skill at negotiating salaries," Bavasi said.

Television revenue was a trickle in Brooklyn, and early Dodgers games in Los Angeles were rarely televised. The national TV package boiled down to one Saturday Game of the Week, featuring Dizzy Dean and Buddy Blattner, who was replaced by Pee Wee Reese. It almost never originated from California and often involved the Yankees, who became the weekly attraction when CBS bought them.

The bucket would become a meteor crater and the drop would become a flood to an extent no one could imagine in 1966. Spurred by the Braves' move to Atlanta, an antitrust trial in Milwaukee required Walter O'Malley to testify. In response baseball would add four more teams in 1969 to make 24 and split each league into two divisions, adding an extra layer of post-season play. In what would become a familiar cry of victimization from the American League franchise down south, pitcher Dean Chance said Koufax and Drysdale had agreed to their contracts long ago and that the holdout was a hoax all along designed specifically to overshadow the grand opening of Anaheim Stadium.

None of this would be allowed to rain on this parade. With Koufax and Drysdale aboard, there seemed to be no obstacle to a third World Series championship in four years. "The gimmick worked," Bavasi said later. "But be sure to stick around for the fun the next time somebody tries that gimmick. I don't care if the whole infield comes in for a package. The next year, the whole infield will be wondering what it is doing playing for the Nankai Hawks."

There would be a day when a Dodgers infield made up of Steve Garvey, Davey Lopes, Bill Russell, and Ron Cey would be muscular enough to carry a team to the postseason. But in the mid-1960s, only two pitchers had that power. The sight of players actually sensing power and wielding it was unfamiliar to men in Bavasi's generation. But the power came directly from those two arms, not from their decision to band together. "This would have been a miserable season without them," said Bavasi.

Plenty of misery, though, was waiting for one.

*　　*　　*

On June 25 Don Drysdale lost at Atlanta 4–3 in the second game of a doubleheader. His record was 4–10, and his ERA was 4.47. The next day Sandy Koufax also pitched at Atlanta. He won 2–1. It was already his 14th complete game of the season. His record was 14–2, and his ERA was 1.56. The Dodgers were tied for second place four games behind San Francisco. Guess who was getting blamed? In the *New York Daily News*, Dick Young wrote, "Maybe Drysdale can hold out with Nate Oliver next time." Oliver was a reserve infielder who hit .226 for his career and never played in more than 99 games in a season.

In the *San Francisco Examiner*, Prescott Sullivan wrote, "His imposing height suggests he could command respect as a gateman or a guard. They could put him on one of the hot dog counters. A place might be found for him as a groundskeeper. Unless the situation improves, it is possible that big Don will be asked to sell tickets, sweep out the stands, or work in the regular lot between his regular turns. You've got to admit that anything O'Malley can get out of the big guy is better than nothing."

In the *San Pedro News-Pilot*, Van Barbieri wrote, "Big D is no longer. Don Drysdale is no longer the highest priced right-hander in the majors. He's the highest priced right-handed pinch-hitter. At the rate he's doing, he should hit the 20 mark without too much trouble…20 losses, that is."

In the *Long Beach Independent*, George Lederer wrote, "The season is one-third old today, which means Don Drysdale has collected $35,000 at the rate of $8,750 per victory. The stats qualify Drysdale for assistance from the pitchers' anti-poverty program. Is he as poor as the record indicates?"

And from Sixth Street in Long Beach, reader Ray Peavy wrote to the *Independent*, "You said you could not understand why Don Drysdale was being cast as a villain in the holdout this spring while Sandy Koufax was getting the red carpet treatment. This is easily explained, and I'm sure you realize the reason yourself. Had Koufax gone through the holdout alone, it would have been settled much faster, and more than likely, Sandy would have ended up with a bigger piece of the pie. Drysdale was just hanging on like a tick, knowing that, whatever the asking price, with Koufax alongside, it would be met."

That was becoming a majority opinion. To Dodger fans who were biting off an extra fingernail per loss, Drysdale had ridden Koufax's superior coattails. He was nowhere near the equal of the Left Hand of God, and the fact that Koufax had included him in the holdout gambit began to look like a needless favor for a buddy. After a 4–2 loss to Houston on June 20, Drysdale lamented to reporters, "You tell me what's wrong. I certainly don't know."

But he had a pretty good idea. It wasn't just that Drysdale was being compared to a left-handed teammate who was in the midst of the most phenomenal pitching run that the National League had seen in modern times. Koufax was also a physical freak who could have leaped out of a New Year's Eve bed to throw low-hit games. Spring training was a contrivance for Koufax. It was necessary for almost everyone else. "Sandy had the longest fingers you ever saw," Joe Moeller said. "They could completely enclose a baseball. He threw so effortlessly. Wayne, our trainer, had been in Cincinnati, where they had Ted Kluszewski. Ted was huge, a big power hitter. Wayne said Sandy had bigger lats than Klu did."

But Koufax could not transfer his powers to Drysdale now that Drysdale finally needed them. "I've pitched lousy," Drysdale said. "Nobody knows it better than I do. What it gets down to is: some pitchers can miss spring training, and some can't. I need the whole six weeks, throwing almost every day. I learned that this year. Sandy is different. There's such a contrast between his fastball and curve that all he has to do is work the ball up and down on each hitter. But I don't have Sandy's stuff. I have to work around two inches on each corner. If I can hit those spots, I've got command."

It all had to do with the triceps muscle. With each outing, it "toned in," as Drysdale said. It was the last muscle to fall in line, and as it changed, Drysdale's release point had to change. That was the reason a bad game always seemed to be lurking behind a good game. "Normally, all of this would've been worked out in spring training," Drysdale said.

Yeah, but Jim Maloney also missed the bulk of spring training and at the end of June was 9–3 with a 2.74 ERA. Juan Marichal was 13–3 with a 1.92 ERA.

Along came Buzzie Bavasi to pick at the scab. "Drysdale doesn't look like he's in shape to me," he said. "And he's making too many mistakes. He lost a game because he didn't cover first base, lost another because he dropped a ball, another because he pitched carelessly on an 0-and-2 pitch. Nobody should lose a game on an 0-and-2 pitch. I don't know what it is. He seems to have too much on his mind."

Then Bavasi brought the ultimate weapon. In those days players did not necessarily get richer with every year of service. Their paychecks could shrink, too, depending on performance. Clubs could not cut salaries more than 25 percent, but if Bavasi was looking to economize, there was only one target, standing nearly six-and-a-half feet tall. "It would be difficult to cut someone 25 percent if they were making $20,000," Bavasi said, momentarily revealing his warm and fuzzy side. "I couldn't do it. However, if other players have a good season, someone has to gain, and someone has to lose."

Really? Drysdale's salary could actually be reduced to $82,500? "It looks like he's worried more about cutting me 25 percent than winning

the pennant," Drysdale replied. "That's his prerogative. It's also my prerogative to refuse it. Anyone in the front office can put a padlock on my
locker anytime they think I'm not giving 100 percent or I'm not in shape."

His locker remained accessible. As slowly and doggedly as a Mack truck
climbing a mountain pass, Drysdale began saving his season. On June 29 he got
through six innings with nine hits but only three runs, and the Dodgers won
at Cincinnati 9–5. "You don't know how good a win feels right now," he said.

In the next start, he pitched nine innings, but his fate was sealed from the
moment the Cardinals chose their starting pitcher. Larry Jaster was a left-hander
who compiled a career record of 35–33. But in 1966 he threw sleeping pills
at the Dodgers. They faced him five times, lost five times, and did not score
a run over the course of 45 innings. They had 24 hits—all singles. It was the
first time a pitcher had shut out the same team five times in a season since the
Phillies' Grover Cleveland Alexander had done it 50 years prior to Cincinnati.
"I just hope the big guy doesn't get his dauber down," Walter Alston said with
a sigh. The Dodgers were in fourth place, five-and-a-half games out.

A win over the Mets, a 4–0 loss to the great and powerful Jaster, back-
to-back complete games, a 4–2 loss to Marichal and San Francisco when
Jim Lefebvre missed a pop-up, an old football knee injury that popped in
the second inning and took Drysdale out of a start against the Reds, and a
palm thorn that wedged inside Drysdale's foot as he was trimming trees at
home…if it wasn't one thing, it was four or five others.

When Drysdale started against the Giants on September 6, two days
after his knee disorder, and couldn't escape the sixth inning, his record sank
to 9–16. Koufax was 22–8, but he had just told someone that a bone spur
in his elbow had grown to a half inch. "If I were 20 instead of 30, I'd be
worried," Koufax said.

The Dodgers already were. They were tied for second, a game and a half behind Pittsburgh. Along the way Bavasi had sent a conciliatory note to Drysdale. At least Bavasi thought it was conciliatory. "I read it," Drysdale snapped. "I'm going to keep it for a year and then I'm going to throw it away. I've never needed any needles to give 100 percent. I didn't think Buzzie would do that to me. I resented it."

On September 10 Drysdale was mountainous again. He allowed Houston four hits in eight and one-third innings. In the ninth Alston removed Drysdale in favor of Phil Regan, who was known as "the Vulture" for his knack of swooping in from the bullpen just in time for the Dodgers bats to awaken and get him a win. Regan retired Chuck Harrison, then retired Houston in the 10th inning. Al "the Bull" Ferrara singled in the 10th off Mike Cuellar, and the Dodgers won 1–0. The Vulture improved his record to 13–1.

Ferrara put on a 20-gallon hat that he'd purchased for $1.98 on Olvera Street, just down Sunset from Dodger Stadium. "This is my Super Sombrero," he said.

Drysdale seemed perturbed over the arrival of The Vulture in that game, but Alston said he kept the grumblings to himself. "It wouldn't make any difference if he did object," Alston said. "But I appreciate it that he's never once complained. There is no better team man than Don Drysdale."

September was starting to feel familiar. On September 15 Drysdale faced off with Vernon Law, traditionally the Pirates' best pitcher. Drysdale won 5–3, though Roberto Clemente and Willie Stargell homered in the ninth and drove him out. "I hope nobody got hurt out there," Drysdale said brightly. "And Stargell must be in a slump. He hit three homers last time I faced him."

The Dodgers now led by two-and-a-half games. Koufax followed with a five-hitter and a 5–1 win. On September 19 Drysdale went the distance and beat Jim Bunning and the Phillies 6–1. The lead was a game and a half as the Dodgers got to Chicago with an off night before a doubleheader. "We were having a tough time winning that pennant," Claude Osteen said. "I was rooming with Ron Fairly. We got a call from Don that night. He was at the bar downstairs. He told me that me and the Fox [Fairly's nickname] should come downstairs. He obviously had something on his mind. We got down there, and he was in deep thought. When he was like that, he'd take two fingers and put them on his lips and start tapping them. He wanted to talk about winning the pennant. He said, 'Hey, we can win this thing.' I remember thinking we needed to win several in a row. We weren't that kind of a club, not that year. But we all had a get-together. And then we kinda stole it."

Drysdale led off the doubleheader by allowing one Cubs hitter to reach third base in a complete-game, 4–0 win. Four days later the Dodgers got to St. Louis, and Drysdale managed to dodge Jaster and face Ray Washburn. He won 2–0, and L.A. led by three. Only then did Drysdale realize he had forgotten his eighth wedding anniversary. Without a card or a gift for Ginger, he had nothing to deliver but an apology, which he did on the postgame radio show.

Then that same sign on the same freeway asked, "Whatever became of Don Drysdale?"

"I've been wondering that myself," Drysdale said.

"We can smell the money," Lou Johnson said, but Jaster could smell the Dodgers. He shut them out 2–0 the next night. Asked to explain Jaster's particular brand of voodoo, Alston said, "I'd ask the players, but I'm afraid they'd hit me over the head."

But Koufax won 2–1 the next night, and the Dodgers took a two-game lead into the final weekend in Philadelphia with three games left. The

Pirates were in second place, and the Giants were a game and a half behind them. They played each other in Pittsburgh, and if the Giants could get within a half-game of the lead by Sunday night, they had a makeup game in Cincinnati Monday. It would only be played if necessary. But if it was, the Giants could force a tie with a win. "We've been in worse spots and won," Drysdale said. "We've been in better spots and lost."

They found themselves in discomfort, a spot they knew well. They lost Friday, as Chris Short won his 19th for the Phillies, and were rained out Saturday. The Giants swept the Pirates Saturday after the Friday game was rained out. So the Dodgers needed one win in a Sunday doubleheader at Philadelphia with Drysdale and Koufax lined up. "I have a funny feeling they're going to lose both of them," said Herman Franks, the Giants' manager.

Drysdale got little chance to win or lose the first one. He was down only 2–0 when Alston gave him the hook six outs in. The Dodgers went on to lose 4–3 on errors by infielder Dick Schofield and reliever Bob Miller. Meanwhile, the Giants were trailing 3–2 in the ninth when Ozzie Virgil's single tied it. Willie McCovey's two-run home run in the 11th inning led to a 7–3 win. With radios in their ears to listen to the Dodgers' nightcap, the Giants headed to the Pittsburgh airport. They were either flying the short way to Cincinnati or the long way back home.

Koufax, on two days' rest, made sure the Giants' vacation began on schedule. He didn't give the Phillies a run until the ninth. By then Willie Davis had homered for a 3–0 lead, and John Roseboro's sacrifice fly augmented that, and the Dodgers were up 6–0 in the eighth. In Pittsburgh an airline employee told Giants pitcher Ron Herbel, "I guess it's tough, not knowing where you're going."

Herbel shook his head. He had been listening to the game. "Superman isn't giving up seven runs," he said.

The crew that Pittsburgh pitcher Alvin McBean had called "a Triple A team" won, and the Dodgers left shaving cream, champagne, and the stress of a long, long season on the clubhouse floor in Connie Mack Stadium.

Drysdale finished his regular season with a 13–16 record, though his 273 ⅔ innings ranked fifth in the league. Koufax finished his regular season with a 27–9 record. For the fifth consecutive year, he led the league in ERA (1.73). In those five years, he won 111 games and lost 34.

For one month they were equals. "I imagine every person who gets a large salary has a feeling this is something to protect," Drysdale said. "But I did not let my difficult days in the summer throw me. When things were going bad, I didn't see the bad mail I received. They cut that off before it got to me. Sure, it was embarrassing to lose that much, but I knew that when the adhesions had time to break loose, when I fixed up my rhythm and command of pitches, I wouldn't be horseshit any longer. When you are done in this game, you are the first to know it. I never believed I was done."

* * *

While the Dodgers were toiling in Vero Beach, Florida, without Sandy Koufax and Don Drysdale in the spring of 1966, a less recognizable figure dropped by. Marvin Miller had been a negotiator for the United Steelworkers. In 1966 he visited every spring training site and campaigned to become the leader of the new Major League Players Association, an idea that was significantly supported by a player vote of 489 to 136.

Two years later, Miller and the owners reached a collective bargaining agreement with a significant raise in pay and a structure to have grievances heard. Two years after that, they signed another agreement, establishing an independent arbitrator to handle those grievances.

After the 1969 season, Curt Flood, the outfielder whom the Cardinals tried to trade to Philadelphia, sued baseball in hopes of making himself available to every team. The Supreme Court denied Flood in 1972, as Miller had told Flood it would. By then Flood had sat out the 1970 season, played only 13 games for the Washington Senators in 1971, and then retired. But the players were on the verge of a long winning streak. When the Oakland A's failed to fulfill an annuity payment to star pitcher Jim "Catfish" Hunter in 1974, arbitrator Peter Seitz declared him a free agent, which set up a wild invasion of Hertford, North Carolina, by executives from all corners of baseball. The Yankees signed Hunter for the flabbergasting sum of $4.5 million over five years, counting a signing bonus.

Dave McNally of Montreal and Andy Messersmith of the Dodgers played out their contracts in 1974 and then filed a grievance against the existence of the reserve clause, which bound each player to the team that had signed him. Seitz sided with them, too. In doing so he became perhaps the leading rainmaker in the history of baseball.

A liberated Joe Rudi left Oakland and signed a five-year, $2.1 million deal with the Angels. Reggie Jackson was right behind him and signed a five-year, $3.5 million deal with the Yankees. Oakland reliever Rollie Fingers began negotiating with Buzzie Bavasi, who was now the president of the San Diego Padres. "He said, 'I'll give you $250,000 a year for five years and then a $500,000 signing bonus,'" Fingers recalled. "I said, 'Give me the pen!' I was making $63,000 a year at the time."

Bavasi's next post was with the Angels, and when Nolan Ryan decided to leave the Angels after the 1979 season, Bavasi was blamed for this primarily because he said the Angels could find "two 8–7 pitchers" to replace the man who had gone 16–14 but was the first true gate attraction the Angels ever had. Actually, Ryan and his wife, Ruth, still lived near Houston and considered it a homecoming. The Astros rewarded him with a four-year, $3 million contract, and Ryan was the first player to make $1 million per season.

Only 12 seasons later in 1992, the average major league salary was $1,028,667. In 2000 Alex Rodriguez signed a 10-year, $252 million deal with the Texas Rangers. In 2023 the average salary would rise to $4.9 million. Concurrently, MLB revenues were $10.3 billion in 2022. Eight clubs were valued at $2 billion or higher, and 29 of the 30 were valued at $1 billion or higher. (The Miami Marlins were the exception and valued at $900 million.) That's a long way from the $311 million that FOX paid the O'Malley family for the Dodgers in 1997, and that deal had been twice the size of the previous high team transaction and terrified fellow owners.

It's difficult to draw a direct line from the K&D holdout and the money torrent of today. But at the very least, the pitchers showed their contemporaries that power existed in the clubhouses and dugouts, depending on who the players were and whether they worked together. The specter of more players teaming up in the offseason probably made Miller a stronger negotiator. "The best thing I ever did," Drysdale declared at season's end, "was to join Sandy and have Bill Hayes represent us together. We just thought about what we'd meant to the club the last 10, 11 years."

With Koufax and Drysdale remaining in the fold and Drysdale rounding into form, a World Series vs. the Baltimore Orioles awaited. The Orioles won 97 games in 1966. They clinched the American League pennant on

September 22. They had traded pitcher Milt Pappas to Cincinnati for Frank Robinson, whom Drysdale had often used for target practice, and Robinson not only won the Triple Crown by hitting .316 and clubbing 49 home runs with 122 RBIs, but he also led the American League in runs, on-base percentage, and slugging. Robinson said it was a relief to escape National League gas-pumpers like Koufax, Juan Marichal, and Drysdale.

Robinson, third baseman Brooks Robinson, shortstop Luis Aparicio, and pitcher Jim Palmer would make the Hall of Fame. Palmer was 20, Wally Bunker was 21, and Dave McNally was 23, and together they were 38–22. Yet the Dodgers hadn't lost a World Series since 1956, two years before they moved to California. National Leaguers walked around with a smug superiority borne out largely by truth. Most Dodgers fans assumed K&D would rule this World Series as they had the previous year and the one in 1963.

Wes Parker, the first baseman, was not among them. "We were exhausted," he said. "We had to come from behind. We hadn't been in first place the whole season. We just hung on. We had to wait until the last day to win the pennant and now we had to fly right back to L.A. for the series. Suddenly, we were there. Our goal had been the pennant. Nobody was ready."

That included Drysdale. Both Robinsons launched home runs off him in the first inning. Walter Alston pulled him before the third. "They were both high fastballs," Drysdale said. "I just couldn't get the ball where I wanted to. People have made mistakes to those guys all year, and I've been seeing it on the scoreboards."

The Orioles led 4–1, but McNally, struggling with Dodger Stadium's steep mound, loaded the bases on walks in the third inning. Manager Hank Bauer removed McNally and brought in Moe Drabowsky, a world-class prankster and veteran of nine clubs who had been demoted to the minor leagues by the Kansas City A's just the year before.

No one imagined that Drabowsky would be the one to show all the actors, singers, and dancers in attendance what a Hollywood ending really is. The Dodgers got to within 4–2 when Jim Gilliam walked. Then Drabowsky got John Roseboro to foul out. He pitched six and two-thirds innings and gave up one hit. He struck out 11, and Baltimore won 5–2. "Moe showed us what to do," said Palmer, who was trying to calm himself before his Game Two matchup with Koufax. "High fastballs and breaking balls away, they couldn't hit them."

Drabowsky once called Hong Kong on the bullpen phone and ordered a full Chinese dinner to go. He had been famous before, as a foil to the more famous. He was the losing pitcher when Early Wynn won his 300th game and he gave up Stan Musial's 3,000th hit. But that night in his Connecticut hometown of Windsor, the homefolks staged a parade through the streets.

Game Two is best remembered for fly balls that kept attacking Willie Davis in center field. He misplayed one of them and threw another one away. No one had committed three errors in a World Series game before, but three other Dodgers made errors, and no Dodgers player scored. It made a prophet of Alston, who had wondered before Game One why World Series games were played in the afternoon since few regular-season games were. Palmer and the Orioles won 6–0, as Koufax had a streak of 22 consecutive scoreless innings snapped in World Series play. But Frank Robinson said Koufax had been "50 percent as effective as the Koufax that I know" and that he seemed "tired."

The Dodgers travelled east for the third and fourth games and then returned to California, but they couldn't bring the Orioles with them. Claude Osteen gave up just three hits to the Orioles in Game Three. One was a home run by Paul Blair. Thus, Baltimore won 1–0 since Bunker was silencing the Dodgers. Drysdale came back for Game Four and pitched one of his best games of 1966. He needed only 84 pitches. Baltimore had four hits. One was a home run by Frank Robinson. Thus, Baltimore won 1–0 since McNally thwarted the Dodgers.

No previous team had failed to score in more than 28 consecutive World Series innings. The Dodgers failed to score in 33. They hit .142 with 17 hits, and 13 of them were singles. Drabowsky in Game One was the last reliever Baltimore was forced to use. "A couple of days ago, we told you the Dodgers looked dead," wrote Charles Maher in the *Los Angeles Times*. "We regret to announce at this time that their condition has deteriorated."

"They got some great pitching," Drysdale said. "They deserved everything they got."

More to the point, Al Ferrara dared to look into the future. It looked bleak to him. It would be worse than it looked.

"The party's over," he said.

*   *   *

Capsolin is a devil's bargain. It is a red ointment that is so incendiary that when Cleveland traded Gaylord Perry to Texas, its trainers told the Rangers' trainers to wear gloves when applying it. "Sandy used so much of it," Claude Osteen said, "it would turn his black T-shirts red."

"He needs a lot of it, more than any pitcher I've ever seen," trainer Wayne Anderson said. "We give him a whole tube of it."

In Sandy Koufax's final regular-season game of 1966, something popped in his neck. From the fifth inning on, the trainers were lathering on the

Capsolin. Koufax also used Butazolidin, which would become familiar to sports fans two years later. An athlete was disqualified for using "Bute." His name was Dancer's Image, the apparent winner of the 1968 Kentucky Derby. Human beings who used "Bute" were leaving themselves open for aplastic anemia. There was arthritis in Koufax's elbow, too, along with that burgeoning bone spur.

So, on November 18, those who looked backward could see it all clearly. Koufax had held out because he had known 1966 would be his final year in baseball. He announced it at the Beverly Wilshire Hotel. There was little advance notice, and no Dodgers officials were in the room. Buzzie Bavasi was agitated because Koufax wouldn't delay his announcement to let Walter O'Malley and the rest of the club return from their exhibition tour of Japan. Koufax said he already felt guilty enough about the way he'd concealed his decision.

It was the end of one of the most arduous journeys to one of the greatest careers in the history of pitching. Koufax had gone from Brooklyn to the University of Cincinnati on a basketball scholarship. In fact, Ed Jucker was his baseball coach and also the junior varsity basketball coach and later coached the Bearcats' varsity to two NCAA basketball championships. His main problem in the winter was trying to find someone willing to catch Koufax's sizzling baseballs in the dark campus gym.

Koufax did have games of 18 and 17 strikeouts on the varsity level, but he had thought of himself as a first baseman. The Dodgers gave Koufax an $18,000 bonus, even though he had only pitched 10 games in a Coney Island semi-pro league and five games for Cincinnati. He came to Brooklyn when he was 19 years old and forced by the bonus rule to pitch before he was anywhere close to ready. His ripening years went by slowly. There were startling games like a 6–3 win against Milwaukee on May 20, 1958. He went 11 innings that night and gave up two hits.

He also threw a league-high 17 wild pitches and walked six batters per nine innings. His home record in the four Los Angeles Coliseum years was 17–23 with a 4.33 ERA. From 1958 through 1960, Koufax walked 297. But few could figure out a way to hit him, not even then. The league's batting average against Koufax in 1960 was .208, just three points higher than his career mark. The Dodgers had enough pitching to indulge Koufax's development, and besides where was he going to go? There was no reason to trade a man with such nuclear stuff. In 1961 it began to click. Koufax led the league in strikeouts for the first time with 269, which broke the league record. He went 18–13 and led the league in fewest hits permitted over nine innings.

He wasn't necessarily one of the guys since he had grown up with ideas of becoming an architect, enjoyed museums and classical music, and took classes at Columbia University. There was no assimilation into the hard-elbowed professional world because Koufax never rode those buses, never played in the minors. But occasionally he would surprise people. In 1961 he and Larry Sherry stayed out late in Dodgertown and missed curfew by two hours. Walter Alston, who usually wasn't up that late himself, spotted them and asked them to explain. Koufax and Sherry dashed into their room and locked the door, whereupon Alston, whose well-hidden fury was a sight to behold, bashed the door so hard that he knocked a couple of diamonds out of his 1959 World Series ring.

That was more like a Don Drysdale situation. Koufax and Drysdale were opposites who attracted, and that magnet was hard to deactivate, as Bavasi and Walter O'Malley found out. "Koofoo and Donnie were really close," Ann

Meyers Drysdale said. "He would come stay with us, and they'd stay up all night, laughing and telling stories. People didn't see that side of him very often."

Koufax knew he was retiring in the spring. The only person he told was Phil Collier, the beat man for *The San Diego Union* and a cherubic fellow who was unanimously liked and known to his friends as "the Phantom." Collier often joked that he was working on a memoir of his days on the road to be called, *The Bases Were Loaded and So Was I.*

Koufax told Collier that if he could hide the news for all those months, the retirement announcement would be his exclusive scoop. Collier did, and it was. "I've taken a few too many shots and a few too many pills," Koufax said. "I'd be high half the time from the pills. My stomach would hurt from the pain pills. I think I had one game last year where I didn't have pain."

Drysdale didn't go to Japan with the Dodgers. From home he said the announcement "leaves me with an empty feeling. It was a privilege to pitch with Sandy."

Bavasi wasn't in Japan either. He and Evit were preparing for a vacation in Hawaii. They went to a nightclub. To their surprise they saw Maury Wills on stage playing guitar with Don Ho. Bavasi already knew Wills had left the Dodgers in Japan with some sort of leg injury. Apparently, his strumming hand was okay. Before long, Wills was a member of the Pittsburgh Pirates.

The Dodgers got to the holidays with no illusions. Their sum would no longer be bigger than their parts. They had lost Koufax and Wills, the architects of the 1–0 wins, the main drivers in the Dodgers experience, one of the few that everyone in Los Angeles could share. The 1966 season had drained and changed the organization. The Dodgers would not visit another World Series for eight years and would not win another one for 15 years.

One day in the mid-1980s, Koufax was helping pitchers in Vero Beach, Florida, and decided to cut it loose himself. He put a 90 on the radar gun. Drysdale saw him a few days later and said, "What the heck are you doing? If you're throwing that hard, you can make a comeback."

"I don't think so," Koufax said. "I can do that for a while. But once I stop, I can't start again."

Koufax and Drysdale had leaned on each other to become the highest-paid pitchers in the history of the game, the only ones who were making more than $100,000 a year. As the season ended with the high of a pennant and the low of a World Series sweep, the holdout was pretty much forgotten.

But not by everyone. Bavasi opened a note from O'Malley at Christmas. O'Malley thanked Bavasi for keeping the team together well enough to win the National League pennant. He congratulated him for surviving the holdout and keeping the roster strong. "And thank you," O'Malley concluded, "for giving up your $10,000 bonus this year."

8

Summer Wind

It was a spring day in 1913, and Walter Johnson, known as "the Big Train," felt slightly off-track as he rolled into St. Louis. He had ridden the rails from his home of Coffeyville, Kansas, to join his fellow Washington Senators. When he got to Sportsman's Park, he mentioned a bothersome headache. Still, there were fans to entertain—11,000 on this afternoon—and there were St. Louis Browns to strike out. Johnson needed two outs in the first inning to set the all-time record for consecutive scoreless innings previously held by Jack Coombs.

This was notable because Coombs had thrown 13 shutouts for the Philadelphia Athletics three years before. Coombs had a chance to study chemistry as a postgraduate student at MIT but opted for baseball. Later in life he would coach Duke's baseball team for 24 years, and one of his students was Dick Groat, the famed Pittsburgh and St. Louis shortstop. Coombs also is credited with telling one of his players, "Don't think. It will only hurt the ballclub." Crash Davis would later immortalize the phrase in the movie *Bull Durham*, which was set in Duke's hometown of Durham, North Carolina.

Coombs was respected. Johnson was mobbed. At one home game, paperboys walked into the ballpark waving copies of *The Washington Times*, proclaiming that Johnson and his fiancé, Hazel, would be married that night.

Tales from his boyhood were breathlessly repeated, including reports that no one could actually see his fastball, and any wooden contact with it was a happy accident. Yes, this was in the midst of the deadball era with huge ballparks, legal spitballs, and emery balls, and a baseball itself that was not replaced until it began to come apart. Still, Johnson was supreme. In 1913 he would win 36 games, lose seven, and be named Most Valuable Player of the American League. He would lead the league in strikeouts for the third time. He would do it nine more times.

It was May 14. Johnson had not allowed a run since Opening Day on April 10, a game witnessed by President Woodrow Wilson at Griffith Park, when Johnson beat the Yankees 2–1. Since then the Big Train had pitched seven times, including five times as a starter, with four complete-game shutouts. He tied Coombs' mark of 53 consecutive zeros when he struck out Pete Compton, the leadoff man, in the first inning. The next hitter, Johnny Johnston, flew out to center fielder Clyde Milan. The Senators led 6–0 after two innings, and Johnson stymied St. Louis through three. Then, with the 56-game streak in his pocket, the Big Train began playing with his food, as he sometimes did when he wasn't challenged, like the day when he threw a 15-hit shutout.

Gus Williams doubled to left field in the fourth, and Del Pratt singled him home. Pratt would collect 1,996 big league hits and became a part of the Yankees' Murderers Row later in the decade. The Senators won 10–5, and Johnson's streak was done. Despite that, almost 25,000 fans turned out in Detroit to see Johnson's next performance.

Johnson won 417 games. He remains—and it's likely that he'll always remain—the only pitcher in baseball history to win 400 games and strike out 3,500 batters. Evidence abounds to support the opinion that the Big

Train was the best pitcher who ever lived. His streak would live through two World Wars and a Korean conflict, through Great Depressions and life-changing inventions. It ended 55 years later, by which time baseball had established itself on the shores of the Pacific, and fans sat in a magnificent stadium and listened to narrators on their transistor radios. Some would stay home and watch the games on images transmitted through a tube. More and more of those images were coming across the screen in color.

*   *   *

In 1968 the Dodgers returned to Vero Beach, Florida, a grapefruit haven on the Atlantic coast. Even in turbocharged times, it was leisurely. During most of March, the unchanging sun and the whispering breezes would protect Vero Beach from the world. That enforced a condition called Vero Hypnosis. If you stayed there for the entirety of spring training, you logically concluded that all upcoming possibilities were good, and the world was merely waiting for the Dodgers to arrive.

Most of the rookies stayed in barracks on the Dodgertown site. When you walked in the main building, you immediately saw a photo display of Jackie Robinson confounding four Philadelphia defenders in a rundown between third base and home. The paths from there to the field were named after Dodgers greats: Jackie Robinson Boulevard, Roy Campanella Avenue, Sandy Koufax Lane. Golf carts would roll by with those very players inside.

Vero Hypnosis would take hold in 1968, as always, and convince all bystanders that the Dodgers were invincible. And why not? Since they moved to Los Angeles, the Dodgers had won the World Series in 1959, 1963, and

1965; appeared in another one in 1966; and nearly won a National League playoff to enter another one in 1962. Families of the players were always nearby. There were Western nights, movie nights, barbecues, everything else you'd expect on a landlocked cruise. Traffic, fire, war, protest, and stress all seemed far, far away.

But when the Dodgers left Vero to play the season, the hypnosis lifted. Koufax had retired after the 1966 season. Suddenly, the Dodgers couldn't win games with four singles and three stolen bases anymore. The 1967 team had the worst batting average in the National League (.236), hit the fewest home runs (82), and made the most errors (160). Without Maury Wills, they were eighth in stolen bases, better than only two National League rivals. Their RBI leader was Ron Fairly with 55. He ranked 35th in the league.

The Dodgers finished 73–89, their worst season since they moved to Los Angeles, and it would be 19 years before they would lose that many games again. They were approaching a rickety bridge between the heroes of the mid-1960s and a re-launch of new stars, heading into the 1970s. It was not the best time to wind down a career.

Don Drysdale arrived in Vero that spring and realized he was the last Brooklyn Dodger standing. Jim "Junior" Gilliam was now a coach. Everyone else from the 1958 migration was gone. Drysdale had turned 30 during the 1967 season and—for a change—wasn't being blamed for the debris around him. He had reduced his ERA from 3.42 in 1966 to 2.74 in 1967. His record was identical to the year before at 13–16, but the Dodgers had presented him with 15 whole runs in his losses. While Drysdale was on the mound, the Dodgers averaged 2.8 runs, but it wasn't personal. They got 3.0 runs for Don Sutton and 3.7 for Claude Osteen. Most notably, the Dodgers were 21–19 when he pitched, and when Drysdale got to Vero Beach, he brought glad tidings. For the first time since the 1966 holdout, he was popping the catcher's mitt again. "He began throwing two weeks earlier this year," said Bill Buhler, the trainer. "I think that made a difference."

This did not deter Buzzie Bavasi from his habitual jabs. "How can you gain weight during spring training?" Bavasi moaned, claiming that Drysdale had zoomed from 210 to 218 pounds since he arrived. He knew that his jabs had always worked on Drysdale before.

But Drysdale refused to shoot back. He was in a serene place. It was difficult to avoid seeing him during the offseason. He appeared in *Cowboy in Africa*, a TV series with Chuck Connors and Tom Nardini. When Jack Benny returned for his only variety special of 1968, he brought heavyweights like George Burns, Bob Hope, Dean Martin, and Danny Thomas. Drysdale was in that cast, too.

Drysdale still had his restaurant, his stock portfolio, and his horses. His wife, Ginger, was in demand for fashion shoots and she sometimes brought daughter, Kelly, along. Drysdale looked at the young pitchers, who were bubbling up through the system, like Alan Foster, Mike Kekich, and John Purdin. He saw Mudcat Grant coming to join Osteen, Sutton, Phil Regan, Bill Singer, and Jim Brewer, and he saw new shortstop Zoilo Versalles. Like Grant, Versalles was a prominent member of the 1965 Twins, who had lost Game Seven of the World Series to Koufax. "I wouldn't be surprised if some of these young pitchers don't do well enough to replace some of the veterans," Drysdale declared. "And I wouldn't blame the management if that happened."

In truth this was an intersection in Drysdale's career. Was he propped up by Koufax, his holdout partner? Was he revered but no longer feared? Was there a Hall of Fame in his future with 190 wins and no 200-strikeout seasons since 1965? "If I pitch the way I'm capable," he said, "I can win 20 games this year and I have three or four good years left."

It soon became clear that the Dodgers had gained no muscle. Drysdale began with a four-hit shutout of the Mets. True to custom, it was 1–0. In his first six starts, the Dodgers gave him 15 runs. On May 5 he pitched 10 innings against the Reds, gave up no walks and one earned run, and left a 2–2 game that Cincinnati won in the 16th inning when Johnny Bench doubled off Purdin.

Five days later in Atlanta, Drysdale singled to lead off the sixth inning and scored on Willie Davis' sacrifice fly. With the game tied at 1–1, Drysdale gave up twin singles to lead off the seventh and came out in favor of Jack Billingham. After manager Walter Alston had intentionally walked Felipe Alou to load the bases, Versalles then made his sixth error of the young season on Felix Millan's grounder, and Sonny Jackson scored. He was Drysdale's responsibility and his run. The Dodgers lost 2–1. They were 13–14, and their starting pitchers had a better batting average than their regular lineup (.230 to .215). Drysdale's record was 1–3, and his ERA was 2.52.

What happened over the next month would turn Jackson into a trivia question and Drysdale into a plaque on the Cooperstown wall. But the nation was a little too distracted to notice Drysdale until the beginning of June. A lot was happening here. What it was…wasn't exactly clear.

*   *   *

On March 30, 28-year-old Marine captain Charles Robb reported for duty. He had prepared for three days at Camp Pendleton and now boarded a plane at Norton Air Force Base in San Bernardino, California. His wife of four months, Lynda Bird Johnson, said good-bye without tears. "I hope I can be as brave as the other women here," she said.

Robb's next stop was South Vietnam to settle at the marine command headquarters in Phu Bai. Lynda Bird's father was the current president of the United States. By the time Robb finished his one-year tour, there would be another one. The war had paralyzed Lyndon Johnson's administration, sent angry college students and sometimes their parents into the streets, and dominated the news to the point of obscuring the memory of the Civil Rights Bill and Johnson's other accomplishments of the mid-decade. In January the North Vietnamese and the Viet Cong had unleashed the Tet offensive.

During that same month, North Koreans captured the USS Pueblo, killed two Americans, and captured the remaining 81 in the crew. The sailors were beaten and tortured periodically for the next 11 months. They were freed only after they signed a document admitting "wrongdoing." The ship itself is still there. Johnson later wrote that the Pueblo was the first sign in his mind of how 1968 would run aground.

During all that it seemed almost a footnote when Eugene McCarthy, a shy, obscure senator from Minnesota, announced a fanciful run for president. Magically, Johnson's opponents gathered at his feet. In a New Hampshire primary that was supposed to be a formality, LBJ only defeated McCarthy by 48 percent of the vote to 42. Four days later, senator Robert F. Kennedy joined the race. That infuriated many of McCarthy's young supporters who had laid the first bricks. It also planted another seed in what had become an orchard of doubt inside the White House.

Kennedy committed to the race after he had visited Delano, California, on March 10 to meet Cesar Chavez, the leader of the United Farm Workers. Chavez was on his 25th day of a hunger strike. This highlighted the struggle to improve conditions for field workers. Physically carried by family and friends, the weakened Chavez celebrated Mass with Kennedy and ate a piece of bread that was about the size of a quarter. Chavez had a statement read to a crowd estimated at 10,000. He was too weak to read it himself.

The night after Robb left for Vietnam, his father-in-law spoke to the nation from the White House. No one knew that Johnson had shown vice president Hubert Humphrey two different versions of the speech that afternoon and told him to prepare to run for President. Nothing seemed untoward as Johnson began to speak. "With America's future under challenge right here at home and with our hopes and the world's hopes for peace in the balance every day, I do not believe I should devote an hour or a day of my time to any personal partisan causes," he said, "or to any duties other than the awesome duties of this office, the presidency of your country."

America began to stir. "Accordingly," LBJ said, "I shall not seek and I will not accept the nomination of my party for another term as your president." Amid the gasps, hardly anyone heard what Johnson said next. "But let men everywhere know, however, that a strong and a confident and a vigilant America stands ready tonight to seek an honorable peace and stands ready tonight to defend an honored cause," Johnson declared, as a strange smile flickered across his face and then disappeared. "Whatever the price, whatever the burden, whatever the sacrifice that duty may require, thank you for listening. And God bless all of you."

The bombing of North Vietnam stopped, and peace talks began. But the war would not end. The American death toll in Vietnam was 16,899 in 1968, easily the most of any year. Full withdrawal would not come until 1975.

Meanwhile, the Dodgers had left Florida. Their groundbreaking issues were Al Ferrara's quiet spring at the plate and Phil Regan's hospitalization with symptoms of arthritis. The club moved West to play exhibitions in Arizona and San Diego. Politics were someone else's problem.

The evening of April 4 would change that and most other things. Martin Luther King Jr. was in Memphis. He was bringing official heft to a dispute by sanitation workers. Two of them, Echol Cole and Robert Walker, had been crushed to death by a malfunctioning truck on February 1. A demonstration was squelched by Mace-spraying garbagemen. On April 3 a federal court passed a restraining order barring King from organizing a march. Three weeks later a demonstration organized by King and his aides was subsumed by violence, and Memphis mayor Henry Loeb called on 4,000 National Guard troops. The next night King prepared for a rally at the Mason Temple Church of God in Christ. He stood on the second-floor balcony at the Lorraine Motel, a short walk from Beale Street, where all the rooms had doors that faced the outside. King looked down and spotted Benjamin Branch, who would be the bandleader at the rally. "That's my man," King said. "I hope you play 'Precious Lord' tonight and play it real sweet."

Minutes later he was shot to death.

Within 24 hours riots in Chicago and Washington, D.C., claimed several lives. Washington hospitals treated 350 who were injured. Other cities burned as well, though Los Angeles was calm. Motorists in Watts shone their headlights during the day as a statement.

The National Basketball Association and National Hockey League postponed playoff games. But the Dodgers, now in San Diego, where Buzzie Bavasi would become president of the new Padres franchise in 1969, observed their exhibition-game schedule. Bavasi said fans needed the entertainment. Washington was the first team to postpone its opener. All the others but the

Dodgers followed. Bavasi said it made no sense to move their game back because King's funeral would be over by the time the West Coast game began. But the Philadelphia Phillies, the Dodgers' opponent on April 10, felt differently. The team was already in Los Angeles when general manager John Quinn flatly stated that the Phillies were prepared to fly home early and forfeit the opener. "We will either be 0–0 or 0–1," Quinn said. Manager Gene Mauch was even more explicit as he addressed his team in Palm Springs, California: "We will open the season 0–1 before we will put a team on the field."

The Dodgers' exhibition with Cleveland was the only pro sporting event held in America on April 8. That did not smooth the waters. "It angered me that a team that pioneered the advent of the Negro in Major League Baseball would take such a stand," said Bill White, a Black first baseman for the Phillies who would later become the president of the National League. "It's an affront to the 150 to 160 Negro players in the National League. If I were a Dodger, I would not play this game. I would tell them where to put their uniforms."

Mudcat Grant said he didn't want to play in that final exhibition and did not want to play Opening Day. "It's not a matter of rebelling," Grant said. "It's a matter of honoring somebody who has been important to a race. But I understand Mr. Bavasi's position. He honors the man. He has no disrespect for the game."

And Jackie Robinson himself was frosted by the Dodgers' intransigence. "Mr. O'Malley is a man of tremendous ability but also a man with a total lack of knowledge on the frustrations of the Negro community," he said. "It grieves me that he did not understand the importance of this thing."

The April 10 game was finally postponed by a night. The Phillies made the best of it with a 2–0 win, as Chris Short gave the Dodgers three singles and a double by Wes Parker. The crowd of 28,138 was the second lowest in Dodger Stadium history, maybe because of the postponement, maybe because of the unease of the times. At least Paul Popovich, who came over from the Cubs and played second base, made some sharp plays.

On May 14, 1968, Drysdale went to the mound against the visiting Cubs, exactly 55 years after Johnson's streak ended. Chicago's starter was Ferguson Jenkins. Even at 25 the 6'5" Jenkins carried himself with the gravity of a walking institution. His father, Ferguson, an immigrant from Barbados, had played outfield for the Chatham Coloureds All-Stars in Ontario, long before integration. His mother, Delores, was a track star whose parents had brought her to Canada through the Underground Railroad. She lost her sight in the effort to deliver her son.

The Phillies signed Jenkins but traded him, along with center fielder Adolfo Phillips, to the Cubs for aging pitchers Larry Jackson and Bob Buhl. The 1966 deal made the Cubs legitimate, and in his first year of starting, Jenkins won 20 games. He would do so in each of the next five years, including 1968, when he lost five 1–0 decisions. He would amass more than 3,000 strikeouts and fewer than 1,000 walks, and his 284 wins got him into the Hall of Fame in 1991, seven years after Drysdale's induction.

Unfailingly genial and kind, Jenkins repeatedly found himself in the crosshairs of heartbreak. His second wife, Maryanne, died in the aftermath of a car accident in 1991. The next year his girlfriend, Cynthia, drove out to an Oklahoma field near an oil well, took a hose, put it on the exhaust, and locked all the doors. Samantha, Jenkins' three-year-old daughter, was in the car. Cynthia and Samantha died of carbon monoxide poisoning.

On this night in May, Jenkins and Drysdale took pitching to celestial levels, as they often did, as many pitchers were doing in 1968. The game took only two hours and 18 minutes. The Dodgers got five hits off Jenkins in seven innings and scored when Ron Fairly's grounder brought home Parker, who had beaten out an infield hit.

Drysdale outdid Jenkins. The Cubs got two hits, both singles. Don Kessinger singled in the fourth inning and wound up on third on Drysdale's wild pickoff throw. In deference to Jenkins, Walter Alston ordered the infield to play on the grass with one out. He knew the Dodgers were unlikely to score again and he couldn't afford to trade an out for a Chicago run. All Drysdale had to do was take care of Billy Williams, Ron Santo, and Ernie Banks. All three are in the Hall of Fame. Williams had 2,711 career hits, Santo had 342 home runs over 15 years, and Banks had 512 home runs over 19 years and was a two-time MVP.

With one out Drysdale struck out Williams, who played 2,488 major league games and struck out in 9.9 percent of his at-bats. He walked Santo, but then he struck out Banks. Drysdale batted in the top of the ninth because starting pitchers often did that in 1968 and grounded out to first against Regan, the ex-teammate who had helped him develop the spitter. It was still 1–0 when he got to the bottom of the ninth and stared at Williams, Santo, and Banks again. They went down in order on two grounders and a fly ball.

Drysdale was 2–3 with an ERA of 2.14. Fourteen of the 24 outs he got were grounders. But he wasn't necessarily happy. "I couldn't stand something like that every time out," he said afterward. "I'm too old for that. You have to be lucky to win a 1–0 game, and it takes too much out of you. I wish we would start hitting."

On May 18, 1968, Drysdale went to the mound against the visiting Houston Astros. Houston's starter was Dave Giusti, who had pitched Syracuse to an unaccustomed spot in the College World Series. He also had a master's degree from Syracuse, and it appeared for a while that he would have to use it prematurely. Going into 1968 he only had one season with a sub-4.00 ERA. But something clicked for Giusti that spring, and he came to Dodger Stadium with an ERA of 2.02. Four days before his duel with Drysdale, he threw a two-hitter and lost in San Francisco.

The ERA would fade to 3.19 by season's end to go along with an 11–14 record. The next year Giusti went to St. Louis, suffered back problems, and was sent to Pittsburgh in 1970 because Roberto Clemente had seen him pitch in the Caribbean Series and recommended him. Suddenly, Giusti's palm ball began working, he got chances in the back of the bullpen, and he saved 56 games the next two years. In 1971 Giusti was the league's Fireman of the Year; in 1974 he gave up two home runs in 105 ⅔ innings.

But his catcher on this May 18, Ron Brand, had just come up from the minors three days before. He was far more familiar with the opposing pitcher. Gilbert Brand worked for Pacific Telephone in the Valley. So did Scott Drysdale. They were foremen, and their desks were adjacent in the office. Their sons played baseball. When Don beat the Phillies during his first start in 1956, Gilbert and Ron listened on the radio at home.

Ron went to North Hollywood High, five years behind Don at Van Nuys. He got to the big leagues in 1963 with Pittsburgh. He was 5'7", and the short guys tended to become catchers back then. His first game against Drysdale was in July of that year. Brand struck out the first time. He took a fastball in the elbow the second time. He was not surprised. "He was telling me I was standing too close to the plate," Brand said. "The next day he asked me, 'How's your elbow?' He was always getting on me. He'd call me Stimp. One day my son and I were warming up in front of the dugout because we had a father-son game, and the Dodgers were in town. Drysdale came over and said, 'How old is your son? Eighteen?' He was five. Don could get on you pretty good."

Brand was the leadoff man for the Astros that night and went 0-for-4. He wasn't alone. Drysdale and Giusti each pitched a five-hit complete game. The Dodgers won 1–0 and again scored a run by rubbing two sticks together. Parker led off the sixth with a base hit, moved up on Willie Davis' sacrifice, moved to third on Fairly's grounder, and scored when shortstop Hector Torres booted Ken Boyer's grounder.

Drysdale led off the eighth and singled. He was on second with two out, when Fairly singled to center. Jim Wynn wound up and threw home, and here came Drysdale, digging toward the plate with a recklessness that would have gotten managers fired in the 2020s. Brand caught the throw as Drysdale barreled into him. "He was late to the slide, and that's what caused the collision," Brand said. "He was on his stomach and he was reaching back for the bag. I yelled at him, 'Your butt is out.' After the game the clubhouse guy came over and said I had a phone call. It was Don from their clubhouse. He said, 'I didn't mean to run into you.'"

There was one more bit of business. Wynn doubled with one out and moved pinch-runner Ivan Murrell to third base. Alston ordered an intentional walk to Bob Aspromonte, which brought up Bob Watson, a struggling kid who would put together two 100-RBI seasons for Houston and later would become the first Black general manager in the major leagues while guiding the Yankees. But here Watson became the 17th Houston hitter to ground out, this time to Versalles. Back-to-back shutouts were not aberrations in those days. Nobody was saying that Drysdale's 18 consecutive zeros were becoming a streak.

On May 22, 1968, Drysdale went to the mound at Busch Stadium in St. Louis. The opposing pitcher was Bob Gibson. At 32 Gibson was crafting one of the classic pitching seasons in baseball history. His ERA of 1.12 was the best since 1911 and remains the best ever among those who pitched 300 innings. He pitched at least nine innings in 26 of his 34 starts and pitched at least eight in his last 32. Gibson also finished with 22 wins and nine losses, even though the Cardinals, defending World Series champs who would lose the 1968 Series in seven games to Detroit, gave him only 18 runs in those starts.

Gibson and Drysdale were the sergeants-at-arms of the National League with one difference. Drysdale would spin a batter at 8:00 PM and drink Scotch with him at 11:00 PM. Gibson refused to speak to National League teammates even at the All-Star Game, a three-day cease-fire in between hostilities. Gibson's career ended in 1975. The Cardinals held a Bob Gibson Day for him in September and displayed a statue. Gibson pitched in relief, and Pete LaCock of the Cubs blasted a grand slam. It was the final major league pitch of Gibson's career. Fifteen years later, LaCock came to the plate in an Old-Timers' Game in Kansas City. Bob Feller was pitching. Suddenly, Gibson bounded out of the dugout and relieved him. His first pitch drilled LaCock. "He was a difficult friend," Tim McCarver said.

McCarver was the Cardinals' catcher and years later would show off his disfigured thumbnail, a casualty of years of Gibson's sliders. McCarver's visits to the mound were usually dismissed with Gibson saying, "The only thing you know about pitching is that you can't hit it."

But then McCarver had already passed Gibson's biggest challenge. While riding a bus in spring training, the 18-year-old son of a Memphis cop was drinking a bottle of orange soda. "Can I get a swig of that?" Gibson asked knowingly as a guy, who had battled his way out of Omaha's tough neighborhoods, now testing a Southern kid with a crew cut.

McCarver thought a minute. "I'll save you some," he replied.

Gibson laughed. "Good answer," he said.

Tommy Helms was with the Houston Astros when manager Harry Walker came to him with an idea. "Step out when you're up there against Gibson," Walker said. Helms was skeptical but did it twice anyway.

Gibson then yelled at home-plate umpire Tom Gorman: "Tell him the next time he does that, I'm hitting him in the head."

What did Gorman say? "He said, 'Get in there and hit,'" Helms said.

"Gibby played with Bill White for years on the Cardinals," Joe Torre said. "He liked to pitch away, and Bill had good plate coverage and could get out there and pull it. He always told Bill that if he ever pulled a pitch at him, he was getting hit. They traded Bill to the Phillies, and Bill doubled down the right-field line off Gibby. Next time up? Sure enough, Gibby got him in the ribs."

It was chilly and wet when Gibson threw the first pitch that night, and only 9,560 fans were there. Thoughtfully, the Cardinals and Dodgers breezed through nine innings in 1:51. It might have been Gibson's top performance of the season, though the L.A. lineup was so feeble that Drysdale's .200 average was the sixth best on the card. Gibson gave up one hit in his eight innings, struck out six, and was nicked only once, when he walked Popovich in the third, and Parker doubled him home with two out. "Somebody in the dugout said, 'There's your lead. Now hold it,'" Drysdale said.

He did. Drysdale gave up five hits, struck out eight, walked no one. He struck out Mike Shannon with a man on third in the seventh. The Dodgers got a second run in the ninth off Joe Hoerner, but Lou Brock led off the ninth with a double. Alston stayed put. Curt Flood, Bobby Tolan, and Orlando Cepeda all grounded out. No one had scored off Drysdale in 27 innings. "It was one of those hang-in games," Drysdale said. "But sometimes it gets a little tiring hanging in. We don't do things the easy way. I haven't been complaining as long as we get one more run than the other team."

"He's faster than he was the first two years," Alston said. "And it's uncanny how he can put the ball exactly where he wants to."

On May 26, 1968, Drysdale went to the mound in Houston's Astrodome. The opposing pitcher was Larry Dierker, who had not yet turned 22. He had thrown his first major league pitch at 18 and struck out Giants star Willie Mays in that first inning. He was from the San Fernando Valley, not far from Drysdale's home, and he went to Taft High. He went to Dodger Stadium occasionally, listened to Vin Scully on the radio. "They had Koufax and Drysdale," Dierker said. "Everybody else leaned toward Koufax. Drysdale was a right-hander and he was from the Valley, so I leaned toward him."

Dierker was not quite the finished product by 1968, but he would become the first 20-game winner in Astros history the next season. He would also make All-Star teams, become the Astros' broadcast analyst, and eventually manage the club for five years. In four of those years, Houston won its division. Dierker fit the stereotype of the carefree Californian who churned underneath. As the Astros manager, he suffered bad headaches, and doctors found an angioma in his brain that demanded surgery to disentangle the blood vessels. Dierker was back in the dugout in four weeks. Later he wrote a book about his career and the game. Its title was, *This Isn't Brain*

Surgery. "People would ask me the toughest thing about being a manager," Dierker said. "I'd say, 'Nothing.' They'd ask me if it was really that easy, and I'd say, 'No, it's not easy, but it's hard to sit there and do nothing. And sometimes to move forward, you have to do nothing. There's a temptation to always be proactive.'"

"Larry was a pleasure to catch," said Brand, the Astros' catcher that night. "He wasn't afraid to go after Koufax and Drysdale. He'd match them pitch for pitch. He was a competitor, too. Had a great curveball. He was one of those guys who liked to come off as not being too smart, but he really was."

This, however, was that rare night in which the Dodgers prioritized runs. Drysdale was involved. He drove in the first run with a single in the top of the third. In the ninth inning while leading 3–0, Drysdale got a base hit off John Buzhardt. Willie Davis and Jim Fairey followed with RBI singles, and a crowd of 21,493 had little reason to hang around. Drysdale, though, had one more zero to post.

In a month of stressful ninth innings, this was another. Denis Menke and Rusty Staub led off with singles. Lee Thomas followed with a hot grounder to Popovich, the second baseman, who ran it down and flipped it to Versalles for a double-play turn. Menke went to third, and Drysdale walked Wynn and then hit Aspromonte, a longtime friend. But then in the first inning, Popovich had scrambled to the bag to relay Versalles' throw on Thomas' double-play ball, which ended the inning and kept Ron Davis from scoring.

Then it was the ninth, and Dave Adlesh approached with the bases loaded. He was a catcher from Long Beach. After baseball he would run a nightclub called The Limit, and Bo Diddley, Jackie Wilson, Ike and Tina Turner, and Linda Ronstadt performed there. He also was a press box attendant at Del Mar's racetrack, and he and his son, Darren, worked together to remodel houses. His career lasted 106 games with one home run and 11 RBIs. Here he grounded to Versalles, and the Dodgers won 5–0.

Drysdale gave up six hits—all singles—walked two, and struck out six. His record was 5–3, and his ERA was 1.47. Of the past 131 hitters in his way, two had doubled, and none had tripled. He was also tired. "I don't know if I even had one pitch left," Drysdale said. "If Pop doesn't make that great play, I don't even know if I could have finished the game. He has one of the greatest pairs of hands I've ever seen."

He also had to endure the usual spitball accusations from Houston's dugout. Umpire Al Barlick came out to inspect his cap and his hair. "He was just admiring my haircut," Drysdale said.

The streak was now at 36 innings. People were beginning to check the record books just in case this would amount to something. "I used to break down the games three ways: pitch by pitch, hitter by hitter, and inning by inning," Drysdale said years later. "You go along that way, and the way I was pitching that year, I felt like I could put the ball anywhere I wanted. I started thinking that I wasn't going to give up any runs. It's like a lot of things. You get on a roll."

On May 31, 1968, Drysdale went to the mound in Dodger Stadium to face the San Francisco Giants. Their pitcher was Mike McCormick, the third Cy Young Award winner who would oppose Drysdale during the streak. He had won it the year before as a rehabbed, reformed power pitcher who was now a precise screwballer. McCormick had pitched at Mark Keppel High in Alhambra, California, graduating two years after Drysdale had left Van Nuys. He was a rare prodigy. Over the course of a high school and an American Legion season, McCormick pitched five no-hitters and struck out

26 of 27 batters in a high school game at Covina. All of this earned him a $50,000 bonus from the Giants, who signed him away from USC, where he would have played with Fairly, a grad of Long Beach Jordan.

McCormick was pitching in New York before his 18th birthday. Before he turned 24, he had pitched 1,000 innings. This wrecked his shoulder, but he managed to win 134 major league games. His 1968 season would be rough with a 12–14 record and 3.58 ERA, but he had little to fear from the Dodgers. He gave them two earned runs in eight innings.

By then he was also a footnote to a famous baseball brouhaha that has spanned a generation. The Dodgers won 3–0, and Drysdale's pursuit continued, but even he wasn't on the marquee. The names that are still remembered are Harry Wendelstedt and Dick Dietz.

Wendelstedt fit the template of the authoritarian umpire. He handled five no-hitters and worked for 33 years. He attended the Somers Umpire School in Ormond Beach, Florida, when he was trying to decide whether to re-enlist in the Marines. He eventually graduated, then bought the school. Wendestedt died at 73 in 2012 and, when he was taken from his house into his final ambulance, he had been watching the MLB Network on TV.

He was working the plate as Drysdale faced the Giants. The Dodgers were ahead 3–0, but the crowd of 46,067, which included McCarthy as he campaigned in the California primary, was looking past the scoreboard. The scoreless inning streak was beginning to grow into L.A. mythology. It had the necessary leading man, standing tall against the odds. Then it was the ninth, and Willie McCovey, one of Drysdale's tormentors, led off with a walk. Nate "Pee Wee" Oliver, a former Dodger, pinch ran for him. Jim Ray Hart moved Oliver to second with a base hit. Dave Marshall followed with a walk. With the bases loaded and nobody out, the streak was tied to the railroad tracks with a locomotive approaching. The 64-year-old record for consecutive shutouts was five set by Guy Harris "Doc" White of the White Sox. In that moment it seemed safe.

Alston moved the infield into double-play position. That meant a grounder to Popovich or Versalles would bring home Oliver and stop the streak. That might seem a needless shame for a team that would finish 10 games below .500 and was treading water, but baseball still adhered to the code. A double play would be the quickest path to a win. The run at that point didn't matter.

Dietz was the hitter. His nickname was "the Mule," and his stubbornness qualified. In 1971 the Giants would win the National League West, and Dietz caught the games in the home stretch wearing a bandage around his head after taking a beanball. After they clinched the division, they celebrated. Dietz told a radio announcer, "The Dodgers can go to hell." He found himself catching for the Dodgers in 1972. Dietz was active in the Players' Association, which called a strike in 1972. He was released after that and he played only one more year with Atlanta. He was done at 32, and some felt he was blackballed.

Drysdale got to a 2-and-2 count and came inside. Dietz did not flinch. He appeared to hold up his left arm, which absorbed the ball. Hit by pitch. Oliver to the plate. Streak over. Catcher Jeff Torborg, who had played at Rutgers, immediately flashed back to a similar play in a game against Columbia. He began yelling at Wendelstedt. "I'll take care of this," Wendelstedt told him.

Wendelstedt quickly told Dietz to stay in the box. He ruled Dietz made no effort to avoid the pitch. Ball three. Dietz and Giants manager Herman Franks besieged Wendelstedt. Torborg went to the mound. Drysdale was coming to the end of a 150-pitch night "Find out what's going on," Drysdale told his catcher.

"I'll try," Torborg said, "but they've got the whole coaching staff out there."

Wendelstedt ejected Franks, and Dietz got back into the box. He lofted a short fly to left field, which was too shallow for Oliver to score. "Harry made it hard on himself," Torborg said. "He could have just called it a strike, and that would have struck him out."

"It was the right call," said Parker, the first baseman. "Dietz made no effort to duck. He just turned his shoulder."

"I never saw that call before," Alston said. "But then it's the first time I ever saw anybody get hit deliberately with a ball."

But there was work left. Ty Cline was the pinch-hitter. The Dodgers' infield remained back. Cline tapped a grounder to Parker's right. Drysdale rumbled over to cover first base. Decisions whizzed through Parker's brain. Throw to second to get Marshall and trigger a double-play attempt? Or go to the plate to stop Oliver? "I would have to turn and basically throw behind me to get the man at second," Parker said. "It was the only time I really thought about the streak. So I went home. Fortunately, it was the perfect throw."

It was almost too perfect. As Drysdale ran to first, he came into the path of Parker's throw. Just in time, Drysdale got down and slid in the grass. If the ball had hit Drysdale in the head, it would've carried the streak into the gutter with it. "I haven't moved that fast in a long time," Drysdale said.

Torborg got Oliver for the second out. "I remember thinking when he was on third, *Pee Wee, you're never going to be standing on this plate*," Torborg said.

As the voices rose on all sides, Jack Hiatt was the Giants' two-out pinch-hitter. He popped up in Parker's direction. "That ball had a lot of spin on it," Parker said. "I got it in my glove, but it almost spun out."

It didn't, and Drysdale had thrown 45 consecutive scoreless innings. The effort had taken his words with it. He sat at his locker underneath a sign that a teammate had made: "Drysdale For President—Shoo-In For The California Primary."

"It's the biggest thrill I've ever had in my life, probably," Drysdale finally said. "I'll admit that pitch to Dietz got away from me. It was a slider, but I didn't think he made any effort to get away. Wendelstedt called it immediately. So he had to be sure."

In the other clubhouse, Franks was just getting started. "It's the worst call I've ever seen," Franks yelled. "If Drysdale breaks the record now, he and Wendelstedt should share it. Hell, put Wendelstedt's name on the trophy first. That gutless Wendelstedt, he said Dietz put his arm out and let it hit him, for God's sake. I don't think Drysdale can be very proud of himself now."

"I'm sure not going to hold my arm up on purpose with that big boy on the mound," Dietz said. "That pitch was hard. I just couldn't move."

Twenty years later, the Dodgers were in New York for Game Three of the National League Championship Series. Wendelstedt went to the mound to inspect baseballs thrown by Jay Howell, the Los Angeles closer. When he found pine tar on the glove, he ejected Howell. The next day commissioner Bart Giamatti suspended Howell for three days, a harsh ruling to be sure, but the Dodgers wound up winning the NLCS and the World Series with Drysdale in the Dodgers' radio booth and with a slight right-handed starter named Orel Leonard Hershiser IV playing a part.

Six years after that, Wendelstedt was walking out of the umpires' room in the right-field corner of San Francisco's Candlestick Park. He was telling his younger mates about Dietz and Drysdale and that Giants fans still hadn't forgotten. They were skeptical until they first stepped onto the field, and someone came to the railing and yelled, "Hey, Wendelstedt, you blew that call on Dietz!"

Harry's son Hunter, or Harry Hunter Wendelstedt III, also became a major league umpire in 1998 and remains so. Every time he comes to San Francisco, he gets booed when his name is announced. "I've seen that call on Dietz," Hunter said. "You might run into it once a year. I've always thought it was the right call. Dad didn't talk about it much. For him, it was settled when he made the call. He was a Marine and a stubborn German. You weren't going to talk him out of it."

Drysdale had given up six hits, all singles. He walked two and struck out seven, though he went to three-ball counts on a dozen hitters. His record was 6–3 with a 1.33 ERA.

On June 4, 1968, Drysdale went to the mound at Dodger Stadium to face the Pittsburgh Pirates. The opposing pitcher was Jim Bunning, who was the third Hall of Famer to match up with Drysdale during the streak. He was 36 and had 195 wins, one fewer than Drysdale. He had one 20-win season and four others in which he won 19 games and he threw a perfect game for the Phillies in 1964, the year Philadelphia had a six-and-a-half game lead with 12 games to go and didn't win. Gene Mauch, one of Drysdale's closest friends, managed Bunning that season. His Phillies would be the next team to visit Los Angeles. Bunning, in fact, would be a Dodger in 1969 and would pitch two more years after that.

Len Gabrielson and Boyer brought home runs with singles in the fourth inning, and Parker homered in the sixth. The bottom half of these innings were window dressing. A crowd of 30,422 paid full attention to Drysdale and the way he was handling the Pirates. By then Drysdale's every move was reported like bulletins from a tidal wave. He, Ginger, and daughter Kelly went to Drysdale's Dugout, his restaurant on Oxnard Boulevard in Van Nuys at 3:30 before the 8:00 PM game. Observant of ritual, they all ordered the same steak sandwiches with cottage cheese on the side that they had ordered before. "By now I think Ginger has forgotten how to cook," Drysdale said.

Before that he rose at noon, had grapefruit, and fired up the record player to listen to Frank Sinatra and Dean Martin.

Around this time Kennedy had finished his surfing at Malibu and was back at his downtown headquarters. This was Election Day. He had lost the Oregon primary to McCarthy. The California winner would head to the Chicago convention with a strong wind at his back, but nobody knew how the delegates would behave, whether Vice President Humphrey would command the stage, or what Chicago mayor Richard Daley had in store.

That afternoon Ross Porter and Rafer Johnson were in the newsroom at KNBC Channel 4. Porter was a sports reporter who would go on to broadcast Dodgers games on the radio, often with Drysdale by his side. Johnson was a national hero and perhaps the most popular and recognizable sports figure in Los Angeles. He went to UCLA and in 1960 won the Olympic decathlon over his college teammate, C.K. Yang, who was from what was then called Nationalist China. Johnson was close to the Kennedys. He would be at the Ambassador Hotel for what he thought would be a celebration. Porter and his wife, Lin, would attend *Cabaret,* starring Joel Grey, at the Dorothy Chandler Pavilion downtown. But Porter also yearned to hear Drysdale extend the streak.

Johnson offered an earpiece to Porter, so he could take his transistor radio into the auditorium. Porter spent the evening watching Grey and listening to Drysdale. Occasionally, Lynn would nudge Ross in the ribs and whisper that he should turn it down. By 10:20 PM Drysdale was done with the Pirates. His sixth consecutive shutout broke Doc White's record. He had gotten an encouraging telegram from White earlier that Tuesday thanks to the industrious work of Dodgers public-relations wizard Red Patterson.

If not for the streak, the game would have been entirely forgettable. Drysdale allowed no hits for four innings and only three overall. He struck out Bill Mazeroski in the second inning, and that broke Carl Hubbell's National League scoreless streak. He gave up two singles, a double from Gary Kolb, and walked nobody. Eighteen of the outs came on grounders.

The 18th happened with two out in the ninth. Former Dodgers star Maury Wills was on first base, and future Hall of Famer Willie Stargell was up. Alston didn't want Wills to steal second effortlessly and score on a blooper, so he had Parker hold Wills at first. Stargell's hard grounder went to Popovich, who again spent the night shagging shots of all types as if retrieving Drysdale's golf balls at a driving range. Dodger outfielders were almost superfluous. There was one fly ball out to center fielder Willie Davis.

The Porters left the theater, and it occurred to Ross that he should check out the election results on the radio. The Drysdales headed for the Stadium Club. As Drysdale left the clubhouse, he asked, "How'd the election come out?"

Pretty well. Kennedy would win California by a 46–42 margin over McCarthy. That gave Kennedy all 176 convention delegates. In the Senator's suite, someone told RFK about the ballgame. "Six straight shutouts," Kennedy repeated. "Good."

Kennedy came down to the hotel's Imperial Room for his victory speech at 12:15 AM. He, or his speechwriters, knew the audience. "I first want to express my high regard for Don Drysdale," RFK began. "He pitched his sixth straight shutout tonight. I hope we have as good fortune in our campaign."

This was not just a casual shout-out. The Kennedys knew the Drysdales. Ginger worked on John F. Kennedy's Presidential campaign in 1960 with the wives of Sammy Davis Jr., Nat King Cole, and Milton Berle. She attended the inaugural in 1961. He and Chuck Connors occasionally visited Washington to work on federal anti-poverty programs, and Don came to Bobby and Ethel's horse farm in MacLean, Virginia. Ginger rode jumping horses there.

As Don and Ginger left the Stadium Club, several young fans were waiting. They had been seeking autographs, but now some were crying with their radios held close. One of them told the Drysdales what much of America already knew: Kennedy had been shot in the kitchen at the Ambassador. "As soon as I turned it on," Ross Porter said, "I heard them talking about Rafer and [Rams defensive tackle Rosey Grier] and something about a shooting."

The Drysdales hurried to the car, drove to Sunset Boulevard, and turned right into the parking lot of a bar called The Short Stop, home to cops, journalists, Dodgers fans, and occasional Dodgers. Johnson, Grier, author George Plimpton, and others had wrestled the assailant, Sirhan Sirhan, to the floor. TV audiences throughout the nation heard a policeman yell, "Get the gun, Rafer!"

After a while Ginger became too upset to stay. Back home at Hidden Hills, Don and Ginger stayed up until 5:00 AM. "I couldn't conceive of anyone doing something like this," Drysdale said. "I completely forgot about baseball."

When Johnson got home that night, he removed his sport coat and quickly realized that Sirhan's gun was still in his pocket.

Robert F. Kennedy died on Wednesday. His body was flown to New York and on Saturday it was taken by train to Washington, passing stations and platforms that were jam-packed by mourners. The House of Representatives immediately passed a bill that banned interstate mail order sales of handguns and prohibited sales to minors and to non-residents of a gun dealer's state. The vote was 305 to 118.

*   *   *

Frank Lucchesi called outfielder Howie Bedell into his office in Reading, Pennsylvania. Lucchesi managed the Double A affiliate of the Phillies, who had just lost shortstop Bobby Wine. "Mr. Quinn wants you to meet the club in San Francisco," Lucchesi said, referring to the general manager of the major league club.

"People were playing tricks like that all the time," Bedell said. "So I didn't believe him."

"Seriously," Lucchesi said.

Bedell knew about Don Drysdale's shutouts. When he got to Candlestick Park, Gene Mauch told him he would probably use him as a pinch-hitter there but that Bedell would get a chance to play in Los Angeles the next stop.

Bedell remembered that Lucchesi had said, "I think you'll get a chance to break that streak." He told Lucchesi that he would try. At that point he was game for anything. He was 32 years old and hadn't been in the major leagues in six years.

On June 8 Drysdale went to the mound at Dodger Stadium to face the Phillies. The opposing pitcher was Larry Jackson, who completed the circle. Jackson was traded for Ferguson Jenkins, the first pitcher Drysdale faced in the streak. Jackson had 194 wins in his career and won 24 games in 1964, most in the big leagues. He also had 27 wins against the Dodgers. Like Jim Bunning, who became a U.S. senator from Kentucky, Jackson got into politics in Idaho and was chairman of the Republican party there.

He and the rest of the Phillies were spectators in a rapidly intensifying drama. The intervening days were long ones for Drysdale. Bill Ford, his high school coach at Van Nuys, died of a heart attack on Thursday, two days short of watching Drysdale's big night. The pitcher was getting ready to putt on the ninth green of Thousand Oaks Golf Course at 7:00 PM when it happened. Closer to home, the Drysdales' three-month-old fawn boxer went missing in Hidden Hills. They got him when the season began, and Drysdale blanked the Mets. His daughter, Kelly, named him "Shutout."

Mudcat Grant, the pitcher who had caught Eugene McCarthy's ceremonial first pitch earlier in the streak, went to New York for Kennedy's requiem Mass. Meanwhile, Claude Osteen was working on a three-shutout streak, partly facilitated by Drysdale's advice to loosen up his knee. The crowd was 50,060 on this Saturday night, and they were there to count seven outs. "Shutout" even returned to the Drysdale homestead that afternoon. If all went well, Drysdale would break Walter Johnson's record with the first out in the third.

It happened just that way quickly and routinely. Roberto Pena, a .209-hitting shortstop, dribbled a grounder to Ken Boyer, who had hit grand slams in the World Series and won an MVP award. Still, he was meticulous in handling the ball and throwing it to Parker, sending Pena to the dugout and erasing Johnson from at least one line in the annals of baseball.

Mauch was disciplined, too. He waited for Drysdale to pass Johnson before he came out and asked umpire Augie Donatelli to go to the mound and check Drysdale's glove, hair, cap, and any available parts of his epidermis for anything wet and greasy. This had become a Greek chorus as the streak went on. A foul ball had gone back into the press box in Drysdale's previous start. It left a large smudge on a scorebook kept by George Lederer, the beat writer for the *Long Beach Press-Telegram*. "At least it wasn't spit," Lederer said.

Theoretically, Donatelli could have ejected Drysdale, but he determined he couldn't prove anything. "He was frisking Don in the manner that he would use for a suspect smuggling dope across the border," said Fresco Thompson, the Dodgers' general manager. "He was exceeding his authority."

After Donatelli ran his hands through Drysdale's hair, Big D said, "Augie, the last person who did that also gave me a kiss on the cheek."

The streak went into the fifth. Tony Taylor led off with a single. Clay Dalrymple followed with another. Pena struck out. Jackson was due up, but the Phillies trailed 4–0. Mauch called on Bedell to pinch hit. "I knew he liked to knock you down," Bedell said. "But I could see the ball well for some reason. It was the third pitch, and he had already backed me off. Now he threw that fastball away. I sort of lunged and hit it to left-center."

The left-fielder was Gabrielson. In 1962 he had been Bedell's roommate in the minors. He had already moved four steps toward center. "I remember you used to hit a lot of balls there," Gabrielson would tell Bedell later. "I guess I didn't move enough."

Gabrielson caught it and twisted his body to get into throwing position. He dived onto the grass in the attempt. It was too late to get Taylor, who scored, and after 58 ⅔ innings and 25 days, something besides a zero was posted on the opponents' row. Bedell came to the dugout, and Bill White told him, "That's the best fly ball you ever hit."

It was his first RBI of the season and the final RBI of his career. His last major league game was July 4 in Chicago. He was 1-for-7 for the season.

Drysdale gave up a home run to White the next inning. By the seventh he was gone, and Hank Aguirre finished up the Dodgers' 5–3 victory. Drysdale was 8–3 with a 1.31 ERA. He got a standing ovation when he came to the mound in the first, got one for each of his two plate appearances, got one when he struck out Dalrymple to tie the record, got another when he retired Pena, and got a sixth one when he left. "Twenty-five years later they had a reunion on the anniversary and they re-created that whole scene at Dodger Stadium," said Bedell, who lives in Pottstown, Pennsylvania. "I couldn't be there. I was coaching third base for the Mariners. They sent me a recording of it and they really played it up. Gene [Mauch] stood in for me. He made me sound like Babe Ruth. Every time Richie Ashburn talked about it on our radio network, he'd say, 'Here's the man who broke the streak.'"

Drysdale ran across Bedell several times over the years. He almost considered him an angel of mercy. "I just went 'blah' after he hit that fly ball," Drysdale said. "I was out of gas. I was glad that it was over. I guess all the things that have happened to me over the last month finally got to me. But I don't have any complaints."

Vin Scully watched it all from above, grasping for perspective. "I've done two perfect games. I don't know how many no-hitters," he had said two days before. "I was there when Gil Hodges hit four home runs in a game and when Maury Wills stole 104 bases. This one I never envisioned. But here's a guy who, even when Koufax was here, was the real leader of the Dodgers. You know what they say about a person being a prophet but not in his own country. Well, Drysdale was a star but not in his hometown. He had never had that one super moment. Taking all things into consideration, this would have to be the most dramatic thing I've witnessed in my broadcasting career."

Scully also said he was growing weary of the road after 19 years. But he said he wouldn't leave for at least two more. He retired after the 2016 season.

The next day, Walter Alston permitted Drysdale to stay home. "The next time he pitches six straight shutouts, I'll let him stay at home again," Alston said.

What most did not know is that the whole Dodgers team preferred to stay home in deference to Kennedy's death. That request was denied.

Drysdale's next game was June 12 against the Mets at Dodger Stadium. Hodges, Drysdale's old roommate in Brooklyn, managed New York. "You sure have slowed down," Hodges teased him. "You never would have let anyone muss your hair a few years ago—and an umpire of all people."

Drysdale faced Nolan Ryan that day and lost 2–1 when J.C. Martin doubled home a run in the ninth inning. As the Dodgers faded, they remembered how to keep Drysdale hanging. He even shut out the Reds for 10 innings on July 5 and didn't win. He ended the season 14–12 with a career-best 2.15 ERA.

How important was the streak? His successful bid to reach the Hall of Fame probably depended on it. The streak was the badge that he wore for the rest of his life, more meaningful than the 25 wins of 1962 or the three World Series championships. It was so unimaginable and was conducted on such a thin tightrope. It was also hard to fathom because the National League was the gathering place for so many legendary hitters, most of whom Drysdale sent down during the streak.

In the six games that preceded the night of Bedell, Drysdale held opponents to a .145 batting average. They had three extra-base hits—all doubles. He walked nine batters and in two games he didn't walk anybody. He struck out 42 and gave up 27 hits in those 54 innings. He stranded 11 runners on third base during the streak. Five were in the ninth inning. Seven of the batters Drysdale retired in the ninth inning became members of the Hall of Fame. Ernie Banks, Orlando Cepeda, and Willie Stargell made the 27th outs. The Dodgers scored 17 runs in those six games. Two were 1–0 games; another was 2–0.

It was the distillation of what Drysdale, his team, and his city meant to the 1960s as a whole. They pushed the boundary of possibility. "He kept the ball down for the entirety of that streak," Parker said. "We played in some big ballparks. He could have pitched up, but he didn't. The whole time guys were beating the ball into the ground."

It must be noted that Drysdale was buoyed by a pitching wave that has not been seen since. The cumulative ERA in 1968 was 2.98, the lowest since 1918. Since then the lowest ERA was 3.26 in 1972. The OPS—on-base percentage plus slugging percentage—was .639 in 1968. It rose to .689 the next year. The American League installed the designated hitter in 1973 and took the bats away from pitchers, and the big-league OPS rose to .704. In 2000 it reached .782.

Denny McLain of the Tigers became the first pitcher in 34 years—and most likely the last one in major league history—to win 30 games. He went 31–6. His ERA was 1.96, one of seven under 2.00. Bob Gibson's

28 complete games tied McLain's for second in baseball. Juan Marichal had 30. Nine starting pitchers held opponents to less than one base runner per inning, which later became a statistic known as WHIP (walks and hits, plus innings pitched). Dave McNally of Baltimore led that group with 0.842. There were 32 starting pitchers who averaged seven or more innings per start. Drysdale averaged 7.7, and Gibson averaged nine. In 2022 there was only Sandy Alcantara of the Miami Marlins who did that.

Drysdale's streak became a mechanical rabbit for others to chase. Gibson was the first in pursuit. In five starts beginning on June 6, Gibson went 5–0 and did not yield a run. The sixth game was July 1 in Dodger Stadium against Drysdale, of course. The Cardinals won 5–1, and Drysdale didn't escape the seventh inning. By then Gibson's bid had ended at 48 innings. Gabrielson and Tom Haller singled, and Gibson fired an 0-and-1 fastball to Ron Fairly. "It was one of the hardest pitches I ever saw, just came screaming in low," Fairly said.

It got past catcher Johnny Edwards and bounced off the foot of umpire Shag Crawford, and Gabrielson scored and danced around as if he had freed the Drysdale clan from a house fire. Parker remembers Gibson being "furious" over the wild pitch, and Gibson's first comment was, "The catcher fouled it up." Later, he said he wasn't serious about that. Like Drysdale, he said he was relieved to see it end. Gibson also said Drysdale's streak "was so great a thing that possibly no one is ever going to break it." If the record seemed so impossible to baseball's most ominous pitcher, what leviathan could possibly challenge it next?

*   *   *

When Orel Hershiser wanted to play Little League baseball in Southfield, Michigan, his dad forged a birth certificate so he could play with the older kids. But Orel IV wasn't big or menacing enough. He was aware of the arms race of 1968, but he identified with the Tigers, with Denny McLain's 31 wins, and with Mickey Lolich's three wins in the World Series. He wanted to climb a mound and look down on the game like they had.

It would take a while. The family moved to Toronto, where he played hockey as well, and then to suburban Philadelphia. Although Hershiser was a solid high school pitcher, he only had a partial scholarship offer from Bowling Green. The Dodgers drafted him in the 17th round.

Hershiser never intimidated his way into a win. He had a young face and didn't appear to have visited a weight room. He was described as owning a "concave chest." He also avoided the postgame bars and read the Bible and he was funny and self-deprecating in interviews. Nothing, in other words, indicated that he would forge a strong relationship with Don Drysdale. Yet they shared more than anyone knew. Both were overshadowed by a left-handed pitcher. Drysdale, of course, had Sandy Koufax, and Fernando Valenzuela was the ace when Hershiser showed up even when Hershiser won 19 and lost three in 1985, his second full season. Valenzuela's starts were cultural occasions long after the "Fernandomania" season of 1981.

Hershiser was an acquired taste. But he threw inside, threw hard, and he could handle a bat. "Don was the one who kept telling me to pitch inside," Hershiser said. "He said, 'Look, you're 60 feet, six inches away. They can get out of the way. They're looser. It's not your fault if you hit them.' I would pitch off the plate on purpose. As a pitcher you're not shooting a rifle. It's a shotgun. You have to understand your spray pattern. He said,

'If you miss, you're going to miss on the corner or on the way in. Your goal is to either get them out or set up the next pitch outside.' My pitching coaches were Ron Perranoski and Dave Wallace, and then there was Tommy Lasorda. Together with Don, they molded my mentality. Don was the living, breathing embodiment of a big, tough right-hander. And they emphasized going nine innings. I'd be in the office with Tommy, and Don would be sitting nearby. Tommy would say, 'Hey, Bulldog, if you're playing poker, do you let another guy come in and replace you just in time to pick up the chips?' Don's in the corner, laughing. But it was that way all the time. To me, they were my committee of toughness."

Indeed, Hershiser played high-stakes poker and got to the quarterfinals of the National Heads-Up Poker Championship in 2008.

The 1988 season was Hershiser's version of Drysdale's 1962 and 1968 all in one. The Dodgers were different. Kirk Gibson won the Most Valuable Player award in his first L.A. season, but they weren't bursting with talent. When Gibson was hurt in the National League Championship Series but still advanced, NBC's Bob Costas said the Dodgers might have had "the weakest lineup to ever start a World Series game," which, of course, was like warm milk to a cat when Lasorda heard it.

They always had Hershiser, who was 16–7 with a 3.06 ERA when he lost to San Francisco on August 14. In the nine starts that would take him to the end of the season, Hershiser gave up four runs total and went 7–1. He pitched nine innings in eight of those starts and 10 in the final one. Then Hershiser went 3–0 with a save in the '88 postseason, pitching complete games to clinch both series. His playoff ERA was 1.05. The Dodgers won a world championship for the first time in seven years, and it would take them 32 years to win another.

And along the way, Hershiser pitched 59 consecutive scoreless innings and took out Drysdale's record. It had only been 20 years. Memories of Drysdale were fresh.

- On September 5 Hershiser won in Atlanta, beating Rick Mahler 3–0 on a four-hitter with eight strikeouts.
- On September 10 Hershiser won at home against Cincinnati, beating Norm Charlton 5–0 on a seven-hitter with eight strikeouts. That was his 20th victory of the season.
- On September 14 Hershiser won at home against Atlanta, beating Mahler again 1–0 on a six-hitter with eight strikeouts.
- On September 19 Hershiser won at Houston 1–0 on a four-hitter with five strikeouts. Nolan Ryan started for Houston but left after two innings with a cramp in his hamstring. "He's such a great kid that I'm having fun watching him," Drysdale said. "I'm glad I'm still around to see this. Plus, it's great to see another guy with a uniform in the 50s. [Hershiser wore 55, Drysdale 53]. That means the clubhouse guys never thought either one of us would stick around."
- On September 23 Hershiser won at San Francisco 3–0 versus Atlee Hammaker on a five-hitter with two strikeouts and 112 pitches.

That led to September 28 in San Diego, but the nostalgia was suddenly bottled up by technicalities. Major League Baseball had suddenly decreed that Drysdale's 1968 record was only 58 innings, not 58 ⅔. Statisticians maintained that pitchers couldn't get credit for a scoreless inning if they didn't finish it in scoreless fashion, and Howie Bedell's sacrifice fly had been the second out of Drysdale's last inning. Hershiser was at 49. A nine-inning shutout would only tie Drysdale, at least officially, and thus postpone resolution until the 1989 regular season.

But the Dodgers offense cooperated. It put together its own nine-inning scoreless streak. Hershiser got a grounder from Carmelo Martinez to end the ninth inning and get his 58 innings. It was still 0–0. Then he had a chance to pitch a 59th scoreless inning.

It began shakily when Hershiser's third strike to Marvell Wynne zipped past catcher Mike Scioscia. Wynne sprinted to first, got to second on a bunt, and then to third on a grounder. Keith Moreland, a dangerous all-fields hitter, came up to pinch hit with two out. On a 1-2 pitch, he hit a fly ball that Jose Gonzalez caught in right field. "I started looking around upstairs to see Don," Hershiser said 25 years later. "I didn't realize he was in the dugout. He was doing the postgame show and he had to plug in, and there was an outlet in the dugout."

Drysdale came out and hugged Hershiser. "You kept it in the family," he said.

Later, Drysdale said he knew Hershiser would rewrite his own history after 30 zeroes or so. "I've been around long enough to see it," he said. "Guys get on a roll. I was proud of him. But I've never really been a records guy. You can't eat them; they don't pay the taxes. I'm sure it helped me get into the Hall of Fame, and that's great."

Hershiser later said he wanted to leave the game after two out in the 10th inning, so he and Drysdale could share the record. That might or might not be true. Drysdale said he wouldn't have let it happen. "I would have kicked him right in the buns," he said.

The Dodgers took out Hershiser after he had broken Drysdale's record. He'd already pitched 10 innings. San Diego won 2–1 after Mark Parent homered off Ricky Horton in the 16th inning.

In real terms Hershiser's streak reached 59 ⅔. On the season's second day in 1989, Cincinnati's Todd Benzinger drove in a first-inning run with two out off of Hershiser, and the Reds won 4–3.

The Cy Young Award winner in 1988, Hershiser finished 15–15 in 1989, though he led the National League in innings pitched for the third consecutive season. In 1990 he suffered a torn labrum and did not return until May of 1991. He lasted three more years with the Dodgers, then pitched for Cleveland, San Francisco, and the Mets before one last song with the Dodgers: a 1–5 misadventure through 10 appearances in 2000. He was 41 with 204 wins, a career ERA of 3.48, and a 8–3 record in his postseasons.

He now sits in a Dodgers broadcast booth these days, as Drysdale did. And, like Drysdale, his streak came the closest to running aground in a game against the Giants. In the third inning of that September 23 meeting in Candlestick Park, Ernest Riles hit a bouncer to L.A. second baseman Steve Sax, who flipped it to shortstop Alfredo Griffin in the midst of a double play bid. Brett Butler, the base runner, ranged outside the base line to hit Griffin. As the ball airmailed first baseman Tracy Woodson, Jose Uribe scored from third. "I thought, *Okay, the streak's over, and we're down 1–0, and I've got Will Clark coming up*," Hershiser said.

But umpire Paul Runge at second quickly ruled that Butler had interfered with Griffin. Butler was out, and the inning was over. No score. "I wanted to get into the dugout as soon as I could, so he couldn't change his mind," Hershiser said.

And, on the way to the dugout, Hershiser yelled something that Lasorda in the dugout—along with a previous generation of Dodgers fans whose hearts rose and fell every four days for a month in 1968—could hear and appreciate. "Dick Dietz," Hershiser shouted, "revisited!"

9

One for My Baby (and One More for the Road)

Almost every professional athlete has a goal that stretches well beyond the championships and the statistics. Get them together, and they all want to control the terms of their disengagement. They want to walk away without being released, injured, demoted, or escorted out of the clubhouse with parking pass in hand.

Few do so. Pitchers are the least likely because their job is dictated by ligaments, tendons, and joints, tenuous body parts that were never meant to work together to fire tens of thousands of baseballs 90 to 100 mph from a position above one's head. It is a design problem. There is no bad luck when it comes to pitching injuries. They are baked in.

Don Drysdale turned 33 on July 23, 1969, the season after he broke the scoreless-inning streak. His final game was on August 5. That was not his choice. Two years younger than the minimum age requirement to become president of the United States, Drysdale found himself announcing that his first career was done. But then Sandy Koufax had retired after he'd won 53 combined games in 1967 and 1968. He was 30. Only six of the 24 major league pitchers who turned in 250 or more innings in 1969 were 30 or older.

It's difficult to compare those days with those in the modern game because in 2022 no one pitched more than 228 innings. Of the 27 pitchers who exceeded 180 innings, nine were older than 30, and Adam Wainwright of the Cardinals was 40-years-old.

Today's pitchers expect to pitch fewer innings in exchange for more years. There is far more of a financial incentive to push into middle age. There is far less demand placed on a starting pitcher, who is not expected to work more than six innings or to face hitters more than twice in a game. Drysdale occasionally pitched complete games in Grapefruit League competition. That, of course, seems absolutely medieval. In 2023 Shane Bieber and Seth Lugo led all 2,032 pitchers in exhibition innings with 23 ⅔. Most of today's pitchers avoid exhibition duty like the plague, particularly when it entails getting on a bus.

The pitcher's best friend is the doctor's office just as an orthopedist's favorite profession is pitching—with mountain biking a close second. But in that office, an encyclopedic amount of cures, remedies, and therapies has replaced the guesswork of Drysdale's time. Orel Hershiser broke Drysdale's streak in 1988. Two years later his shoulder went into full rebellion, and he was sidelined with a torn labrum. The labrum surrounds the shoulder joint, as well as the hip, and holds the ball and socket in place.

Trainers didn't talk of labrums in the 1960s. Sportswriters sometimes wrote about the discovery of the "rotor" or the "rotary cup." Most fans today have at least a vague idea of what a rotator cuff is. It is a group of muscles that attaches the humerus to the shoulder blade. A rotator cuff injury is a disruptive event, requiring one to two years of post-operative recovery time. But it is no longer an automatic ticket to the shuffleboard court, as it was before Hershiser tore his.

Dr. Frank Jobe, the inventor of Tommy John elbow-transplant surgery and thus the savior of thousands of pitching careers, looked at Hershiser's condition as a challenge and knew Hershiser was game for it. He reconstructed Hershiser's shoulder. Thirteen months after Hershiser left the Dodgers, he returned with a shaky start at Houston. He took his next turn and went six and a third innings in St. Louis. "I felt like a pitcher tonight," he said.

In Chicago he won his next start. That was his 100th win. Hershiser later ordered the same surgical tools, had them gold-plated, turned them into a baseball holder, and presented them to Jobe, who said later that he felt like crying every time Hershiser won a game. Hershiser took a regular turn the rest of the season and went 7–2 with a 3.46 ERA. He would win 105 games after the procedure. He would win an American League Championship Series MVP award with Cleveland in 1995 and he would pitch until he was 41. That last year wasn't the greatest, but for the most part, his career was finished business. He got to the fork in the road and took the optional exit. No one else put the turn signal on for Hershiser; no one else pumped his brakes. That, unfortunately, is usually the road not taken.

A rotator cuff or a labrum can still end a career. Johan Santana and Mark Mulder, Cy Young Award winners, were never the same after their rotator cuff surgeries. But Trevor Hoffman, the San Diego closer, pitched five years after his surgery and cemented his Hall of Fame credentials. A 2012 study published by the *Orthopaedic Journal of Sports Medicine* found that 48 percent of pitchers with such procedures returned to competition, but only seven percent matched or exceeded their previous level of performance.

As Jobe recalled, that was still a quantum leap compared to what existed before. Karl Spooner was a sensation for the Dodgers until his shoulder began hurting. In 1954 he struck out 27 batters in back-to-back starts, a National League record. But he made only 16 career starts and was done after 1955. In those days doctors thought tooth infections or abscesses could lead to shoulder problems. Spooner had his teeth removed. His shoulder still hurt. "So now he had a sore shoulder and no teeth," Jobe said. "He probably had a torn rotator cuff."

* * *

Don Drysdale's scoreless streak ended on June 8, 1968. The extraordinary demands of the streak, which consisted entirely of complete games, had not yet registered. He was 4–4 in his next 10 starts, pitched two complete games, and his ERA had risen from 1.31 to 1.63.

On July 28 in Chicago, he pitched the first game of a doubleheader and lost 8–3, though he pitched all eight innings. In the eighth inning with the Cubs leading 5–3, Ron Santo tried to bunt with two runners on. Drysdale fielded the bunt and ran into Santo on the base line, and Santo's shoe hit Drysdale in the right shoulder with force. Al Spangler followed with a two-run double.

Drysdale pitched six times in August, went 2–4, and gave up 10 earned runs in 10 ⅔ innings in his final two starts. His shoulder was hurting, the Dodgers were hopelessly beaten, and he was shut down for September. It was a drastic move since Drysdale had gone 10 years without missing a start, pitching through knee pain, injured thumbs, injured fingers, and that case of shingles. But it seemed to make sense at the time, and besides, if anyone deserved a little R&R, Drysdale did.

Looking back, Drysdale said the collision with Santo was the beginning of his end. He said Santo "knocked something loose in my shoulder" that never could be reassembled. He said he never was felled by overwork or fatigue.

He came to Vero Beach, Florida, in 1969 with a peaceful shoulder and eventually a $120,000 contract for the season. Al Campanis, the general manager after Buzzie Bavasi took over the expansion club in San Diego, said they arrived at that figure "after two beers of talk."

The lords of baseball lowered the mound after the pitchers had ruled the 1968 season, and the arrival of four expansion clubs would spike the run production overall, as it generally does. "I feel like Thomas Edison out there," Drysdale said after his first game on flatter ground. "It was like a stranger out there pitching."

On April 2 in an exhibition at Houston, Drysdale was backing up third base when cutoff man Ted Sizemore threw wildly. Running back toward the dugout, Drysdale raised his right arm to grab part of a fence to brace himself. He said later he heard a pop, which was amplified by a home run struck by Jim "Toy Cannon" Wynn. Once he got to a 2-and-2 count to Doug Rader, he knew something wasn't right and left the game forthwith.

Two days later the Dodgers said Drysdale was merely dealing with an adhesion and would miss no starts. On April 7 he allowed Cincinnati two runs in six innings. Six days later he was driven out of a game when Houston's Denis Menke sent a liner against his ankle. Two starts later he lost to San Francisco 6–0 and gave up seven hits. He was removed one out shy of finishing five innings. His ERA was 5.85. In 20 innings he had struck out only nine. When the home clubhouse at Dodger Stadium opened for the writers, he was sitting on a table. No anger, no excuses. Just a man conducting a negotiation with the cold, hard truth. The other Dodgers moved silently around him. "Maybe that's it for me," Drysdale said calmly. "I'm having trouble getting my arm up. It's that simple. I've got a problem and I don't know how to cope with it. I don't have it and I'm not throwing hard. Well, I'm throwing just as hard. It's just not getting there as fast. There's no use kidding myself. It's just so deep down there [in my shoulder] that it can't be trusted with any degree of success. I don't know. I'm lost. If they want me to go to the bullpen, that's up to them."

Drysdale would not pitch again until June 15. He took cortisone shots. He rested. Then he threw every day. His return was promising, including a win against the eventual World Series champion Mets, when he got 17 outs and gave up two runs. On June 20 he shut out Cincinnati for six innings and won 4–2. Was he back? "Let's put it this way," he said. "I'm throwing as hard as this thing will let me throw."

"He might not have thrown as hard," catcher Tom Haller said. "But he was throwing with fantastic precision."

For a while it seemed Drysdale would get to the finish line. He had an easy complete game on June 28 when the Dodgers punished San Diego 19–0. Then the Dodgers lost while he pitched a two-hitter over seven innings to the Reds. Afterward, the arm seized up once more. "It tore loose again," he said. "It was unbelievably sore tonight. I tried to play catch between innings and I had to quit."

His avocation began imitating his work. One of the thoroughbreds Drysdale owned, High 'N' Tight, swerved into the rail at Hollywood Park and hit Talking Barberob, knocking off jockey Bill Hartack and sending him to Centinela Hospital.

Drysdale was going to miss most of July, always his money month. He beat the Cubs 6–2, gritting his way through five innings. "My fastball was like a rubber band that has been in the sun too long," he said. "When you go to try to snap it, nothing happens. There's still some pain. I simply haven't pitched enough innings to stay sharp. But this was one of the most important games of my career."

He certainly hoped so. "I need four starters," manager Walter Alston said plaintively. "I've got [Bill] Singer, [Claude] Osteen, and [Don] Sutton. I have to have Drysdale."

He wouldn't have him long. On August 5 Drysdale faced Pittsburgh in Dodger Stadium. The fans buzzed about a drive that the Pirates' Willie Stargell hit out of the ballpark estimated at 480 to 500 feet, but that came against reliever Alan Foster. Drysdale had long since left the 11–3 loss, though he did put up what became known as a quality start with six innings, two earned runs, and eight hits.

The leadoff man in the sixth was Manny Sanguillen. At that moment the Dodger Stadium message board was flashing a game of "Guess the Player" with a number of ascending clues. It showed that the answer was Sanguillen. Then Drysdale fed him a hanging curve, Sanguillen hit it out, and the Pirates led 3–0. Drysdale left after six innings. He never pitched in competition again. His final pitch was on a 1–0 count to Matty Alou, who grounded it to shortstop Maury Wills.

So many things were apropos. He hit his last batter in the second inning after the type of adversity that would usually set him off. This time it was an error by Wills and a passed ball by Haller. Gene Alley drove in a run after that. And true to form, the Dodgers put nothing but zeroes on the scoreboard for Drysdale. Willie Crawford pinch hit for him to lead off the sixth. Drysdale left the dugout. No ovations, no tips of the cap. At that point only he knew he was through.

He was listed as the scheduled pitcher on August 9 against Bill Hands of the Cubs. Instead, Foster handled that game. Drysdale met with Peter O'Malley at the stadium. At noon the next day, Drysdale put on his coat and tie and stood behind microphones at the Stadium Club and he spoke without tears as he looked into the rest of his life. He was retiring. The option had been exercised for him. "The pain has come back the way it was at the beginning," he said. "There is no snap in my arm. I can't bring it over the top. I can't sleep. My arm keeps waking me up. I had to use my left arm to brush my teeth."

He was concerned about the cortisone he was taking. Years later he described himself as a "walking drugstore" during that time. "I was afraid the police would have to pick me up on some corner of Sunset Boulevard," he said. "I just can't take any more medication."

At one point in that final game against Pittsburgh, his vision got blurry, and he had to put a hand over one eye to focus on the scoreboard. Roberto Clemente got a base hit on a line drive up the middle that Drysdale didn't see until it reached the outfield. Afterward, Drysdale touched his ear because he thought he felt a gnat buzzing around it. He saw blood on his fingers, where Clemente's hit had clipped him.

Alston couldn't withhold his tears on the day of the announcement. "If he believes he can't pitch," he said, "you have to be concerned. If the Dodgers have been successful in the years I have managed, Don would have to be one of the reasons, one of the big reasons."

Walter O'Malley noted that Drysdale "was our last tie to Brooklyn" and called the day "a nostalgic wrench." Drysdale knew which way he was leaning when he met with Peter O'Malley the day before. But he said it was easier to reconcile it when he sat there and heard pitches hitting catchers' mitts below him. It was a sound he had blocked out during all the days he was pitching. "It had always been a magnetic click for me," he said. "I saw my whole childhood again. At that point I knew my dreams had come true."

Drysdale said his biggest thrill remained the day he first put on a Dodgers uniform on that 1955 morning in Vero Beach. He also singled out the 1959 All-Star Game, when he won the MVP award while his wife, Ginger, was in the hospital, having given birth to daughter, Kelly.

From the safety of the sidelines, Sandy Koufax nodded grimly. He had announced his retirement in November of 1966. He was in Houston, announcing a game for NBC, when he ran into Dick Young of the *New York Daily News*. "It gets to the point where you say to yourself, *Whatever became of that kid with the great natural talent, and the pure unpained body, and the zest to just go out there and do it?*" Koufax told Young. "It gets to the point where you take a cortisone needle. When they say, 'That's enough shots for a while,' and then some other pills come along to offset the side effects of the green pills, and you say to yourself, *Who am I kidding? That's not me out there pitching anymore*. It's the pills. And with Don, the pills are getting to his stomach. You go out there, and your eyes have trouble focusing because of the painkillers. And you start thinking that sooner or later you're going to catch one right here," he said, pointing at his forehead. "They tell you that you can continue to pitch if you aren't competitive. This means you can throw the ball to spots, but don't put any extra on it when you're in a jam. How can you ask a man to pitch that way? Certainly not a man like Don, who has always been such a great competitor."

The Dodgers quickly replaced Drysdale by dealing for Jim Bunning, another future Hall of Famer, who was trying to harness one last push himself. They finished 85–77 and in fourth place behind Atlanta in the new National League West.

Drysdale had one more turn on the rubber. He agreed to pitch in an Old-Timers' Game August 24, a hit-and-giggle exhibition that got funnier when Jimmy Piersall, poking fun at the widespread and accurate perception that Drysdale's knuckle forkball was not entirely dry, brought hair lotion to the mound. Other Dodgers built a temporary fence right behind shortstop to see if Wally Moon could recreate his Moonshot home runs that he'd made famous at the Los Angeles Coliseum. Drysdale got the win 2–0, as he doubled home a run off Art Fowler.

The Dodgers gathered on September 27 to honor Drysdale at Dodger Stadium. Wes Parker, speaking for the club, gave him a ring with his No. 53 inlaid in diamonds. Kelly got a puppy, Ginger got a watch, the family got a car and a stove. Courtesy of Willie Mays of the visiting Giants, Drysdale also got a bottle of Vitalis and a tube of Vaseline. Drysdale had appeared at a banquet honoring Mays earlier in the year. Someone wondered why he would be welcome since he made a habit of knocking down Mays. "He just wanted to see what Willie looked like standing up," came the reply.

Governor Ronald Reagan was there and called Drysdale "the epitome of the value of athletics." Vin Scully spoke and called Drysdale "the spirit of the Dodgers."

Drysdale spoke and thanked Ginger, the rest of his family, Alston, the fans, the media, and the Lord—not in order of importance. By then the Dodgers were seven-and-a-half games behind Atlanta and mathematically eliminated. They had surged briefly after Drysdale retired and even took the lead at the end of August. In the end the man, who was always there, wasn't there anymore, and they weren't sure exactly how to act. Not until 1974 would the Dodgers make the playoffs again.

*   *   *

Don Drysdale never bothered himself with numbers. He even seemed ambivalent about all those scoreless innings in 1968 until they threatened history. But over 14 seasons, he filled baseball's chalkboard like an obsessed math professor. He had eight seasons of 200 innings and a sub-3.00 ERA. Only Tom Seaver, Greg Maddux, Bert Blyleven, Gaylord Perry, and Roger Clemens had done that. Randy Johnson, Steve Carlton, Bob Gibson, Whitey Ford, and Nolan Ryan never did.

At the time he retired, he was the all-time Dodgers leader in innings (3,432), wins (209), shutouts (49), starts (465), and strikeouts (2,486). Nine times he was among the National League's top 10 pitchers in ERA, 11 times in innings, six times in WHIP, six times in wins, and 11 times in strikeouts. Four consecutive times, beginning in 1962, he led the league in starts. In 163 of his 485 starts, he got zero, one, or two runs of support. That's 33.7 percent of his starts. In only 128 of those starts did he get six or more runs. The "quality start," an invention by baseball writer John Lowe that was defined as six or more innings while giving up three or fewer earned runs, came along later, but retroactively Drysdale lost 67 quality starts in his career. He had only 16 "cheap" wins or wins when he didn't post a quality start. The Dodgers were 254–211 in games he started. There was a 36 percent chance Drysdale would pitch a complete game, and he averaged seven and two-thirds innings per start. In 1964, which he considered his best season of pure pitching, he averaged eight innings and put up a quality start 80 percent of the time.

Among his lesser-known talents was the ability to stop the running game, which was important because hardly anyone could keep the Dodgers themselves from running. Only 96 base stealers were successful against Drysdale in 14 seasons, and Dodgers catchers threw out 84 runners when he was pitching.

He had an ERA of 2.95 in games that he started. Right-handed hitters had a .222 average against Drysdale and a very low OPS of .595. Left-handed hitters hit .262 with a .711 OPS. At home Drysdale was 114–74 with a 1.084 WHIP and a 2.53 ERA. On the road he was 95–62 with a 1.219 WHIP and a 3.41 ERA.

His best time of the year was September, lumped in with the first few days of October. He was 36–22 in that frame with a 1.071 WHIP and a 2.29 ERA. He was dominant in July, too, going 44–18 with 32 complete games in 77 starts. His July ERA was 2.76. In the second half of his seasons, Drysdale won 99 and lost 69 with a 2.80 ERA.

He preached the importance of retiring the first hitter and he practiced it. Leadoff men hit .225 against him, and 2 percent of them began innings with home runs (10 in 485 at-bats). His overall batting average against was .239, but it went down to .230 with men in scoring position. He pitched 210 ninth innings—if one can imagine such a thing today. In those the opposition hit .236 with a .622 OPS. When he faced the batting order for a third time, he limited its batting average to .246.

The only team that had a winning record against Drysdale was Pittsburgh, which went 22–19. He was 34–31 against the rival Giants with 28 complete games in 73 starts. Drysdale was 12–16 when Frank Secory was the home-plate umpire, which explains why he and Secory butted heads so often. Drysdale was 20–6 with Stan Landes handling balls and strikes, 12–4 with Ed Vargo, and 13–6 with Augie Donatelli.

To support his estimate that 1964 was his best season of pure pitching, Drysdale gave up an OPS of .538, the best of his career. Houston had the lowest team OPS in the league that year at .599. The notoriously punchless

Dodgers were at .645. In 1968, the year of the streak, the OPS against Drysdale was .573. For his career it was .645.

Hank Aaron had 17 home runs, the most of any opponent, off Drysdale. Willie Mays had 13, and teammate Willie McCovey had 12. Bill White had seven, most of any player who is not in the Hall of Fame. Drysdale hit Ernie Banks with five pitches. He drilled Frank Robinson, Orlando Cepeda, Carl Sawatski, and Frank Torre four times apiece. Despite all the celebrated chin music, he only hit Mays twice and never hit Aaron. Although Aaron certainly scored his points off Drysdale, he also struck out 47 times, 15 more than anyone else. Drysdale's most storied battles were with Robinson, who left the National League after the 1965 season. Robinson hit two home runs and had a .215 average against Big D and grounded into six double plays against him, more than anyone else.

Drysdale's hitting feats will live much longer because pitchers no longer hit in the majors. In 1958 he hit four home runs in a span of six at-bats. He homered 29 times overall, which is sixth all time for a pitcher, excluding pinch-hit home runs, and nine behind Wes Ferrell. Only 13 pitchers have hit 20 or more. Adam Wainwright's 10 home runs were the most by an active pitcher before the National League adopted the designated hitter in 2022. Drysdale had 113 RBIs, walked 60 times, and had 69 sacrifices. The Dodgers used him as a pinch-hitter 25 times, and he hit .217 in that role as opposed to .187 overall.

Drysdale hit seven triples in his career. Think about that for a second. In 2022 only five major league hitters had seven or more triples, and only Amed Rosario of Cleveland had more (nine). Three of Drysdale's triples came in the misshapen Coliseum, where outfielders fought off the glare from white-shirted fans. Triples are largely accidents created by a fielder's gaffe or an oddly designed stadium, and the Coliseum was quite accident prone.

Postseasons were shorter in Drysdale's time. Until 1969 the regular-season champs of each league went straight to the World Series with no league championship series, wild-cards, or any of the preliminaries that push our postseasons into November today. So Drysdale only had six postseason starts. He went 3–3 in those starts with a 1.2 WHIP, giving up 36 hits and striking out 36 in 39 ⅔ innings.

He was excellent in All-Star Games, recording a 1.40 ERA and allowing only 10 hits and four walks to a total of 69 batters. By working the eighth and ninth innings and giving up only one hit, Drysdale saved the 1963 victory for the National League.

That seems a preponderance of accomplishment. But the Baseball Writers Association of America, whose members elect the Hall of Famers, were reluctant to initiate Drysdale into the Cooperstown Club and had defensible reasons for it. Drysdale got only 21 percent of their Hall of Fame votes in 1975, his first year on the ballot. In 1977 his share rose to 51.4 percent, but he didn't break the 75 percent threshold until 1984. In those days most writers recognized that a pitcher's win total was not the most reliable barometer of his performance, that it depended on too many uncontrollable phenomena. But it was given more weight than it is today. As Nolan Ryan said, "My job is to be better than the other pitcher," and in those days pitchers were given the opportunity to settle that score no matter how many innings it took.

Even in that context, Drysdale's win total was a concern. His 209 wins rank 103rd in major league history, and there are a slew of pitchers who were his contemporaries or came along later who surpassed 209 and have no shot at getting into the Hall—at least not without Ticketmaster. Less celebrated Dodgers such as Jerry Reuss (220) and Charlie Hough (216) had more wins. Tommy John had 288 and remains the top winner who hasn't been enshrined. Jamie Moyer, Andy Pettitte, and CC Sabathia have more than 250 victories, and Curt Schilling just got through 10 years of eligibility without success despite 216 wins.

Only 13 starting pitchers have won fewer games than Drysdale and gotten buzzed into Cooperstown. But one of those was Koufax with 165. He got there with a magnificent five-year run at the end of his truncated career, and he and Drysdale were twinned by their 1966 holdout and the way one man's brilliance played off the other's.

The writers were also much more vigilant guardians of the Hall of Fame back then. In Drysdale's first nine years of eligibility, they never elected more than two players in any year. Duke Snider, for instance, made the top 10 in Most Valuable Player voting six times and exceeded 100 RBIs six times. But Snider had to wait 11 years to get in. When Aaron and Frank and Brooks Robinson became eligible, they were approved immediately, and that delayed Drysdale, too. In 1984 he finished third on the ballot but passed the three-fourths barrier, finishing behind Harmon Killebrew and Luis Aparicio. Later, he was heartened to learn that Pee Wee Reese, the captain of the first Dodgers team he made, got into the Hall on a vote from the Veterans Committee and would be inducted in the same ceremony.

In the end all candidates need something to set them apart from everyone else's wheelbarrow of decimal points. Drysdale had the endurance stats, the complete games, the shutouts, and the stingy WHIP and ERA numbers. But he became a Hall of Famer because of the scoreless streak and his total lack of compromise. It's easy and lazy to cite a player in the Hall of Fame who has, say, 425 home runs and maintain that your favorite candidate should be inducted automatically because he has 426. Numbers are important, especially when they convey consistency. But a Hall of Famer should have an impact on the game. He should stamp a memory that belongs to him alone. Drysdale was a symbol of his time. He made hitters wake up in the middle of the night. He kept fans rooted, watching for a kinetic moment that could erupt at any time. He was as much of a brand as he was a pitcher. That's why the door swung open at last. "My biggest thrill was the first day I walked into the clubhouse in Vero Beach, Florida, and realized I was wearing the same uniform as all those great players," Drysdale told the Cooperstown crowd at his induction ceremony. "That was enough for a kid from the San Fernando Valley."

On the same day in Atlanta, baseball found a more specific way to commemorate Drysdale. Pascual Perez of the Braves began that Sunday's game by hitting San Diego's Alan Wiggins with a pitch. One plunk led to another, and after they sorted out all the brawlers and ejected four pitchers and nine others, the umpires ridded both dugouts of anyone who wasn't actually playing in the game. Such an all-comers brawl would have been Drysdale's Lollapalooza. Atlanta manager Joe Torre called San Diego manager Dick Williams "a fucking idiot and spell idiot with a capital I and spell Williams with a small T."

"There isn't enough mustard in Georgia to cover Mr. Perez," Williams replied.

Unfortunately, Drysdale couldn't be in two places at once.

*   *   *

For the unprepared and for the unfulfilled, a forced retirement can be a head-on crash. For Don Drysdale it was different. There was really nothing left for him to chase, not with a Cy Young and three world championships and two 20-win seasons. He had invested well—both with his money and his interests. There would be no long aimless stretches in his life. When he was pitching, Drysdale functioned on emotion, adrenaline, and disdain. When he wasn't, he was a calculating pragmatist with a knack for rolling the dice.

When Ginger Drysdale filed for divorce in 1969, she listed the Drysdales' assets at $500,000. At their ranch in Hidden Hills, Drysdale was establishing a horse racing business called Hickory Hills Farms. He bought Greek Money, the 1962 Preakness winner, to stand at stud, though Greek Money's progeny had little success, but he did well with Honey Bern, who won 10 races and finished second 11 times, mostly with Wayne Freeman in the saddle. Don B. also won 10 times and brought home over $225,000, and Drysdale had bought him for breeding purposes as well. Drysdale's horses won six of their first 26 starts, mostly at Hollywood Park; Agua Caliente in Tijuana, Mexico; and Golden Gate Fields in Berkeley, California.

The ranch, east of Hemet, was called Rancho Rojo, and Drysdale was its president. It was a subsidiary of Upton Enterprises, which was mostly a lumber company. Eventually, Drysdale soured on the whole business and agreed to work for Upton as a public-relations representative for three years. When they dismissed him nine months later, he sued and won a $100,000 settlement in 1973.

It was hard to avoid Drysdale. At least when he pitched, he only surfaced every fourth day. He remained a favorite of TV producers. He appeared on episodes of *The Flying Nun* and *Then Came Bronson*, in which he played a major league scout. He signed up for variety shows. He was attending his usual Little League and Boys Club clinics. He was playing tennis with Ginger and lost occasionally, "which always ticks me off," he said.

Even in his minor league days, Drysdale would find a quiet place on days he wasn't pitching and narrate the live action out loud. He was practicing on a microphone to be named later. Tommy Lasorda, his Montreal teammate, once told him to do two innings of a game in which neither was pitching, and Drysdale did. He would do the same in Brooklyn and he recorded himself in hotel rooms. Sometimes teammates would see him holding a spoon to his mouth and talking to it. "If he's going to go into broadcasting," Rusty Staub, the gifted hitter for Houston and Montreal who was getting tired of Drysdale's hard breaking stuff, told the *Los Angeles Times*, "I wish he'd go ahead and do it."

The Montreal Expos called Drysdale to do limited broadcasts, and in 1972 he became the full-time analyst for the woebegone Texas Rangers. He said he had to work to keep his voice light when the Rangers were in the middle of a losing streak, which they often were. "I don't like it when you can hear the announcer's voice and tell who was winning the game," he said. "A few times this year, I slipped up and said, 'We' and I got very mad at myself."

He also had a self-imposed rule against second-guessing. He was successful enough that it became clear he wasn't headed toward managing. If he was going to be involved in baseball, it would be in an office far above the field. But he wanted the game he loved to remain his livelihood. "I wasn't going to go live in Lard Lake, Iowa, and sell insurance," he said. "Baseball is all I've ever known."

He joined a group that attempted to buy the Seattle Mariners and another that was angling for an expansion franchise in Orlando. As those bids fizzled, Drysdale came home and took the analyst's chair beside Dick Enberg, broadcasting California Angels games for Golden West Broadcasting, the property of club owner Gene Autry. Enberg, Drysdale, and Dave Niehaus did Angels games through the 1979 season and were part of their march toward relevance. Those were the years when Nolan Ryan was a no-hit threat every time he pitched, particularly in those ABC Monday night games that began amid the 5:00 PM shadows in Anaheim. Los Angeles fans, who had been spoiled by Vin Scully's broadcasting, now knew they had another top-notch team living on their dial.

But Drysdale lived in Palm Springs, California, and began to get weary of the commute, at one point asking for a chauffeur-driven limousine for home games. As it was often said, "Autry's radio station vetoed Autry's ballclub when it came to negotiations," and Drysdale left. This allowed him to do more work for ABC, and he became a staple of its postseason baseball coverage. He also worked college football and teamed with Enberg to do Rams radio.

His next and most famous stop was Chicago. Harry Caray and Jimmy Piersall had been an incendiary broadcast team for the White Sox, overshadowing the team at times. The Cubs swept in to hire Caray, and White Sox owner Jerry Reinsdorf hired Drysdale and Ken Harrelson, formerly the Red Sox announcer. They developed an authority of their own. Harrelson was the nickname artist, the one who called Frank Thomas "the Big Hurt" and who called out umpires whom he felt were damaging the White Sox.

But in 1986 Harrelson was named general manager of the club. He later called it "the worst job in baseball" and he only had it for one season. Reinsdorf returned "the Hawk" to the booth full time. One of Harrelson's ideas was to hire Drysdale and several other retired stars as consultants.

The problem was that manager Tony La Russa was steadfastly loyal to Dave Duncan, the pitching coach who would follow La Russa to Oakland and St. Louis and win World Series in both places. Moe Drabowsky, the Orioles' hero in the 1966 World Series win against the Dodgers, was also a pitching advisor. Harrelson said all these opinions would bump up against each other and create a better product. La Russa publicly went along. When it eventually blew up, Harrleson fired La Russa in June and promoted Doug Rader from his cast of coaches to be the interim skipper. Then he hired Jim Fregosi, who had managed the Angels when Drysdale was on their broadcast team.

All along, people kept tripping over the chain of command, which now had Dick Bosman as the pitching coach. "I had named Don my director of pitching," Harrelson said. "He did a hell of a job. He was great at it. He'd set up tackling dummies in spring training and put them on both sides of the plate and showed the pitchers how to drill somebody. He wanted them to grow some balls and be accountable. I remember one guy, we were going to take him to the bullpen and teach him the spitter. We were walking to the bullpen with Fregosi, and Don was ripping into this kid to the point that it was a little embarrassing. He was saying, 'You're a gutless motherfucker, you don't have a single gut in your body.' And I didn't know what this might be doing to the kid. He never let up on him. Well, the kid turned it around and became a double-digit winner for us that year."

The White Sox had only three double-digit winners that season: Rich Dotson, Floyd Bannister, and Joe Cowley, none of whom pitched in relief. Dotson had been injured the previous year. Cowley had just come to the Sox from the Yankees, where he had been 12–6 the previous year. He was 11–11 in 1986, though he did pitch a no-hitter. All the bureaucratic bulge didn't help the Sox avoid a 72–90 season, but the club did rank third in American League ERA.

Fregosi kept the job in 1987, and Harrelson gladly rejoined Drysdale in the broadcast booth. But after that season, Scully's partner, Jerry Doggett, retired in Los Angeles. An opening arose for Drysdale to describe the exploits of young players who never had known Brooklyn but wore the uniform that Drysdale prized so much. Reinsdorf agreed to let Drysdale join the Dodgers broadcast team. He knew that there was another team back home that Drysdale couldn't wait to rejoin and a role that would become his all-time favorite.

10

LOVE AND MARRIAGE

It was a summer league basketball game in Huntington Beach, California, like hundreds of others every weekend. DJ Drysdale was playing. His mom, Ann Meyers Drysdale, was in the bleachers. He knew by then that you can't take your gene pool into the game with you. Still, this one opposing kid was being particularly disrespectful. "He took a running start and he elbowed one of my teammates in the back," DJ said. "This had been going on for a while. He had been really obnoxious. So his team got a rebound, and they're coming downcourt, and I took a little bit of a wide turn. And I tripped him up."

Ann came out of the bleachers like a rocket. Everything stopped. She demanded that DJ's coach remove him from the game. "She was so mad that she left," DJ said. "My coach said, 'Well, she said to take you out of the game, so I can't put you back in.' The game ended, and I went to the car, and she wouldn't speak to me. We're on the way home, and she finally says, 'I saw what you did. I can't believe you would do that.' On and on. Finally, I said, 'Who do you think I learned it from?' I mean, she taught us how to step on people's feet if you thought it would give you an advantage. I grew up hearing all the stories about how my dad was so competitive, and then when the games would be over, he would be a completely different person. The same was true for my mom."

Maybe more so.

Ann Meyers became one of the essential figures in the history of women's basketball with an Olympic silver medal and a national championship at UCLA. Ross Porter, the Dodgers' broadcaster, was introducing her at a function one day and asked, "Annie, how many Halls of Fame are you in now?'"

She blushed and said, "Put it this way: it's nearly 20."

To this day she probably has more close friends among a wider spectrum of athletics than any other living American. She has been the general manager of the Phoenix Mercury of the WNBA, a broadcaster on several different levels, and a player so determined and fearless that she nearly made the roster of the NBA's Indiana Pacers.

On a Venn diagram, the tangible data of her life and Don Drysdale's life would have barely bumped each other. Drysdale was 19 years older and was married. His life was bound up with baseball, show business, thoroughbred ownership, and many places Meyers never had been. She had played almost every sport except baseball. Drysdale was one of two children; Meyers was one of 11. Drysdale had a structure, a clean pathway into the sport of his choice if he was good enough. Meyers felt she had to slay dragons on a daily basis. Drysdale was married and quite experienced in the ways of romance. Meyers had dated but never had a relationship that could equal the magnetic pull of sports.

And yet Drysdale and Meyers might have had more serendipity in their relationship than anyone suspected, including her. She came to realize that each of them could understand the Jekyll/Hyde forces that churned inside the other in a way no one else could. Because of their age gap and their different backgrounds, they also connected as people, not line scores or trophies. Competitiveness does not burn like a blast furnace inside most people. It takes a warrior to appreciate one.

Meyers Drysdale sat in a Seal Beach restaurant in May of 2023 and talked freely, wistfully, sometimes puckishly about her husband. Someone mentioned that Drysdale had played football and baseball at Van Nuys High but not basketball despite his height. Wonder why not? Meyers Drysdale grinned and said almost in a stage whisper, "Not good enough."

* * *

Patricia Meyers was one of those saints on earth, who in the words of John Prine, "can do 14 things at once, and then the phone'll ring." She was a driver, referee, organizer, ringmaster, chef, custodian, psychologist, researcher, teacher, and whatever else you can fit into the definition of an 11-child mom. There was never a time Ann Meyers could recall the washing machine and the dryer sitting dormant at the same time, but there were plenty of times she would see her mom carrying those clothes at midnight or so.

Pat somehow gouged out enough hours to volunteer for Meals on Wheels twice a week and was basically on call for whatever was needed at her church, Our Lady of Guadalupe. Bob Meyers had played basketball at Marquette, then played on a professional team called the Shooting Stars. He worked at Sears, and Ann's earliest memories came from growing up in Wheaton, Illinois, before the family moved to Orange County, California. They were all Green Bay Packers fans. If the Dodgers were ever on TV, they were background music.

Pat and Bob had to sign the form that would allow Ann to play after-school basketball with and against the boys. There were parameters in the house, but there were no limits. Pat had met Bob at Marquette when she joined the Nursing Corps during World War II. But Bob became more remote as the years went on and eventually he moved away from the dozen people in his house who were finding it difficult to reach or understand him. Later, daughter Kelly had a car accident in Mexico and was killed. Somehow Pat soldiered on, and Ann lost herself and shelved her anger by pursuing all those bouncing balls.

They all played something. David would become an NBA power forward with the Milwaukee Bucks after he'd helped John Wooden win his final NCAA championship. Patty, the oldest, played AAU softball and was on Cal State Fullerton's national championship basketball team. She also was Ann's merciless volleyball coach for one high school season. Mark played football at Cal.

Ann played nearly everything from setting state age-group records in the high jump to soccer and tennis and field hockey and badminton. At UCLA she was an All-American basketball player—in fact, the first four-time All-American of any gender at any college in any sport—who played varsity volleyball and also played intramural rugby until the athletic department blew the whistle on that.

Basketball was the lure, maybe because Ann was trying to keep up with David. In her mind he could be an obstacle, too, like the skeptics who kept popping in front of her, trying to draw the charge. "Why do you always have to follow me?" Dave asked her with some irritation, as Ann recalled in her book, *You Let Some Girl Beat You?*

"You're a girl, Annie," Dave would say. "Act like one."

That didn't smooth the waters, of course. Ann once hit a referee with a basketball, wasn't above chucking one into the seats, and wasn't always the easiest person to coach unless the coach had already earned her respect. Her avatar was Billie Moore, who had carved her own name at Cal State

Fullerton and was at UCLA when Ann, then a senior, finally led the Bruins to the national championship.

Ann was the first woman to get a full athletic scholarship at UCLA. She also was on the first U.S. Olympic women's team, a squad coached by Moore. It went to Montreal and won a silver medal in 1976. But she still remembers walking against the winds of sexism, particularly at Sonora High, when she felt she'd played her way onto the boys' varsity. She had earned her way, she felt, against the boys in the summer. Now the parents were up in arms, people were questioning her sexual identity, and all sorts of g-forces were taking hold. She gave up the fight. "It was the last time I would let anybody else's opinions dictate my decisions," she wrote.

She met Wilt Chamberlain at the famous Mt. SAC track and field meet one spring, and he counseled her on high jump technique. Chamberlain was at UCLA quite a bit, and the two had a fairly regular racquetball game. When the strongest and most physically indomitable player in professional sports—and one could argue in American professional sports history—hit a shot Ann couldn't return, she became, in her words, "terribly angry."

Ann tried out for the Indiana Pacers of the NBA, got $50,000 out of it, and survived until the last cut, when coach Bob "Slick" Leonard told her she might have made it if she'd been taller than 5'9". That stung—and still does. She had held her own in pickup games against the best NBA players like Magic Johnson and Calvin Murphy, one of the guys she could post up. She also had to fight the assumptions and prejudices of those who enjoy putting the lance to another person's dream. A writer smugly asked her if she could envision taking a charging foul from 6'11" Bob Lanier. "Nobody in the NBA takes a charge from Bob Lanier," she replied.

Meyers played in the Women's Basketball League (WBL) for the New Jersey Gems, where she signed a nice contract and never saw $83,000 of it. She recalls living in a dreary Howard Johnson Hotel near the Newark airport in 1979. Team chemistry was difficult since she had come to the league as a celebrity. She knew teammates weren't thrilled to learn she was flying to the Bahamas to enter ABC's *Superstars* competition, in which famous athletes from all sports would swim, bowl, run obstacle courses, and frolic for bragging rights and a few bucks.

Well, some of them may have frolicked. After the first day, Meyers was in fourth place, having shown up "as white as a handkerchief" from spending all that time in gymnasiums. The sun had gotten to her a bit. But that's not why her blood was boiling. She wasn't winning. Pat was along for the ride, and so were Ann's brother, Mark, and his wife, Frannie. When Ann's luggage didn't make the trip, they went to the wardrobe room to get her some clothes.

Don Drysdale and Bob Uecker were there, too. They were announcing the competition for ABC Sports. Pat knew who Drysdale was. Ann did not. Since this was an ABC function, Ann thought maybe he was Don Meredith of *Monday Night Football* fame. "I'm Ann Meyers," she said.

"Yeah," Drysdale said, "I know."

It might be exaggerating to say that sparks began flying. Ann's first reaction was bewilderment. *She had been recognized on the flight to the Bahamas, but now these famous broadcasters knew her, too?* Her second reaction was a little more nuanced. Something about Drysdale's smile and general carriage was intriguing. For so many years, Meyers had sensed that she was a threat to most men. There was an acceptance that she spotted in Drysdale's eyes. Frannie later told Ann that she could tell almost immediately that a relationship was brewing.

The *Superstars* competition ended the next day. Ann finished fourth. The Meyers family was invited to an ABC staff get-together, and Pat got a huge kick out of Uecker, who had played for the Milwaukee Braves and, of course, had parlayed his mediocre career into big bucks as a guest on *The Tonight Show* and a comic actor. A piano bar, cocktails galore…a fine time was had by all. "They were having their drinks, and I was having my 7UP," Ann said.

Ann stayed over an extra night. So did Drysdale. He asked her to dinner, which seemed innocent enough. "I did wonder, *What am I getting myself into?*" she said.

Somewhere between the drinks and the check, Drysdale said, "So what would you say if I asked you to marry me?"

There are several ways a woman can react to such a question. One would be to scurry out of the restaurant. Another would be to get angry and maybe fling a glass of water in his face. A third would be to haltingly decline, making sure that she expressed how flattered she was while leaving the door open to friendship. That is what Ann did. After all, here was a man with ultimate confidence. And, obviously, no commitment issues.

Ann returned to the WBL and its frustrations. Two days later Drysdale called her to make sure she'd made the trip with no problem. They talked for half an hour and even got to the part that neither had said out loud yet. Drysdale told Ann that he considered his marriage over, even though it wasn't. As she hung up, she realized she'd at least have something to anticipate on lonely nights in bad hotels after connecting flights.

But first she had some business to finish. Ann was invited to a special women's *Superstars* competition and she won that one three consecutive years. "I worked six to eight hours a day," she said, "running, swimming, hitting golf balls, lifting weights, playing tennis. The *Superstars* competition was something that came along at the right time."

In other words, she was recreating the purity of her childhood back when she wasn't just juggling sports but manipulating them.

The late-night conversations with Drysdale got longer, the vibes stronger, the relationship closer. She began taking golf lessons from Lou Rosanova, a teacher Drysdale had recommended, so they'd have something else to share. Rosanova had taught Ken Harrelson, White Sox broadcaster and Drysdale's booth partner. Rosanova also had taught Hollis Stacy, who won three U.S. Women's Opens.

Drysdale was a pitching legend to many—but not to Ann. "People don't realize," Ann said, "Don started pitching in the major leagues the year after I was born. He had a lot of his big years when I was just a kid. Besides, I didn't follow baseball at all. The only use I had for baseball cards was to put them in between the spokes on my bicycle with clothespins…I didn't look at him as this great pitcher, although I certainly enjoyed learning about that as we went along. I loved being with his friends and hearing all the stories. I loved being in Vero Beach for spring training. And I was always impressed when we'd be out, and people would react to him, and he would always treat people with the utmost respect. That's just part of how easy it was to be with him. He never acted like he had anything to prove."

Ann also didn't realize that Drysdale was quick to form opinions and quicker to make decisions. He had married Ginger Dubberly in 1958, three-and-a-half months after they met during batting practice at the Los Angeles Coliseum. "I knew he was dating Ann, but we hardly ever talked about that kind of stuff," Harrelson said. "One day we're out playing golf, and he says, 'I'm in love, Hawk. I'm going to marry this woman.'"

Drysdale was just as effusive when he ran into Sonny Jurgensen, the Pro Bowl quarterback for Washington. "She can beat me shooting free throws," Drysdale said almost in wonderment. "She can beat me at tennis. She can run faster than I can."

Jurgensen harrumphed. "Sounds to me like that's ample grounds for divorce," he said.

Drysdale retired from pitching in 1969. Ginger and daughter Kelly accompanied him to Don Drysdale Night on September 27, which happened to be the Drysdales' 11th wedding anniversary. Willie Mays attended the ceremony and presented Drysdale with a bottle of hair tonic in honor of Drysdale's mysteriously moist knuckle forkball. Ginger kissed Don. The papers ran the picture.

On October 28 Eula Eugenia D. Drysdale filed for divorce in Santa Monica Superior Court, maintaining that Drysdale had beaten her "30 times," including once on October 27. She sought a restraining order.

On May 14, 1970, the Drysdales attended Father Garrett's Boys Ranch as honorary chairmen of Terry's Teenage March. The function honored the late Terry Lanham, who had founded a door-to-door drive to raise money for the ranch. By then the gossip columns were whispering about a reconciliation, and Ginger and Don visited Hollywood Park together to watch Don's ponies run and they chaired the same march in 1971.

But Drysdale was spending his baseball seasons broadcasting Texas Rangers, Chicago White Sox, or California Angels games and all kinds of events for ABC. Don moved out of the Hidden Hills ranch house and to the Club at Morningside in Rancho Mirage, California. In 1982 the young lovers, who had been the most visible of all the Dodgers couples, were officially divorced after 24 years. "Ginger was a wonderful mother to Kelly,

Ginger had good business sense, Ginger was a terrific person in many ways," Drysdale wrote in his book. "What happened? I detested all the arguing. I fell out of love with Ginger. I have never been able to deal with petty stuff in my life. I'd rather just walk away from a bad situation."

Don and Ann began spending more time together, especially on the golf course. Ann had picked up the game as quickly and as intensely as anything else. She got down to a six handicap. Don was a 10. "I had to start cheating to beat her," he said.

"We were playing in Bob Lemon's tournament in Jamaica," Meyers Drysdale said. "I was just learning how to play. I was tending the pin, and Don had a putt. I didn't know you were supposed to pull it out. The putt is on his way, and he starts yelling, 'Pull the pin!' When I tried to pull it, the cup came out. No, he wasn't happy. But I didn't know."

She also didn't know how to stop. She found herself hitting balls for eight hours a day. In her mind she was aiming for the LPGA Tour. Why not? She had reached the top in everything else. "I thought I could do it. I was still in my 20s," Meyers Drysdale said. "But it really wasn't going to work for me. I had to go through the process of getting my tour card, competing with the best players in the world who had been doing this for years. I could see that it would be a lonely life. I wouldn't be part of a team. Did I really want that feeling? Plus, more than anything else, I was falling in love."

In 1986 she was chosen to broadcast the Goodwill Games, a Ted Turner brainstorm that would provide programming for his networks and maybe start to soften the Cold War. Back then, an American athlete performing in the Soviet Union was a curiosity and vice versa. Meyers, Rick Barry, and Bill Russell made up the broadcast team for women's basketball, and Meyers was already friends with them. Team USA then defeated the mighty Soviets 83–60 and ended their 152-game winning streak.

But while she was in Moscow, Meyers could only reach Drysdale through letters. Drysdale had proposed often. Meyers had resolutely turned him down and finally told him to quit asking. With the marriage out of the way and with long days and nights to consider everything, the only obstacle was her wariness. Eventually, the rewards surpassed the risk. When Meyers landed at Los Angeles International Airport, Drysdale picked her up, and as they drove away, he presented her with an engagement ring.

The wedding happened on November 1. Gene Mauch was Drysdale's best man.

On July 23, 1987, Donald Scott Drysdale Jr. was born. It happened to be on his dad's birthday. Instead of referring to him as Don Drysdale, Jr., Annie and Don decided on DJ. "We knew what Mickey Mantle's son had gone through, bearing that name," she said.

When Jim Fregosi, the White Sox manager, heard about DJ's arrival, he smiled. "I wouldn't mind having the breeding papers on that one," he said.

The unanimous perception, among their acquaintances, is that the marriage of Don and Ann represented the happiest days in both their lives. "I know people heard about us and were probably scratching their heads," Drysdale said in 1988. "But the truth is that every day is like a honeymoon."

Another perception is that Meyers Drysdale—with her undeniable will—somehow reformed Drysdale, maybe even domesticated him. Sure, Drysdale already knew how to run a squeaky-clean house. But the drinking had become problematic. In January of 1991 on the way home from a tournament sponsored by USC coach Rod Dedeaux, he blew a 0.19 on the breathalyzer, over twice the legal limit, after he had collided with a woman's car in Universal City. She was hospitalized for abrasions and cuts, and Drysdale was arraigned for felony drunk driving. He pleaded no contest and was fined $2,320 and had to perform 200 hours of community service with a youth baseball agency. Soon after, he curtailed his drinking.

Two years before he had suffered chest pains, and doctors performed an angioplasty. Drysdale began to realize he had quite a bit to lose. "I didn't straighten him out," Ann said. "But obviously his life was different with me. We were starting a new family. That weighed on him a lot. He knew he had to start doing things differently. But he had his routines, and so did I. He would come home from Chicago after he'd spent the year broadcasting their games, and it was a little different. I'd say, 'Don't you have somebody to go play golf with?' He'd ask me if it was okay if he went and played golf with Gene, and I'd say, 'Please, go. You don't have to hang around.'"

When DJ was born, Drysdale's sister, Nancy, and her husband, Ed, held a baby shower. Nancy told Ann, "Thanks for bringing my brother back."

"That's the thing about my family," Meyers Drysdale said. "You get one of us, you get us all."

*   *   *

Providentially, the Dodgers needed a new broadcaster in 1988. Jerry Doggett retired. Chicago White Sox owner Jerry Reinsdorf, who had grown up watching Dodgers games in Ebbets Field, understood the lure. Don Drysdale signed a five-year contract with the Dodgers in September of 1987. He was coming home to do the radio games with Ross Porter. Rather, that's what he wanted to do. He wanted to be on the air *with* Porter. The Dodgers preferred that Porter and Drysdale split up the innings and do them individually. That had always been Vin Scully's preference.

Drysdale and Porter began working an exhibition game at Holman Stadium in Vero Beach, Florida, and they were sharing the same microphone. That lasted for a half inning. The phone rang in the booth, and Dave Van de Walker, the engineer, handed it to Drysdale. "It's for you," he said.

Club president Peter O'Malley told Drysdale what the club policy was. "Don was livid," Porter recalled. "He couldn't get out of the booth fast enough. Don raced across Dodgertown to make his case."

When Drysdale got there, O'Malley said, "Don, we don't do two-man broadcasts."

"Are you telling me you are right, and every other owner is wrong?" Drysdale demanded.

"That's the way it is," O'Malley said.

Big D stormed out. Then he was a major part of the broadcast for five-and-a-half years, just as he always returned to the mound after something had driven him over the edge. "He told me more than once, 'All these starting pitchers are wimps these days, going just six innings,'" Porter said. "That was his attitude. He had his opinions and he was going to express them. We got along famously."

Nearly every baseball fan can memorize Scully's call of Kirk Gibson's home run that won the first game of the 1988 World Series: "She is gone… In a year that has been so improbable, the impossible has happened."

Scully made that call on the NBC broadcast. Those, who were listening to Drysdale on Dodgers radio, heard a call that was just as crafted: "If there ever was a preface to 'Casey At the Bat,' it would have to be the ninth inning. Two out, the tying run aboard, the winning run at the plate, the bottom of the ninth inning, and Kirk Gibson standing at the plate…Davis standing at second, a full count to Gibson: three balls and two strikes, and the crowd on their feet, and Gibson calls time and backs out. So the battle of minds starts to work a little bit. Gibson, a deep sigh, regripping the bat, shoulders just shrugged, now goes to the top of the helmet as he always does, steps in with that left foot. Eckersley working out of the stretch. Here's the 3-2 pitch. A drive into right field! Way back! This ball…is gone!"

And for the next minute and 56 seconds, Drysdale said nothing. He sat there and let the most joyful noise in the history of Dodger Stadium reach crescendo after crescendo. Finally, he broke in: "This crowd will not stop! They can't believe the ending. And this time mighty Casey did *not* strike out!"

Drysdale was nominated for the Frick Award given to a broadcaster for his meritorious service and would have been part of an exhibit at the National Baseball Hall of Fame just down the hall from the gallery that contains his baseball plaque. Scully won the Frick in 1982, Bob Uecker in 2003, Ken Harrelson in 2020. Drysdale hasn't—at least not yet. No Hall of Fame player ever has.

In the early 1990s, Don and Ann welcomed son, Darren, and daughter, Drew, and they kept pursuing goals the only way they knew how. Meyers Drysdale expanded her impressive broadcasting career to handle the first weekend of the 1992 NCAA men's basketball tournament for CBS. Drysdale worked to expand his Hall of Fame charity golf tournament, luring enough Senior Tour players to make it an event within an event. On May 10, 1993, Meyers Drysdale was inducted into the Basketball Hall of Fame, joining friends like Bill Walton, Julius Erving, and former seven-foot Soviet star

Ulyana Semyonova, who always had been a fascinating figure for Meyers Drysdale. "My buttons are popping," Drysdale said proudly.

Meyers Drysdale praised her husband's skill as an announcer. "I remember when Donnie told Pedro Martinez he was tipping his pitches and helped turn his career around," she said. "They don't give Donnie enough credit for being a broadcaster. He could recognize things like that. He had a great eye for the game. I loved watching games with him. At first I couldn't recognize pitches. The only thing I could tell was whether it was a fastball or a breaking ball, at least at first. He had such a good time with Dick Enberg when they did the Angels games. Dave Niehaus was there, too. I just wish ABC had let him work with Ueckie on the Monday night games. That would have been something. But he enjoyed so many simple things, just being by the pool with the kids, just hanging around at home. He loved going to Boys' Clubs, working with young pitchers."

She shook her head. Being Don Drysdale's wife was a ticket to acceptance. Being Ann Meyers' husband was also a validation for Drysdale. He had been bruised in a relationship. Meyers just wanted a chance to be on that battlefield. Too many guys couldn't get past her superstardom or handle her obsessiveness. "To have someone like that pay attention to me like that," Meyers Drysdale said, "I kept telling him no. Sometimes I wonder if I wasted too much time. At the time I wasn't impressed with his Dodger accomplishments because I didn't know them. Now I realize there is so much I still don't know about him."

Meyers Drysdale is now a vice president of the Phoenix Suns and Phoenix Mercury. She spent the early part of 2023 getting through a well-earned knee replacement. She is a grandmother. Jekyll has taken the wheel. Hyde is in hiding. But maybe not permanently. "I remember the day I beat her in golf for the first time—by one stroke," DJ said. "She didn't speak to me for 30 minutes. And I remember a story Tommy Lasorda told me. There was a basketball court in Vero Beach, and Mom was playing Dad one day and killing him. According to Tommy, she was going to the basket one time, and Dad just clotheslined her. She had so much energy, too, and still does. Every Tuesday and Wednesday, she had a regular game at Seacliff. Two of her partners would be in the cart, and she and another partner would play speed golf. She'd get finished in two hours and 30 minutes. Then I'd get in the car, and she'd take me to school."

11

WE'LL BE TOGETHER AGAIN

It was late in the evening of July 2, 1993, and Dave Van Horne was seeing Don Drysdale for the last time. He didn't know it, of course, when he waved good night to Drysdale, who was walking toward the Pie-IX station of the Metro train system in Montreal. The train stopped just inside the framework of Olympic Stadium, where the Expos played against the Dodgers, and the Dodgers had managed to squeeze out a 4–3 win on this Friday night.

Van Horne was the Expos' play-by-play man. Long ago, and for not very long, he and Drysdale had been partners. On this night Drysdale boarded the train and got off at the Peel stop, the closest one to Le Sheraton Centre, where the Dodgers were staying. Athletes, and those who hang around them, rarely go straight home when the games end in Montreal, especially on a Friday night. The bars and the hangouts and the *jeunes filles* on Crescent Street call out persuasively. But Drysdale was a 56-year-old father of three young children. DJ turned six on July 23, which was also Don's birthday. Darren was four, and Drew was three months old. Last calls, for the most part, were in his past. Lord knows he hadn't missed many.

On Saturday the first team bus left the hotel at mid-afternoon. Drysdale wasn't on it. He usually was. When he played, most everybody rode the bus because it was (A) free and (B) a symbol of togetherness. The worst thing you could say about a team was, "25 guys, 25 cabs," which indicated dissension. The next bus would get to the ballpark at about 5:30 PM. When Drysdale wasn't on that one, the broadcasters took note. "We didn't know where the hell he was," Vin Scully said. "I figured, well, he's probably seeing some friends because he used to play there."

The minutes went by. You always knew Drysdale was in the room. Then his colleagues were keenly aware that he wasn't. When the game started, Ross Porter manned the radio microphone, and Scully began his telecast. "There was this big glass door behind the booth," Scully said. "You could see a lot of reporters gathering there. I began to realize what was happening."

In an adjoining booth was Rodger Brulotte, one of the Expos' announcers. He remembered 1955, when Drysdale was playing for the Triple A Montreal Royals. On days he wasn't pitching, Drysdale would sometimes come to Rouen Park and play extemporaneous baseball with the kids on the sandlot. Brulotte grew up near that park and was one of those kids.

Bill DeLury, the elfin traveling secretary who had also come west from Brooklyn with the club, decided to return to the hotel. He was followed closely by Ken Daley, who was covering the Dodgers for the *Los Angeles Daily News*. DeLury called Peter O'Malley, who told him to get into Drysdale's room. DeLury found the hotel manager, who called the police and the paramedics, and they broke the door open. Drysdale was lying there, bloody. A drawer was open; perhaps he had banged his head against it when he fell. As Daley got there, he saw the paramedics wheeling Drysdale out on a stretcher.

Among the possessions they found in his room was a cassette tape of Robert F. Kennedy's speech in 1968, the one after he won the California Democratic primary, which he led off by congratulating Drysdale on a shutout shortly before he was assassinated at the Ambassador Hotel in Los Angeles. As best they can tell, Drysdale had died around midnight. DeLury called O'Malley again but added another complication. "He told me he couldn't find Annie," O'Malley said.

The Dodgers president got Pat Meyers' number and told her the news and asked where Ann was. She and the kids were at Huntington Beach and they were headed to the house of Ann's sister, Kelly, to celebrate her birthday. It was 1993. Not everyone was tethered to a cell phone back then. Ann was looking forward to watching the Dodgers at Kelly's house, but Kelly preferred to leave the TV off with guests there. Finally, Cathy, another sister, called to tell Ann that Drysdale was in a hospital. Ann called O'Malley, who told her Drysdale was gone.

In the booth Scully was seized with dread. His energetic baritone was muted and almost rote that night, a foreign timbre for all his listeners. DeLury came in sometime in the third inning and whispered, "He's dead." But Scully would not and could not mention it on the air until he was sure that Ann knew.

When he was assured of that in the seventh inning, he said this: "Friends, we've known each other a long time, and I've had to make a lot of announcements, some more painful than others. But never have I ever been asked to make an announcement that hurts me as much as this one. And I say it to you as best I can with a broken heart. Don Drysdale, who had a history of heart trouble—you may remember a couple of years ago he had angioplasty—was found dead in his hotel room, obviously a victim of a heart attack."

Not every outlet was as solicitous. ESPN Radio reported it before Scully did. Harrelson was broadcasting the White Sox game. "In 19 years of broadcasting…" Harrelson began, then paused to clear the grief from his throat. "This is the toughest thing I've ever had to say. Don Drysdale is dead at the age of 56."

Tommy Lasorda, the Dodgers manager and a longtime Montreal Royals pitcher, heard the news at 7:00 PM as he sat in the visiting manager's office. "I heard him yelling, 'Oh my God, oh my God,'" Orel Hershiser said.

Kevin Gross was the starting pitcher for the Dodgers. He was almost in the process of his warmup when he and everyone else on the field were called back into the clubhouse. "That's when I knew it was serious," said Felipe Alou, the Expos' manager.

"One of the hardest parts of a ballplayer's life is spending all that time alone in your hotel room," said Dennis Martinez, the Expos' pitcher. "You don't want to think about dying alone in that room."

Later, Al Michaels, Drysdale's play-by-play man on ABC telecasts, remembered how Drysdale had committed himself to a cleaner lifestyle after he and Ann had started their family. "Of course you're glad he did that," Michaels said. "But when you think about it, you wonder: *What if Don had not quit drinking?* He probably would have been in the hotel bar when it happened. And maybe he could have gotten some help."

Instead, Drysdale was searching for something when he first felt the pains and he did travel with nitroglycerin pills in case his heart flared up. Doctors had performed an angioplasty in 1989. Two of his uncles had died of heart problems. His mother, Verna, would also die of a heart attack in 1994. "But I'm convinced she died of a broken heart," said Scott Fieux, her grandson.

Sorrow ran through baseball and Los Angeles. Roy Campanella, Drysdale's first catcher, his Dodgers mentor, and a three-time Most Valuable

Player, had died a week earlier. It was sad, but then so much of Campanella's life was sad after he was paralyzed in a car accident three months before the Dodgers' first game in Los Angeles. It also was anticipated.

Then Drysdale was gone. A game or a bus or a press box without Drysdale's hearty "ah-ha-ha" and his pastel Hawaiian shirts was beyond the imagination. The fact that three young children would be left behind, along with the wife, whose arrival in Drysdale's life channeled it so positively, was haunting to everyone.

Jim Lefebvre was managing the Cubs at Colorado that night. "I remember that date as clear as can be," he said. "It broke the hearts of everybody. He was the guy you always wanted to be."

Jeff Torborg was driving in Pennsylvania, coming back from a college summer baseball league game with his son, Dale, in the passenger seat. Dale was playing for Northwestern. He did a turn as a professional wrestler known as "The Demon" and is now the strength coach for the White Sox. "We're driving along, and I turn on the radio," Torborg said. "They're playing Vin, who's doing the last game of the scoreless streak. I'm getting fired up just listening to it. Then the guy explains why they're playing it. Don Drysdale has just passed away. I started getting sick to my stomach. I had to pull off the road for a while."

"I couldn't go to the funeral," Harrelson said. "I knew I wouldn't be able to handle it."

"The last time I saw him, he walked into the radio booth with us," Porter said. "He had a cup of strawberry ice cream with him and he was laughing. I'll never forget that."

Jerry Reinsdorf was at the White Sox ballpark, watching a game against the Orioles. "I remember Jack Gould, one of our partners, coming into our box, and he was crying," Reinsdorf said. "I remember thinking, *We're only a few months apart.* I remember watching him in Ebbets Field."

Sportswriters shelved their plans and began gathering thoughts of the surviving friends. Buzzie Bavasi and Gene Mauch both answered their calls, even though they were crying. "He was the same man on the day that he died that he was when he was 17 years old," Bavasi said. "I loved him. I loved that right arm."

Mauch and Drysdale had a golf date lined up for July 14, a week from the upcoming Wednesday. Those were more frequent during the fall and winter. "I remember his dad bringing us to the old L.A. Angels games," Mauch said. "He wanted to be a second baseman then. But he had bad feet and a great arm. He took those bad feet and that great arm and he went to the mound time and time again. He had a broken bone in his hand one year and he still pitched 300 innings. This is hard, it's tough. There's not enough room in the newspaper for what I think about Don Drysdale."

The funeral was at Forest Lawn Cemetery in Glendale at the Hall of the Crucifixion-Resurrection. It was July 12, the day before the All-Star Game in Baltimore. Lasorda was a National League coach. So he took a red eye after the service to get there. "It was the saddest funeral I've ever been to," Michaels said. "I'll never forget seeing Annie come into the chapel. She had the two little boys with her and she was holding Drew with her arms around Annie's neck."

"I was sitting there holding Darren," Scott Fieux said. "He was sleeping."

The estimated crowd was 850. John Werhas, a former major league third baseman and now a pastor, conducted the service. A pretty respectable batting order of former Dodgers attended, including Sandy Koufax, Johnny

Podres, Pee Wee Reese, Duke Snider, Norm Larker, Don Zimmer, and Ron Perranoski. Current Dodgers were there, too, including Eric Karros, Jody Reed, Tim Wallach, Dave Hansen, Cory Snyder, and Jim Gott. The speakers were those who were closest to Drysdale in some fashion. They were Lasorda, Scully, Porter, Mauch, Dick Enberg, Bob Uecker, and Hershiser.

Porter talked about the idyllic marriage that propelled Drysdale through his final years, though Drysdale surely would have wanted to know how final they were. "We can take credit for the fact that when he left us he was the happiest he'd ever been in his life," Porter said. "How many people are able to say that they went to their maker at the happiest time of their lives? We are not grieving for Don Drysdale. We are grieving for ourselves."

Mauch told the crowd that Drysdale indeed was a "giant man who walked among giants. And if he could hear me, he would say, 'Either sit down or start over. I never had anything to do with Giants in my life.'"

Bill Bavasi remembers it being "just a horrible day...and then Uecker got up."

Uecker came to the lectern at the service. "The one thing about Don Drysdale is that he had a way of touching everyone he ever met," Uecker said before pausing. "I remember the first time that he touched me." Uecker raised his index finger and pointed it at the side of his neck. "It was right here."

The laughter brought a tidal wave of oxygen into the room. "The whole thing changed," Bill Bavasi said. "Everybody cracked up."

It's not a surprise Uecker made everyone at the service laugh. He played six major league seasons for three different teams, but he started in his hometown, playing for the Milwaukee Braves. He hit an even .200 with 14 home runs. One of them was off Koufax. Uecker said later that he apologized because he feared such an accident would keep Koufax out of the Hall of Fame. Koufax later begged Uecker to quit saying that. Uecker also said that the Braves originally said he could play for them for $500. His parents balked because they didn't have that kind of money. Uecker was wrapping up his career for the Braves (now in Atlanta) and he was telling his usual jokes when Al Hirt, the famous trumpet player from New Orleans, heard him. Hirt was so amused that he called some agent friends and arranged for Uecker to appear on *The Tonight Show*. Neither Johnny Carson, the host, nor Ed McMahon, the sidekick, knew anything about him. When Uecker's bit was over, Carson asked McMahon, "Did that guy really play baseball?"

McMahon replied, "I think so."

Uecker's absolute deadpan expression and his spotless timing got him several return invitations, and then the TV shows began calling, and pretty soon Uecker was one of most recognizable baseball people in America and an A-list actor. Typically, he never forgot where Milwaukee was. He continued to work as the Brewers' play-by-play man, where he hardly ever trafficked in comedy and in 2023 was doing those games for the 53rd season.

Over the years Uecker and Drysdale became close primarily because Drysdale always was partial to those who didn't take themselves seriously and yet were dead serious about the things that mattered. When Drysdale became interested in Annie, he asked Uecker if he'd be interested in watching a basketball game. He had a particular player in mind, he said. They were in New York at the time, so Uecker thought Drysdale was taking him to a Knicks game. When they crossed the New Jersey line, Uecker thought, *Okay, maybe Rutgers or Seton Hall.* Instead, they wound up at Thomas Dunn Center at Elizabeth High School, home of the New Jersey Gems of the WBL. There was the young woman who was in that wardrobe room in the Bahamas.

But after Uecker's amusing eulogy, the issues remained. "Our family is sitting there and saying, 'What do we do now?'" Scott Fieux said. "We know that Annie is going to need help. How can we do that without getting in the way of the huge family that she had? Fortunately, Annie has been great throughout. She was helping us out when our mom died." (Nancy Fieux passed away in 2023.)

There is the logistical, and then there is the emotional, and the Drysdale children faced a challenge that few others ever do. What happens when everyone seems to know your father better than you did? It is difficult enough to duplicate a legend. The kids were suddenly being asked to walk inside footprints that they had never seen imprinted. Drysdale was such a transparent figure that his fans felt he belonged to them. When he was angry or indignant or happy, the world knew it. Now everyone's assumptions would be transferred to two boys and a girl who were saddled with the name but never heard the voice. "I remember one of my baseball coaches saying, 'Well, your dad is in the Hall of Fame and your mom is in the Hall of Fame, so what happened to you?'" DJ said. "He was joking, but it's something that you don't forget. It got to the point that I didn't enjoy playing team sports anymore. I'd rather play golf. I could really play shortstop at one point. I was very natural at it. But I didn't play travel ball because Mom wanted me to play all the sports. I was also 5'9". So the coaches at Huntington Beach said I was too small to play shortstop, and they wanted the travel ball guys to keep the positions they were playing."

Slowly, as Drysdale's friends and teammates began to surround the family, DJ began to understand. He does have a few memories of Don. He remembers the day when Ann got into the Basketball Hall of Fame, and Don draped a big "Congratulations, Welcome Home" banner across the front of the house. There were also the days of watching fireworks on the Fourth of July. "Mostly, I can recall the days of him just being a dad," DJ said. "But I'm not going to lie. It's tough enough not having a dad in the first place and then dealing with all the people who have all the memories that you don't. As I kept hearing about what he meant to people, my attitude changed. I became very proud to be his son."

Ann was the driver of all that. She took the kids to spring training in Vero Beach, Florida. She made sure they were at Dodger Stadium. The club cooperated fully. Every year the Dodgers sent Ann four tickets for every game and parking passes. "We had the run of the place," DJ said. "We'd run up and down the stairs. We'd be in the clubhouse. I'm not sure that was the best place for kids that age to be, but we got to be good friends with Eric Karros, Chan Ho Park, Darren Dreifort, Raul Mondesi, all those guys."

Meanwhile, the pictures stayed up, and the clothes stayed in the closet. It wasn't that Ann couldn't bring herself to bring them down. She had no interest in ridding the house of the residue of her Donnie, particularly when there was a story to tell to an audience of three. "Geno [Mauch] said that the biggest shame of all this is that the kids will never know how much he loved them," Ann said. "People would come over and say, 'Annie, you're in mourning. You've turned this into a mausoleum.' I'd say, 'Yeah, this is what I want to do right now. I want to keep all of this alive.' I'm sure the kids did resent it for a while, but when people would come up and tell us things Don used to do for people, it all began to change."

And the name still resonated. When one of DJ's teams ran into a pitcher, who was either helplessly or creatively wild, and two teammates got hit, the coaches brought DJ to the mound. "Sure enough," DJ said, "I hit a guy."

* * *

Don Drysdale would be a grandfather today. Darren and his wife, Sam, had a daughter, Danielle Patricia, in January of 2023. They live in Huntington Beach, California, where Sam is a lawyer, and Darren is in the Gymboree business. DJ and wife, Kelsey, are in Gilbert, Arizona, where he's in the mortgage business. In late 2010 his car was smashed in the driver's side by a driver who ran a red light. Eventually, he had to have bones fused in his neck, which, among other things, sidelined his golf game for a while. "When he was at Arizona State, he got a job with the Diamondbacks," Ann said. "Derrick Hall and Josh Rawitch were both there and they had worked for the Dodgers. DJ caught some heat from some people. They'd say, 'You're not a D-back; you're a Dodger.' DJ would say, 'My dad was a Dodger. I never was.' He would run into that type of thing."

Drew, like her dad, is a talented singer. She has performed the national anthem in eight different major league parks. She has had ambitions of a singing career based in Nashville but lives in Huntington Beach now. One of her recordings, "Blue Dream," begins with her father's voice at the Hall of Fame induction ceremony, saying, "It seemed like an impossible dream."

After she graduated from UCLA, she lived in Van Nuys, California, briefly to get the feel of the schools and the town where her dad had grown up. "It was really important to her," Ann said. "She's so talented. She has quite a few balls in the air right now. She was working in a flower shop in Westwood and wanted to start a business like that at home. We got a dog for her during Covid-19, and she would go to the dog park and she'd have bouquets there for people to buy. Mother's Day was perfect for her."

Kelly Drysdale, Don's daughter who was born during the 1959 All-Star Game, lives on the Big Island of Hawaii and runs several restaurants, according to Scott Fieux. She and Ann had a cordial relationship until Ann put Don's memorabilia up for auction. His 1963 World Series ring sold for more than $110,000, and his 1962 Cy Young Award went for more than $100,000. The collection brought in more than $1 million. Kelly criticized Ann publicly, and their relationship ended. "The Cy Young Award was the one thing that was proudly and prominently displayed in every house I ever lived," Kelly said. "It's the first thing that I asked for, and there never was a reply. These are things that my family had long before she ever met my father."

"It wasn't an easy decision," Ann said. "Things were going on where I decided I had to do that. I know it was difficult for Kelly. Would I do things differently? Probably."

Ginger Drysdale is living in Hawaii, but Scott Drysdale, Don's father, died in 2002. Scully died in 2022.

Van Nuys is no longer the same sanitized American ideal, as defined by half-hour segments with laugh tracks. The things that evoke Don Drysdale's name are dwindling, a natural process. It's fortunate that archives are more elaborate and available than ever.

Essence, however, is difficult to preserve. That's why Ken Harrelson still carries the memory of the days in a Chicago broadcast booth with his friend. "DJ was visiting. He was about 10 or 11," Harrelson said. "I was doing the lineups, writing them down. He noticed that I had a toothpick in my mouth. He wanted to know why, and I said, 'Well, as a matter of fact, that's what your dad did when he wrote down the lineups. It's the same reason I've always got a rubber band around my cash and credit cards. That's what Don did.' DJ nodded his head. The next night he's in the booth, and he's got a toothpick in his mouth."

SOURCES

I knew Don Drysdale from the days he was on the Dodgers broadcasts. I would talk to him during spring training in Vero Beach, Florida, and at Dodger Stadium and sometimes on the road. We were cordial acquaintances. I used the Drysdale file at the National Baseball Hall of Fame. They had clippings from *Sport* magazine, *True* magazine, *The Sporting News*, *The New York Times*, and the *Los Angeles Times*. They also had the original scouting report on Drysdale written by Branch Rickey. The Hall of Fame archivists provided excerpts from the *Cultural Encyclopedia of Baseball* for the chapter on brushbacks. Courtesy of YouTube, I watched Drysdale's appearances on the TV shows *Lawman*, *The Rifleman*, *To Tell the Truth*, *The Donna Reed Show*, and *Leave It to Beaver*, and the appearance Don and his wife, Ginger, made on *You Bet Your Life*. I also saw Drysdale's appearance on Roy Firestone's *SportsLook* interview show.

I got quotes from Vin Scully, Tim McCarver, Don Sutton, and Stan Williams in 2013 and 2014. I extensively used Baseball-Reference.com for the many statistics in the manuscript. I used *Sports Illustrated* archives, particularly when it came to the Sandy Koufax/Drysdale holdout and the background on Buzzie Bavasi. I used the California State University, Northridge library for the collection of copies of the Van Nuys High School newspaper.

Newspapers

Los Angeles Times
Valley Times
Long Beach Independent
New York Daily News
The New York Times
Los Angeles Herald Examiner
The Ponca City News
San Francisco Examiner
San Francisco Chronicle
The Cincinnati Enquirer
The Montreal Gazette
Detroit Free Press
The Boston Globe
The Bakersfield Californian

Books

Once a Bum, Always a Dodger
You Let Some Girl Beat You?
Set the Night on Fire
Lords of the Realm

Personal Interviews

Peter O'Malley   Joe Moeller
Fred Claire   Sandy Koufax
Wes Parker   Ron Brand
Ralph Mauriello   John Edwards

Bob Aspromonte

Tim Tschida

Joe Torre

Hunter Wendelstedt

Howie Bedell

Larry Dierker

Jeff Torborg

Jerry Reinsdorf

Ken Daley

Chuck Harris

Claude Osteen

Stan Williams

Vin Scully

Ken Harrelson

Carl Erskine

Kelly Fieux

Scott Fieux

Ann Meyers Drysdale

DJ Drysdale

Orel Hershiser

Dave Van Horne

Ross Porter

Al Michaels

Bill Bavasi

Dennis Lamp

Jim Lefebvre

Rene Lachemann

Frank Howard

Tim McCarver

Joe Amalfitano

Phil Regan

ACKNOWLEDGMENTS

I had begun gathering material on Don Drysdale for a book in 2013 and 2014, but the project fell through. In late 2022 I got a call out of the blue from Bill Ames of Triumph Books. He told me they were looking for projects and wanted to know if I had one. Indeed I did.

Thanks to Bill, Jeff Fedotin, and the editing crew at Triumph Books for their diligence.

Thanks to my wife, Robyn, and my son, Philip, for their support and interest in this project. Robyn was an outstanding sports journalist and had many useful suggestions.

Thanks to Ann Meyers Drysdale—without whom this would not have come to fruition. Her willingness to go through the extreme highs and lows of her days with Don were invaluable. And she enjoys hearing the many stories about Don as much as anybody does. Thanks also to family members DJ Drysdale, Scott Fieux, and Kelly Fieux.

Thanks to Peter O'Malley, who provided many of the resources you see in this book.

Thanks to Mark Langill and Steve Brener of the Dodgers for providing phone numbers and arranging interviews, especially the one Steve arranged with Sandy Koufax.

Thanks to the folks at Baseball-Reference.com, whose unique website has been as necessary as plasma for everyone who writes about baseball.

And thanks to the memory of Don Drysdale himself. I hope I've been able to convey how he managed to be such a symbol and yet retained the common touch. He had a spirit that could warm the hearts of Frank Sinatra and a bystander at an airport bar, sometimes on the same day. I wrote this book in hopes of making sure his life would be commemorated and remembered.